Critical Social Studies

Editors: JOCK YOUNG and PAUL WALTON

The contemporary world projects a perplexing picture of political, social and economic upheaval. In these challenging times the conventional wisdoms of orthodox social thought whether it be sociology, economics or cultural studies become inadequate. This series focuses on this intellectual crisis, selecting authors whose work seeks to transcend the limitations of conventional discourse. Its tone is scholarly rather than polemical, in the belief that significant theoretical work is needed to clear the way for a genuine transformation of the existing social order.

Because of this, the series will relate closely to recent developments in social thought, particularly to critical theory – the emerging European tradition. In terms of specific topics, key pivotal areas of debate will be selected – for example, mass culture, inflation, problems of sexuality and the family, the nature of the capitalist state, natural science and ideology. The scope of analysis will be broad: the series will attempt to break the existing arbitrary divisions between the social studies disciplines. Its aim is to provide a platform for critical social thought (at a level quite accessible to students) to enter into the major theoretical controversies of the day.

Marxism, Ideology and Literature

Cliff Slaughter

HUMANITIES PRESS
Atlantic Highlands, New Jersey 1980

First published 1980 in the U.S.A. by
HUMANITIES PRESS INC.
Atlantic Highlands N.J. 07716

Printed in Hong Kong

Library of Congress Cataloging in Publication Data

Slaughter, Cliff.
    Marxism, ideology, and literature.

    (Critical social studies)
    Includes bibliographical references.
    1.   Communism and literature.   I.   Title.
HX531.S58   1979   335.43'8'8   79—16392
ISBN 0—391—01190—1

To the memory of my father

Contents

Acknowledgements

The quotations from Karl Marx, *Grundrisse: Foundations of the Critique of Political Economy*, translation © Martin Nicolaus 1973, are reprinted by kind permission of Penguin Books Ltd and Random House Inc.

I must also thank Jonathan Cape Ltd and Harcourt Brace Jovanovich Inc for permission to quote from Walter Benjamin, ·*Illuminations*, edited by Hannah Arendt and translated by Harry Zohn, copyright© 1955 by Suhrkamp Verlag, Frankfurt a.M., English translation copyright © 1968 by Harcourt Brace Jovanovich Inc.

Special thanks are due to Mrs Margaret Ellis and Mrs Jean Lister for their typing of the manuscript. Steven Kennedy and Timothy Fox were extremely patient and helpful in guiding the book through the press. My wife Vivien Slaughter shared the development of every theme in the book.

I cannot possibly single out individuals from the many friends and students whose work and comments have encouraged and contributed to whatever may be of value in these pages. It goes without saying that responsibility for its defects is mine and not theirs. Readers of the book will understand why I say that my greatest debt, shared with so many, is to those who gave their lives in the long battle for Marxism against its Stalinist and reformist enemies as well as against capitalism.

1
Introductory

A confrontation between Marxism and the sociology of literature is long overdue. This is especially so because sociologists so often assume that what they take to be Marxist insights into literature can be grafted on to their sociology. A critical survey of the results of this misapprehension might be interesting, but it would contribute little to demonstrating any unity in the subject matter, and would consist of no more than a series of more or less interesting individual essays. An introductory glance at three texts, in many important ways very different from each other, will help to clarify the need to go beyond such an essentially abstract and academic manner of presentation.

In his book *Goethe and his Age*[1] Georg Lukács showed how the ideas on art and beauty as well as the literary practice of the great writers and thinkers of the flowering of German culture (Lessing, Schiller, Goethe, Hegel, Schelling, Hölderlin) could not be understood simply in terms of their consistency and applicability to specific works or schools of art, nor as 'ideological reflections' of class interests, but rather as the highest peaks of the struggle (a struggle forced by the backwardness of German economy and politics into a concentrated philosophical and artistic development, as Marx and Engels had long ago pointed out) to grasp the essence of emergent capitalist forms of life, with all their implications for the nature of mankind. When these German writers paid so much attention to the classical models of Greek art and literature, it was in the service of a struggle to overcome the hostility of the capitalist division of labour and separation of public from private life to any integral development of human individuals. This was understood to be at the same time a struggle to understand and so take the first step beyond the limits imposed by modern society on art, the true function of which is to express this integrity of human life, men's conscious mastery and development of their own nature through the purposive activity of transforming the natural world. Lukács was surely right to assert (echoing Goethe himself) that *Faust* was the summit of this particular development, and was a work which could not serve as a model for the future: its meaning was that society had entered a necessary phase which excluded henceforth such a combination of drama and epic. *Faust* was the very self-consciousness of the transition to this new epoch, in literature and art as well as in social relations. Lukács's political positions prevented him from drawing from this work all the conclusions so obviously relevant for the critique of Stalinism and its policies on art and literature, but within the limits of his purely 'historical' treatment of the German Enlightenment he was able to illustrate the insights of Marx and Engels on these matters. This is in general characteristic of the 'orthodoxy' affected by Lukács.

Trotsky, writing about a historical turning point even more decisive, the opening up of the epoch which followed the October Revolution of 1917, was not restricted in the same way. On the contrary, his writings on art and literature of the 1923–6 period (the best-known of which is *Literature and Revolution*[2]) are only comprehensible as an inseparable component of the historic struggle which he led for the continuity of Marxism against the rise of Stalinism. Behind Stalinism was the state bureaucracy, strengthened immeasurably by its role as policeman in the conditions of economic and cultural backwardness in the isolated Soviet state. Its influence worked first, and fatally, through what Trotsky called the 'theoretical corrosion' of the Bolshevik Party, whose reduction to pragmatism and empiricism soon produced a series of blunders and betrayals after which the bureaucracy, more and more free from control from below, struck out to liquidate physically all opposition, especially the revolutionary generation of 1917 and all those who rallied to it. Trotsky's analysis of post-revolutionary Russian literature stands at the beginning of this process.

Literature and Revolution is sometimes grudgingly praised in passing by liberal critics as a work which is more generous and tolerant to writers, more ready to recognise the merits of pre-revolutionary literature, than was Stalinism. This type of comment misses the point. Trotsky in fact takes the discussion of 'proletarian culture' on to a level much more fundamental than that of labels and prescriptions for literary products. He argues against Stalin and others that the proletariat is not the bearer of some new society conforming to its special nature as a class, which is that of an exploited, oppressed and revolutionary majority. It is, on the contrary, engaged in a struggle to abolish itself along with the bourgeois society it must overthrow. The period during which this revolution is completed and during which the conditions are created for a future 'truly human' culture is a lengthy transitional one, transcending the national boundaries of the first Soviet state. In this transitional period the vast majority of men and women will for the first time have any chance to appropriate the cultural heritage of all past societies. What 'proletarian culture' could there be, particularly in the conditions of the Soviet Union of 1923–4, which revived every day 'the struggle for individual existence', and with it 'all the old crap' (Marx)? Trotsky knew that to dress up the cultural products of this period as 'proletarian culture' was an imposition of the interests of a bureaucracy. When the spokesman of the bureaucracy a few years later hailed as 'socialist realism' the insufferable banalities of 'illustrative literature', it was then a conscious and deliberate cultivation of works which accorded with the bureaucracy's own definition of the achievement of socialism in the USSR. That this phase coincided with the purge trials and liquidations (including the deaths of many writers) was a striking confirmation of Trotsky's analysis of 1924.

In the same book Trotsky drew the conclusions for policy from his analysis. The literary tendencies in Russia were the products of the relation of the various classes, sections of classes, and their 'spokesmen', to the revolution. In cultural policy the 'fellow-travellers' among Russian writers should be appraised and encouraged from the standpoint of their artistic contribution to the future 'truly human' culture, and not according to some abstract yardstick deemed the

cultural equivalent of the revolutionary nature of the proletariat. Within all these tendencies, as well as in those which
opposed the revolution, Trotsky analysed the disintegration
of that celebration of individuality which had inspired literature since the Renaissance.

The critic René Girard attacked the problems of literature[3]
in a context and manner quite foreign to those of Trotsky or
indeed Lukács. And yet, despite his sarcastic and embarrass-
ingly ill-informed asides about Marxism, certain of his remarks
about Proust and Stendhal bring to the foreground something
which is implicit in the main points extracted from Trotsky
and Lukács and fundamental to a critique of the 'sociology
of literature.' Marxists have suggested[4] that sociology's basic
concept of 'role', far from being 'value-free', is an ideological
reflection of and apologia for the division of labour and alienation of capitalist society, and not a scientific notion for
grasping that society. The particular emphasis of Girard's
work on 'mediated desire' helps to crystallise the implication
of this criticism of sociology in the field of sociology of literature: sociology must be dealt with not merely as an adversary
to be debated with about interpretation of the novel or
drama, but as itself a specific product, of course under definite
conditions and by a different path, of the same class, its relation to other classes, its reactions to the class struggle, and its
characteristic forms of consciousness, as the novel itself.

> Proust calls 'Selves' the 'worlds' projected by successive
> mediations. The Selves are completely isolated from each
> other, and are incapable of recalling the former Selves or
> anticipating future Selves.
>   The first signs of the hero's fragmentation into monadic
> Selves can be seen in Stendhal.[5]

Stendhal had sought the fulfilment of the French Revolution's promise of individual liberty and fraternity, the happiness which was to have resulted from the removal of absolutism
and obscurantism, and forced himself in his novels to show
how the individual must surrender integrity and happiness to
the demands of bourgeois, post-revolutionary reality. Proust,
three-quarters of a century later, did not flinch from the truth

of the reduction of the bourgeois individual in Paris to a chameleon-like existence of successive impotent surrenders to the absurd requirements of snobbish conformity to a decayed 'nobility'. And he demonstrated in his own perverse way the necessity of the artist's sacrificing any real mutual being with his fellow men in order to carry out the work of facing up to this truth, through the struggle, in memory, to rescue experience from its falsifications and rationalisations.

In an important sense sociology of the twentieth century is related to the truth of the great realist novels of the last century in the same way as vulgar economics is related to the classical economists of the eighteenth and early nineteenth centuries. The great novelists, like Smith, Ricardo, Ferguson and Millar in political economy, discovered and presented decisive truths about the fundamental tendencies of bourgeois societies, within the limits of a bourgeois individualist world outlook (specifically, they could not attain the level of comprehending — in the one case scientifically, in the other in images — the historical significance of the rise of the organised working class). Vulgar economics was a mere apologetics, rejecting the conquests of the classical economists. Sociology, instead of negating and integrating on a higher level the philosophical, economic, political and historiographical attainments of bourgeois culture, falls below them, just as it throws away the insights into human relations under capitalism which had been achieved by the realist novelists. Sociology reduces social life to the interaction of 'roles' or 'social personalities', Any reality higher than the interplay of these fragments of humanity is endowed with an entirely mystical nature (Durkheim's 'le social en soi', Parsons' 'central value system', etc.). The great novelists' impassioned struggle against the alienating results of the capitalist division of labour is replaced, in sociology, by the acceptance of men's fragmentation into 'roles' as the 'facts' of which society is composed, to be classified, quantified, categorised, subjected to tests of significance, rendered 'operational', made fit for consumption by a well-behaved computer, which will turn out to be that of the state power or the international corporation. Of all the social functions announced by this pseudo-science, only that of sociology itself is crystal clear. What the novelists combated as the destruction of true individuality and true community through alienation and 'mediation', the sociologists celebrate as the positively given data of 'orientation', 'internalisation', 'role-conflict', 'cultural conditioning', 'socialisation', and a hundred other plangent barbarities. That a book could appear with the title *Sociology as an Art Form*[6] only goes to show the extent of the destruction achieved.

The problem is therefore to make some contribution to rescuing literature from sociology. For a Marxist this means proceeding with the understanding that defending mankind's literary heritage depends upon success in the struggle to free humanity from the oppressive, historically outplayed society of which sociology constitutes one of the ideological defences. Sociology regards such statements as mere 'ideology'. There is no meeting point. It is necessary, in considering the Marxist view of literature, to make a critical appraisal of the development of the theory and practice of Marxism itself, within which views of literature have evolved. A book like the present one can hardly claim to do more than make an exploratory redefinition of the problems for future research.

These introductory remarks might thus help to explain why it has been thought possible to treat in one volume matters which may be considered by sociologists properly to belong to the separate disciplines called history, literary criticism, philosophy, sociology and political science. Historical materialism does not substitute itself in some mysterious way for the detailed work of investigators in specialised fields, but it does reject those a-historical divisions between the different social sciences and between social sciences and humanities which obstruct a critical and materialist analysis of society and culture. Literary criticism has suffered no less than history and sociology from these divisions, but the problem cannot be overcome merely by piecing together the products of the separate disciplines. The questions need to be formulated in new ways. We may begin with a familiar example from Erich Auerbach's outstanding work[7] in breaking down the traditional divisions between literary and historical—social studies.

The contrast between the story of Abraham in the Old Testament and Homer's *Odyssey* has its source in the contrast between two societies and their cultures. Auerbach shows how Homer finds it natural to describe actions and details in a 'uniformly illuminated' landscape. The introduction of a new character or element in the story, with necessary digression to explain whence it comes, is done in leisurely fashion, without a trace of concern about losing tension in the development of the overall action. This 'epic' mode is not found in the Old Testament. Details of time, place and background are omitted or enter only in the direct service of the moral and religious order whose reaffirmation is the sole purpose of the story. The Israelites live by the word of God. Meaning attaches to what they do and say only through God. Every experience, every object of this experience, is approached and absorbed only in terms of the Almighty and the powers attributed to him. Objects, events and actions merit description only if such description is necessary to indicate the divine purpose. This jealous God can permit no freedom, no individuality which experiences the world just as it presents itself naturally to the senses of the developed human being. For the Greeks of the Heroic Age there is the beginning of freedom, and not yet the presentiment of the new unfreedom which the future contains. For a time men feel themselves able to confront the world in a 'natural' manner, where the meaning of life is not more than that one lives to enjoy the sense of how the whole man feels in finding his place in the world, a world in which he sets out with his purposive activity. Auerbach points to the consequences for 'realism' of the Israelite contrast:

> What he [the Biblical narrator] produced ... was not primarily oriented toward 'realism' (*if he succeeded in being realistic, it was merely a means, not an end*); it was oriented toward truth. Woe to the man who did not believe it! [Emphasis added] [8]

While the life of the Greeks of the Archaic and Classical periods produced a consciousness which fought free of the religious authoritarianism exemplified by the Old Testament, the feudalism of medieval Europe was later certainly able to find in it a suitable ideological form. That the Greeks who constituted Homer's audience did not understand anything of the contradictions within private property, the beginnings of commodity production, and the dire social consequences of the escape of the product from the producer's control, is not relevant at this point. This very naivety proves positive, from the point of view of what it was able to produce in literature and sculpture, not only for the Greeks but for all subsequent generations. For this historically short space of time, men's feelings were fashioned and expressed in a way which could anticipate, for the men and women of future millennia, the striving to transcend the limitations of the social division of labour in class societies, of oppression and ignorance, of alienation and the split between public and private lives, of the feeling of powerlessness and meaninglessness induced by the development of capitalism. When later generations, or the writers and artists who wrote and acted and painted for them, returned to the Greeks for inspiration, it was because the creative work done in the Archaic and Classical periods was able to make genuine discoveries, genuine conquests in the arts as paths to freedom, upon which every artist of subsequent generations must build. One reason was that the language of the people had not yet been separated from 'literary' language.[9]

Marx, as Prawer[10] in particular has noted, was not inclined to separate 'creative' from other literature. He viewed his own journalistic work in the 'revolutionary democracy' of Germany in 1843 from the standpoint of a definite conception of the heritage of antiquity, interesting for the present discussion:

> The self-confidence of the human being, freedom, has first of all to be aroused again in the hearts of these people. Only this feeling, which vanished from the world with the Greeks, and under Christianity disappeared into the blue mist of the heavens, can again transform society into a community of human beings united for their highest aims, into a democratic state.[11]

Even Brecht, seeking a theatre which dissociated the audience from the everyday ideological prison of experience, reaches back to 'epic', with its atmosphere of a 'uniform illumination'. His aim is to 'make strange' the individual events and persons by prising them from their familiar relations one to another and to the subject, thereby forcing on the audience's attention a different possible relation between universal and individual. By this means he strives to present the possibility of freedom, first by giving the audience the chance to think differently and feel differently. Even if not one of his plays was successful, this conscious attempt and its influence, which is only in its beginning, mark out Brecht as a great innovator.

Every revolution brings with it euphoric and even ecstatic moods, expressive of the hope that the day of freedom is at hand. Marx declared that the heroism necessary to achieve the bourgeois revolutions would have been impossible without such illusions: the promise of exploitation through the appropriation of surplus value and the creation of a mass of propertyless wage-labourers would hardly have inspired the revolutionary deeds of the 1640s or 1789. And there was a degree of truth, of 'necessity', within the illusion, in that the step forward taken from feudalism to capitalism was the only one possible for humanity at that stage of development of the productive forces and social relations of production (a foundation of culture still hidden from the actors, who conceived of history and progress in terms of individuals and the satisfaction of their needs, or of divine will, or a combination of both). The flowering of individualism, in its Romantic or its utilitarian and rationalistic forms, was characterised by Marx as a 'historically justified' illusion, because it reflected the contemporary necessity of progress through individual appropriation and enterprise as well as serving the necessity of the great struggles to overturn the feudal order. While it was true that the individuals who carried through this struggle, and their descendants, must be differentiated into exploiters and exploited, yet individuals had to be freed from feudal ties if modern industry and the modern proletariat, the prerequisites of a social revolution which could end class society and provide the material conditions for true individual liberty, were to be created.

In the resultant bourgeois society the novel came to predominate as a literary form. To all outward appearances the novel is the equal of epic in so far as we consider only the points made above about epic: it purports to describe realistically the worldly experiences — the actions, thoughts and feelings — of individuals. Characteristically, however, the objects and persons encoutered by the hero of the novel constitute a *hostile* environment. It is by now a commonplace that the history of the novel is one of a progressive break-up of the normality of relations between the individual and his world. The inner turmoil of the hero comes to structure the universe of the novel, in contrast to the 'naturalness' which is assumed to prevail in that universe at an earlier stage.

What is the relevance of Auerbach's Greek—Israelite comparison to this development of the novel? The Greeks of the Homeric period (and, with differences which are unimportant for this stage of the argument, of the Classical period) felt quite spontaneously the birth of an individuality freed from the ancient commune and with the universe open before it. Where tragedy entered, its character derived from the individual's confronting the awesome necessity of the break from the limitations of gentile society and its kinship-bound solidarity, and not at all from any sense of the trauma in store for humanity in the new world of class society. When, by contrast, the writer in bourgeois society creates his work, he does it at that point, historically, where class society has almost run its historic course nearly two and a half millenia after the peak of Greek civilisation was reached. The individuality which was released upon the world then has developed to an extreme but only to the accompaniment of the degradation consequent upon the exploitation of man by man.

In art and literature men find images to communicate and share their apprehension of the wholeness of that eternally renewed battle to master feeling, will, thought and action, the battle which constitutes human life in its distinctive relation with nature. It is a relation which is a qualitative development beyond the determinism of the biological evolution that was necessary for *homo sapiens* to emerge, but it does not signal the beginning of some abstract realm of pure freedom or of the reign of the spirit. Man's purposive activity is one which must learn to proceed on the basis of the laws of nature—freedom must be won, through the process of making the laws of nature work in accordance with men's needs. But to this struggle is added a mediation which complicates, obscures, and gives new contradictory forms to the artistic comprehension of men's life and work: the social division of labour and relations of production in class societies divide men one from another, separate material production from most spheres of consciousness, and in this way provide more or less fixed idealist forms of answer to the problems of knowledge thrown up by men's struggle for control and cognition of the ever-changing material world.

When humanity reaches a historical impasse like the present one, then the depth and intensity of the conflicts concentrated into the transitional epoch produce characteristic responses in forms of consciousness. In particular ways, according to the particularities of the national culture (which, it goes without saying, are related to the specific conditions and tempo of the emergence of capitalist relations and of earlier systems in the particular country), though with the increasing influence of a world literature, men and women see their lives in terms of either (1) a romantic—reactionary yearning for some lost idyllic, organic past order, (2) disillusion, pessimism and despair or impatience, indiscriminate rage and violence, (3) a philosophical resignation to what is taken to be 'the human condition', or (4) a confused combination of or oscillation between any of these; alternatively, they may seek, against these moods, a revolutionary theory and practice to overturn the existing social condition. All these conclusions have their expression in the worlds created by writers and artists (some writers express their conviction that one of these conclusions is correct; others are able to show the sources and interrelations of all or some of them).

The interior world of these creative works, in the vast majority of cases, is not the 'uniformly illuminated' and unquestionably 'natural' world such as we find in Homer—a world recognised by every reader as his own. On the contrary, men find themselves more and more unable to feel confident that they can communicate, and wonder if the world they know is some private hell. This 'psychological' chaos is nothing more than a phenomenology of the explicit content of the novel of the late nineteenth and early twentieth centuries, the raw experience of the men and women of the period. There remains the fundamental question, that of the objective source of these very phenomena. What is the 'unfreedom' that confronts men, which divides them while at the same time imposing the same necessity upon them all? Is the everyday world of actions and objects described in the novel as matter of fact as it appears? Can these questions be answered in the terms of sociology, of any system of thought which merely quantifies and compares as 'facts' the elements of the life produced by a 'neutrally' conceived 'industrial society'?

In the novel we seem to find a straightforward description of the individuals living out their lives. Such a literary form did not exist in pre-capitalist societies, where the dominance of ascribed status, legally or customarily defined social rank and position, could allow only exceptionally for the adventurer or relatively free agent. In its distinctive *form*—typically a story of the individual hero's encounters with the world— the novel is a true reflection of the *form* of capitalist social life, where the social—economic—political estates of feudalism have been replaced by equality before the law and common citizenship, and classes exist only 'unofficially'. But this social form contradicts as well as expresses the content of capitalism. Economic relations, the social relations of production, escape legal definition but are the real determinants of social life. Some novels will be written in such a way that they never reveal this contradiction between the form and the content of life in bourgeois society. Others will produce a tension between the novel form and the novel's content which opens up to consciousness the contradiction between form and content in life itself. The commonsense form of one or another variety of biographical description in the novel can either reinforce the illusion that social life is nothing more than an aggregate of such careers, or it can reveal the contradictions brought about in social forms by a content which produces them as its necessary expression and life-form and at the same time continually disrupts them and accumulates the force to break them.

Is not the novel form then a spontaneous literary reflection of the appearance of capitalist social life—the product of the aggregate of self-interested individual actions? Marx showed in *Capital* that in reality these same individuals act as members of definite classes with roles in production and social life which exist independently of their wills. It is not just that men are essentially producers, in such a way that they would only have to be first comprehended as inter-dependent producers of the use-values they need, and on this foundation social life could be understood. In capitalist society nothing is produced without labour's entering into a definite relation with capital. This relation is nothing to do with the necessities of production as such; it is independent of the wishes or ideas of any of the bearers of the relation. It consists of the sale of the commodity labour-power by propertyless workers to owners of capital. Not only suits of clothes, motor cars and loaves of bread are produced every day; the social relations of exploitation and property forms are also reproduced. From the value produced by the labour-er derive all the revenues of all the classes, contrary to the appearance that the capitalist and landlord are rewarded in proportion to their contribution as 'factors of production', as sociology still so naively believes. The direct producers are compelled by their lack of property, their separation from the means of production (a condition to which their fore-fathers were reduced at the dawn of capitalism), to themselves be repositaries of the commodity labour-power, which they must sell in order to have the means of subsistence. Marx thus saw living human labour enslaved by 'dead labour', i.e., by capital, which is the accumulated labour (value) of the past. Man's essential activity of productive labour, purposive activity in society deploying the resources conquered by past generations, is turned against him. And yet the same capita-list system takes to a new height the socialisation of produc-tion and the interdependence of all labours. But this sociali-sation and international division of labour remain within the framework of individual ownership and appropriation and of the world capitalist market, so that the result is greater alienation and oppression.

The novel form rests, in a certain sense, on the assump-tion that the description of everyday reality in the lives of individuals can be truth, can be art. But no matter how pic-torially accurate a description were made of the processes of production and distribution, it could not reveal the value form from which the understanding of capitalism as a system must be developed. It could never reveal the fact that not only capital but also the contradictions of capitalism are reproduced in the act of production. The class relations are reproduced, and also the processes which undermine these relations. In the most general formulation these processes constitute the contradiction between socialised production and individual appropriation of the product as value. Here we arrive at a development of the contradictions of capitalism which is directly relevant to ideology and to literature. It is the socialisation of production on a massive scale which is the basic material precondition for the leap to freedom, beyond capitalism, requiring the conscious direction of the associated producers (in contrast to their unconsciousness and separation as exploited wage-labourers, as well as to their earlier existence as individual petty producers or feudal serfs). The persistence of individual capitalist ownership and appropriation is the barrier to this step to freedom. Yet bourgeois ideology suggests the very opposite: that freedom consists in the individual's defiance of what society prescribes, and that private property and individual business enterprise are the *sine qua non* of liberty.

In the twentieth century serious literature rejects the bourgeois formula for freedom, and the hostility of capitalism and commercialism to art is now a commonplace. The patent mendacity of capitalism's claim to defend liberty has provoked volumes of outraged protest. For this reason there has been one effort after another to find in literature a successor to the traditional novel. What was once a 'historically justified illusion' is now a cheap ideological falsehood. And it is to be expected that if literature is to embody man's striving for truth and is more than ideology, then the old novel form must be called in question. It does not necessarily mean that no creative literature can be written in the traditional form. A novelist may find ways of using that form precisely in order to seek to express the extreme tension between the outworn forms of capitalist society and culture on the one hand and the growth of productive forces on the other. Another novelist may feel it necessary to experiment radically with new forms, in the conviction that persistence in the old form is collusion with forms of perception and expression which cannot but defend capitalism. To insist on the 'correctness' of one or the other would be empty dogma. Literary tendencies are not born out of such abstract oppositions. What we actually find is works in both directions, hundreds of attempts to modify the novel form in such a way as to be able to respond to the shattering experiences of our century of wars and revolutions.

In the chapters which follow it will be suggested that the degree of success of various Marxist critics in attempting a social or sociological explanation of literature is related to the extent to which they are able to recognise and hold fast those profound historical and philosophical questions which transcend the horizons of sociology and which, Marxists maintain, cannot be comprehended outside of what Marx called revolutionary—practical activity. It is evident that from such a standpoint, which must aim always to begin from the necessity of recognising and overcoming the world-historical social crisis, those 'sociologies of literature' which think it possible to begin from 'the text' or the *langue* or some other structuralist fetish must be opposed. The same critics have created a climate in which such words as 'creative' and 'human' are considered metaphysical and mystificatory. They consider any emphasis on the element of feeling in literature and art as inimical to scientific comprehension. This smacks of rationalism rather than Marxism, despite the claims of some of these structuralists to be Marxist and scientific. They view literature as an object of thought ('theoretical practice') rather than as the product and property of men who must act, must concentrate their passions, must make decisions, as well as think.

For the Marxist, can any serious meaning be attached to the notion of a vital element of 'feeling' in the work of art? One of the most illuminating contributions in this context is that of Max Raphael in *The Demands of Art*.[12] Analysing the painting and writing of Cézanne, he shows how the artist makes the reality 'produce itself' by the working through of its internal contradictions. This is contrasted to the artist's selecting from reality in accordance with the criteria of his 'world-vision' (as Goldmann might put it) in order to compose a picture. Here is an extremely important emphasis by Max Raphael, drawing upon Cézanne. It serves to prevent the relative truth contained in the assertion that art is a free activity of creating original worlds and works from becoming an untruth, a false absolute. This it does by defining the limits, which are *at the same time* the fundamental sources, of true realism in art. In Max Raphael's (and Cézanne's) formulation we see artistic-literary labour as one which strives for creative freedom not as self-expression but rather as the consciousness of necessity in the object and in the activity and cognition necessary to master the object. Such striving can constitute the essential character of a writer's work without necessarily informing his explicit philosophy (in Cézanne the degree of explicit commitment to this view is very striking). The notion of 'creativity' is freed of its usual subjectivist mystique, if it is used in this way, where art is seen as a concentration of the quintessence of that historical necessity to which mankind as a species is tied.

Men in the course of history learn to make nature work according to their needs. This means learning to court nature, to coax nature, and not to suppose that an arbitrary will can be imposed on it to make it render up its wealth. Men's unity with the rest of nature, constantly rediscovered and developed in struggle, and in the first place through productive labour, is the essence of human fulfilment. How can the worlds of feeling and thinking be separated? Passion, to paraphrase Marx,[13] is man bent with his whole being on a definite object. Art seeks to reproduce this passion of the whole man striving for harmonious application and fulfilment in the achievement of freely decided objectives. This wholeness of man engaged on his own becoming, through labour on the rest of nature which successfully brings together the work of his forefathers and of his fellow men, is—however obscure or hazy in the artist's consciousness—the potential reality which art extracts ever anew from the vale of tears which is man's life. The artist does this even when to do so means engaging in mortal combat with existing conditions. This struggle, at one with every movement for the emancipation of mankind, is the fount of the 'element of feeling' without which there would be no art. To summon it up and express it in images is a very different thing from the common resort in literature to generic biological needs as somehow the properties of a 'natural' man in defiance of social constraints. The element of feeling in art, which so embarrasses some 'structuralist Marxists', is indeed the principal content of art. It is the replenishing of men's resources for the unending struggle to fashion nature, including man's own nature, in accordance with historically formed human needs. This is not an 'aspect' of humanity, but the meaning of humanity, its mode of existence. (Marxism suggests an explanation of the element of feeling in art consistent with the characteristic and fundamental activity of human beings in society. This is of course in contrast to the stress on emotion in art by a philosopher like Alain, for whom the artist's style reveals his emotional life, so that through this emotional life is gained an insight into the universal condition of human individuals.)

Hegel had already elaborated a history of culture as the life-work of the 'Absolute Spirit'. When Marx 'turned Hegel on his head, or rather, on his feet', he came to see Hegel's Absolute Spirit as an inverted image of the labour of all humanity. To comprehend the intellectual as well as the material products of men, Marx now thought it necessary to begin, not from some generic human nature inherent in each individual man, but from the character of human social activity taken as a whole, with its specific internal contradictions and laws of motion. This point is clarified if we contrast it with what would be the result of inverting *subjective* idealism rather than Hegel's 'objective idealism'. In such an operation, rejecting the subjective idealist interpretation of culture as a product of the individual mind or spirit, we would substitute a theory of culture as the creation of the natural, real, sensuous individual in his material environment, influenced more or less by the opinions and pressures of other individuals, or perhaps possessed of some natural feeling for social intercourse. It was precisely for such a materialism that Marx and Engels criticised Ludwig Feuerbach—it did not go beyond 'the standpoint of the isolated individual in civil society'. Inverting Hegel, Marx arrived at

historical materialism, seeking in science (political economy)
a theory of the actual functioning and development of organised human activity and not a theory of individual motivation
(or even 'interaction'), however materialist. It was not
enough to understand that men confronted the world and
were differentiated from the rest of nature by labour. The
specific forms of development of social labour, the relations
between producers, means of production, non-producers,
etc. must be grasped in every case: 'These [social] relations
are not relations between individual and individual, but
between worker and capitalist, between farmer and landlord, etc. Wipe out these relations and you annihilate all
society.'[14] Summarising the views he had expressed in the
same book, Marx wrote to Annenkov in December 1846:

> Monsieur Proudhon has very well grasped the fact that
> men produce cloth, linen, silks, and it is a great merit on
> his part to have grasped this small amount! What he has
> not grasped is that these men, according to their powers,
> also produce the *social relations* amid which they prepare
> cloth and linen. Still less has he understood that men, who
> fashion their social relations in accordance with their
> material productivity, also fashion *ideas* and *categories*,
> that is to say the abstract ideal expression of these same
> social relations . . .

In his later work Marx gave very precise expression to the
implications of this *historical* materialism for the understanding of ideas and literature:

> In order to examine the connection between spiritual
> production and material production it is above all neces-
> sary to grasp the latter itself not as a general category but
> in *definite historical* form. Thus for example different
> kinds of spiritual production correspond to the capitalist
> mode of production and to the mode of production of the
> Middle Ages. If material production itself is not conceived
> in its *specific historical* form, it is impossible to understand
> what is specific in the spiritual production corresponding
> to it and the reciprocal influence of one on the other.[15]

[For 'what is specific in the spiritual production corresponding to it', Prawer prefers the translation 'the concrete nature of the intellectual production corresponding to it'.[16]]

Anticipating those 'scientific, Marxist critics of our own day who interpret literature as 'ideology', or as something which 'makes us see' ideology,[17] Marx made the following distinction in qualifying the passage just quoted:

> Because Storch does not conceive material production itself *historically*—because he conceives it as production of material goods in general, not as a definite historically developed and specific form of this production—he deprives himself of the basis on which alone can be understood partly the ideological component parts of the ruling class, partly the free spiritual production of this particular social formation.[18]

Let us summarise. Against those who want to reduce literature and art to ideology, it is necessary to emphasise Marx's theory of knowledge, and the fact that labour, practice, working on nature, makes the world of men and produces real knowledge. But that practice takes place in the specific forms bequeathed by past practice. To discuss literature in terms of the labour process abstracted from these specific forms would make 'impossible' an understanding of its 'concrete nature', what is 'specific' about it. Most interesting is the fact that at the point where Marx is most insistent on historical specificity, he makes a clear distinction between 'the ideological component parts of the ruling class' on the one hand, and 'the free spiritual production of this particular social formation' on the other. (Naturally, we are not proposing that these distinctions be accepted as correct simply because Marx made them. For the moment it is only a matter of establishing just what was Marx's position, showing that some 'Marxists' have misinterpreted this. The consequences are discussed in later chapters.)

Not only Marx's historical objectivity but also his understanding that men produce their own life, their social relations and their ideas, were derived from the critique of Hegel.

Hegel saw the history of mankind as the process of objectification of Spirit, of thought, and in this way he introduced practice into logic and philosophy. Now logic and philosophy must comprehend the material realisation of thought through actions. This is what Marx meant, in his *Theses on Feuerbach,* when he wrote that the 'active side', neglected by the old materialism, had been developed, though of course in abstract form, by idealism. Those who, following Althusser, want to correct Marx's and Engels' opinion about their debt to Hegel are obscuring fundamental questions—the centrality of practice and the historical objectivity which Marx understood by 'standing Hegel on his feet.'

2
The Legacy of Marx

The interpretation of the relevance of Marx's theories to literature and art is a matter of dispute not merely between Marxists and non-Marxists (sociologists, literary critics, philosophers), but has been and is still the subject of bitter controversy between those claiming to be Marxists. It will be one of the principal concerns of the present work to show that the divisions on these problems can be understood only in connection with divergences concerning the general development of the theory and practice of Marxism. Here again, these divergences are at least as significant among Marxists as between Marxists and non-Marxists. In this chapter some features of the general social and philosophical theories of Marx are outlined, in order to lay some basis for the subsequent analysis of the continuities and discontinuities in the development of Marxism and their relation to interpretations of the nature of literature.[1]

In Marxist terms these continuities and discontinuities are not simply stages in a debate or a journey of discovery, but rather moments of the long struggle to develop theory in the way that Marx conceived: in the creation of a revolutionary working-class movement. In the course of that history it has proved necessary time and again to return to and rework the basic problems of Marx's philosophy—dialectical materialism. These philosophical questions are the very ones which are at stake in comprehending the relation of Marxian theory to art and literature, and it is to them that we return in our concluding chapter. We do not mean to say, of course, that there is a 'correct' Marxist 'line' which will tell us what in literature is to be enjoyed and what is not! On the contrary, we might be led to understand better how and why the art and literature of present and past times provides such an endless variety of inspiration and enjoyment. (It would be an achievement to write a book which convinced author and reader of the enlargement of freedom to be gained from the enjoyment as well as the production of artistic works, and the consequent deliverance from sociology of literature. History, biography, philosophy and psychology would then be appreciated as a culture which enriches the receptivity of every individual to the creative work of others.)

Marx and Engels achieved a revolution in philosophy, in political economy, and in political theory. In the very nature of that transformation these fields of inquiry had to be taken beyond their previous abstract character, and could now develop as part of the self-conscious historical comprehension by men of their own present, a comprehension having as both subject and object men's own practice in changing nature and society. The rich literary culture of Marx and Engels themselves shows through in all their writings, in their style as much as in their allusions to literature in many languages. There is no doubt that they saw this literary culture as vital to the enterprise of critically appropriating and negating bourgeois civilisation. However, in contrast to their work in economics, philosophy and politics, they never worked on a Marxist 'aesthetics' or developed systematically their ideas on any branch of literature and art. Like the great revolutionaries who followed them in Russia, their responsibilities for expounding and developing the new world outlook and method, and the fact that these could in no way be separated from the tasks of revolutionary leadership, did not allow the time, if such a mundane expression may be permitted. Only Trotsky found it necessary to turn briefly to a rather more detailed treatment of these cultural questions (see Chapter 3). However, it is evident that the dialectical-materialist method and the theory of history developed by Marx and Engels have profound implications for the interpretation of literature. The first requirement is a clarification of these implications, before any interpretation of the familiar remarks in passing made by Marx and Engels.

Marx followed Hegel and all the great German Enlightenment thinkers, not to mention Rousseau, in his conviction that capitalist society was fundamentally hostile to art. It is possible, however, to over-emphasise the continuity between the Enlightenment and Marx in this matter, so that such questions as 'What are the possibilities for literature under capitalism?' and 'In what sense can capitalism give rise to its own characteristic literary form, the novel?' appear insoluble. It is only on the basis of what was original and distinctive in Marx's view of modern society that such questions may be posed in historical terms, through a consistent critique of the consequences of class society rather than through declarations for humanism in the manner of Rousseau or later Romantic critics. Nor was Marx satisfied with Hegel's demonstration of the *logical* necessity of the attainment of the rule of true morality by self-consciousness, in which the Spirit transcended the manifest contradiction between 'civil society' and art.[2]

Marx, as a materialist dialectician, conceived of the 'transcending' *(Aufhebung)* of capitalist alienation as a necessity born of objective contradictions, to be effected by an objective revolutionary force produced by these very contradictions and not simply by mastering them in consciousness, from the outside. If we pursue the implications of this standpoint for our present concerns, we can dispense with the eternal arguments about the word 'reflection', which Marx himself did not use in relation to literature and art. Art does not 'reflect' a given class structure such as capitalism. It is a product of the men thrown into struggle by the specific contradictions of the given social formation. In their literature and art men do not produce some mysteriously congruent copy of the social structure; rather they express the content of the fundamental struggle with nature and with their own nature which that society, at its particular stage of development, carries forward or inhibits, or does both at the same time. They express the struggle for consciousness of what they must do to survive against the dangers of these particular contradictions, whether they can be overcome or merely resisted with nobility. They express the frustrations that arise and achievements made in defining and tracking down the enemies who must be overcome. They educate the sentiments necessary to continue to live but at the same time rise above the everyday ideological conceptualisation of experience, and where necessary carry through revolutions.

Understanding literature and art and the nature of their appeal from the Marxist standpoint, therefore, means first to bring into as sharp a focus as possible the specific character of social relations, including the relation between society and individual, in each social formation, and in particular capitalism, to the analysis of which Marx's scientific endeavour was primarily devoted. One aspect of this, among several which have been misunderstood or given a completely wrong emphasis by 'Marxist' literary critics, is that Marx's view of the specificity of capitalist social relations is one which is not merely individual—contemplative but is itself historical; it is engaged; it is 'the standpoint of socialised humanity' *(Theses on Feuerbach)*; it is the viewpoint of the class of direct producers who must abolish class society, armed with an objective understanding of its historical contradictions. For this reason any outline of Marx's distinctive characterisation of capitalist society and its specific type of 'individuality' must indicate clearly what is meant by the standpoint of the proletariat. It will be argued that this question is of paramount importance in explaining the limitations and contradictions of the systems developed by Lukács and Goldmann as well as other, more recent professed disciples of Marx of a structuralist persuasion.

When Schiller, Goethe, Lessing, Hegel and other writers of the Enlightenment looked to the city—state of Classical Greece, it was not only to find the model for art but for the social relations which could provide individuals with the possibility of producing and appreciating such art. However, the social and historical outlook of these men did not go beyond a philosophical equivalent of the political and social ideals of the French Revolution of 1789. German philosophy was able to take to its furthest limit this world view, even laying bare many of its contradictions, but the same German social and political backwardness which concentrated the concerns of the intelligentsia into philosophical abstractions also inhibited any break from these abstractions to the historically concrete contradictions of capitalism. Marx saw all the insights of German philosophy, culminating in Hegel, imprisoned in the dead system of idealism. Marx's concept of the social revolution to end capitalism was not in any way separate from his verdict on the essential abstractness of the appeal to antiquity by these German idealist philosophers:

> The all-round realisation of the individual will only cease to be conceived as an ideal, a vocation, etc., when the impact of the world which stimulates the real development of the individual is under the control of the individuals themselves, as the communists desire.[3]

Paradoxically, then, the assertion, against the capitalist division of labour, of the ideal of the all-round development of the individual by the German Enlightenment was at the same time, by virtue of its very abstract and 'ideal' character, itself a product of the capitalist ideology, reflecting as it did social relations which dominate the individual as forces alienated from him in the form of his own product, the commodity, its obedience to the laws of the market, its transformation into capital, which stands over and against the producers, etc. According to Marx, the only way in which the heritage of classical civilisation could actually be rescued, reappropriated, and developed on a higher level, was through a revolution in which men placed themselves in a position to control their own historical destiny. In this passage (in 1845) Marx and Engels write in a very exact, deliberate and uncharacteristically pedantic style, in order to state everything in terms which (as they expressed it later, looking back on the text) settled their philosophic conscience. Thus Marx's materialism is here very explicit ('the world which stimulates the real development of the individual') and is shown to be in its implications the very opposite of an external and rigid determinism: 'the individuals themselves' are in a concrete and developing way responsible for and must come to control the 'world' and its 'impact'.

It was the same concept of man as producer of his own world (of course under conditions that were not matters of his choice) which informed Marx's entirely original theory of revolution. He did not proceed from the conspiratorial method of the Blanquists, who thought (and acted as if) individual enlightenment, heroism and organisational skill on the part of a tiny minority (whose acquisition of these qualities remained totally unexplained) could liberate the benighted masses from the weight of oppression. This was no different in essence from the old Utopian socialists' model communities and hope of socialism through moral education. Behind Marx's aphorism, 'The emancipation of the working class is the task of the working class alone', lay a philosophical revolution. For Marx capitalist economy produced the material preconditions for classless society, and it produced the class of men who would be forced by exploitation to overthrow it. But there remained the question of how the new men and women to build the communist society of the future would be made, if 'the individual's real development', as Marx himself put it, is the product of the 'impact of the (present) world'? How could men formed by the conditions of capitalist production and ideology consciously create a society based on collectivist norms? Clearly Marx could not proceed from a theory which simply saw men as the product of something called 'the environment'. Marx's scientific socialism meant a break with mechanical materialism:

> Both for the production on a large scale of this communist consciousness, and for the success of the cause itself, the alteration of men on a mass scale is necessary, an alteration which can only take place in a practical movement, a *revolution*; the revolution is necessary, therefore, not only because the *ruling* class cannot be overthrown in any other way, but also because the class *overthrowing* it can only in a revolution succeed in ridding itself of all the muck of ages and become fitted to found society anew.[4]

These are not isolated remarks about revolution, but are integral to the whole development of Marx's philosophy and conception of history. As we have seen, these assertions about revolution also connect directly to his critique of those idealist theories which contrasted the inimical relations between capitalist society and art with the classical ideal. At the very least, it is difficult to see how there could be a Marxist theory of literature and art which did not place the revolutionary role of the working class at its centre. Yet this is the case with Goldmann, Adorno and, in different ways, Lukács. It is not just that their actual positions on political questions involved the rejection of that role. Even more important is the fact that their interpretation of literary works tends always to be in terms of a closed system of a reified structure of thought imposed on all the members of a social class or even of a whole society. Such a view will oscillate between seeing the working class as a particular interest group with an 'ideology' of its own—like the oppositional and therefore one-sided world view attributed to it and to Marxism by Karl Mannheim[5] — and conceiving of the working class as a helpless victim of the fetishism and reification of bourgeois ideology. The latter idea can predominate whether its advocate is formally 'orthodox' in affirming in general the revolutionary role of the proletariat (Lukács) or openly rejects it (Goldmann).

Marx entertained no such notion of an ideological straitjacket. Whatever the constrictions of bourgeois ideology, he saw as decisive its disruption by developments in the material base upon which it depended:

> Since the abstraction of all humanity, even of the semblance of humanity, is practically complete in the full-grown proletariat; since the conditions of life of the proletariat sum up all the conditions of life of society today in all their inhuman acuity; since man has lost himself in the proletariat, yet at the same time has not only gained theoretical consciousness of that loss, but through urgent, no longer disguisable, absolutely imperative need — that practical expression of necessity—*is driven directly to revolt* against that inhumanity; it follows that the proletariat can and must free itself.[6]

By 'the standpoint of socialised humanity' and of the proletariat, then, Marx meant to say that living experience of the dehumanisation caused by capitalist exploitation and division of labour produced at the same time a recognition in theory and practice of the destructive limits of capitalism and of the necessity of revolution. And this 'criticism of weapons' (i.e., an actual revolutionary overturn) would be the real matrix of the criticism of capitalist culture, in contrast to the 'weapon or criticism', the moralising protests of the idealists:

> The criticism of the French and the English is not an abstract, preternatural personality outside mankind; it is the real human activity of individuals who are active members of society and who suffer, feel, think and act as human beings. That is why their criticism is at the same time practical, their communism a socialism which gives practical concrete measures and in which they do not just think but act even more, it is the living real criticism of existing society, the discovery of the causes of 'the decay'.[7]

Thus the working class, not for moral reasons but by compulsion, *rejects* the rule of reification, rejects capitalism's reduction of men to the commodity labour-power, to a thing, rejects the illusory freedom arising from the free sale of labour-power, and proceeds to assert the rights of labour as 'the *living source* of value'[8] (thus not as the 'contribution' of a one-sided element in the total society or 'factor of production' with its own partial point of view).

Working his way out of the idealist shell in which was contained the 'rational kernel' of Hegel's philosophy—the dialectic, the understanding of the world as a complex of internally contradictory and interrelated processes, the historical world as the product of human activity—Marx had been able to extract from French political life and thought and historiography, and from English political economy and the workers' movement, the notion of the revolutionary role of the proletariat. From this standpoint he was able to criticise and go beyond not only the abstractness and even mysticism of German idealist philosophy but also the mechanical determinism of Feuerbach and all previous materialism. When Marx seemed to follow Hegel and Schiller in summoning up the classical ideal in art against capitalism, it was from the standpoint of this new outlook, which embraced human purposeful activity in a fashion which was quite alien to either idealism or the existing materialism. It is not difficult to conceive of the magnitude of the implications for theories of art and literature, if Marx was right in now grasping intellectually what, according to Max Raphael, 'Goya had already seen, viz., that the course of history can be changed only by historical means and only if men shape their own history instead of acting as the automatons of an earthly power or an allegedly eternal idea'.[9]

If we now turn to Marx's characterisation of capitalist social relations as relations inimical to artistic production, it is easy to fall into the trap of seeing only the oppressive, objective, almost 'natural' character of these relations and their ideological effects. This impression arises especially because we have to hand all Marx's completed work on political economy, without any similarly detailed work on society's totality. It must always be borne in mind that Marx's work is essentially dialectical. The central contradiction in capitalist society is that between the productive forces, increasingly socialised in their operation, and the social relations of production in which private appropriation is increasingly concentrated and centralised in private hands. Of these productive forces, more and more fettered by the outmoded social relations, the most important is the class of direct producers itself. Destructive of the conditions for artistic production, capitalism nevertheless, and by the same token, breeds as its necessary condition the class which can have no other future than the destruction of capitalism, the reappropriation by society of the means of material production and also of the whole cultural heritage of mankind. Because capitalism's own laws demand the development of the means of production, so the modern industrial working class must be produced. The consequent polarisation of society is the source of the process leading to revolution and thence to freedom. But this relation between capitalist and worker

> . . . develops more purely and adequately in proportion as labour loses all the characteristics of art; as its particular skill becomes something more and more abstract and irrelevant, and as it becomes more and more a purely

abstract activity, a purely mechanical activity, hence indifferent to its particular form.[10]

It was this concept of abstract labour which Marx was to develop as fundamental to his analysis in *Capital*, Volume I. It represents the most succinct expression of the historical meaning which Marx gave to the traditional aesthetic criticism of early capitalism. He leaves romanticism far behind by his recognition of the necessity and progressive character of capitalist development. And he locates the origin of capitalism's hostility to art in its most basic social relations of production, the transformation of labour-power into a commodity, rather than simply describing, with however fine a sensibility, the artist's separation from his fellow men and the evils of commercialisation. Henceforward the criticism is not abstract. These relations of production contain objective contradictions which must eventually prove insoluble, resulting in a situation where the productive relations as a whole come into conflict with the further development of the productive forces. And at the heart of the living contradictions, the working class is led by its necessary struggles to assume the role of executioner of the old social order.

It was as early as 1845 that Marx and Engels concluded that 'the key to the anatomy of civil society was to be found in political economy'. While never ceasing to participate in and study the experience of the working class in its struggles, Marx henceforward laboured to the end of his days at the scientific investigation of capitalist economy. By so doing he uncovered the material basis of the moral and cultural problems so compellingly described by his idealist predecessors. The transformation of the negative moral and cultural consequences of capitalism could then be understood as dependent upon the overcoming of the internal contradictions in these material conditions which produced them, rather than in some moral rearming of men. In the best-known example Marx acknowledges that the criticism of religion is 'the beginning of all criticism', but he wants to say above all else that no amount of freethinking 'criticism' will alter the fact that religion is produced by real-life conditions and has a hold upon men. This reality depends upon the continuation

of a social condition in which men's destiny escapes their
control. Thus religion is 'the spirit of unspiritual conditions . . .
the cry of the oppressed creature'. It is not enough to explain
that this is the case. Scientific understanding consists
in grasping the nature of that force within those 'unspiritual
conditions' that will necessarily abolish them. This is only
one aspect of Marx's attitude to the whole question of the
possibility of the formation of an integrated human personality in contrast to the alienation produced by capitalism.

Marx found a social–historical explanation for the phenomenon remarked by Hegel: that modern society provided no
basis for epic poetry, with its 'action ramified into the whole
of its age', combining 'an underlying community of objective
life and action' with 'freedom in this action and life'.[11]
Hegel's closed system, the inevitable consequence of his idealism, could end only in resignation to the necessity of the modern state and economy. Marx exploded the contradictions
in this state and economy and in Hegel's concepts of them.
Hegel saw the resolution of the contradiction he had described as an ideal resolution, i.e. one which takes place in
consciousness, by art's 'recognising' that it cannot reject the
necessity of modern institutions, and particularly the state.
The resignation of art follows necessarily from the self-
consciousness of the necessity of reconciling the ignoble real
individual of the real bourgeois world of competition to the
state as realisation of the social ideal. It is characteristic of
Marx's materialist dialectic that it cannot be so easily satisfied. If contradictions are essentially logical and ideal rather
than material, then 'resolution' presents less difficulty. The
resolution of contradictions of a material character, however,
can result only from the working through of the actual conflict of real opposites, interconnected with all other contradictory processes, and in no way simply from a demonstration
of the necessity of resolution. Once having set foot upon the
road, philosophically, of 'standing Hegel on his feet', Marx
could not avoid arriving very soon at the point where the
contradiction between the ideal state of abstractly equal
citizens (i.e., they are equal in so far as one abstracts from
everything except their political rights, their citizenship) and
the material world of bourgeois or 'civil' society could be

resolved only in a struggle of material forces necessarily thrown into mutual relations of unity and conflict by this society.

Marx did not exactly think out the philosophy first and then apply it to politics. As a 'Left Hegelian', he participated in all the ideological struggles which sought to hammer out the basis of a democratic movement in the Germany of 1841–3. Investigating the reasons for the conservative conclusions of Hegel's philosophy of law and the state, he was led to the conclusion that the contradiction between the democratic state which truly represented humanity and the dehumanising private property at the basis of social life must be *abolished* rather than reconciled. This was the point at which the transition from a revolutionary–democratic standpoint to a proletarian–communist one was inescapably posed. Now the discovery that Hegel's notion of the work of the self-alienating Absolute Spirit was an inversion of the practical revolutionising of conditions by humanity's social labour was within Marx's grasp. It is not difficult to see that up to this point the democratic and humanist view of society and the state could be satisfied with the aesthetics of a Schiller, a Goethe or a Hegel, with their appeal to the classical ideal of integral individuality and the *polis*. But now was developed a theory insisting on the recognition of the historical *necessity* of those social relations which had produced the modern split between public and private life, the isolation of the artist from his life-blood in the community, the dehumanising capitalist social division of labour; and which at the same time directed itself to the forces necessarily destroying those relations from within. There was no avoiding a complete revaluation of the old aesthetics if this historical materialist dialectic were true. It would provide the basis for an entirely original interpretation of the relation of art to society; and it would pose in new ways the question of the possible direction, limits and possibilities of art under capitalism. It raised also the question of what new paths were opened up for art if and in so far as both producers and consumers of art and literature absorbed the new outlook. Marx and Engels, as we have said, did not carry out the specialised work necessary to clarify these matters. But they

did a great deal more than give a general philosophical outline of the dialectical materialist method and outlook. Their
analysis of capitalist social relations, and particularly of the
relation of the individual to society, provides invaluable
pointers to the solution of the many still undeveloped
problems of a Marxist theory of art and literature. (Once
again, however, it is necessary to put up a warning sign: do
not mistake these results of Marx's specialised scientific
investigation, these detailed characterisations of capitalist
social relations and their ideological reflections, for some
purely external and objective reality standing outside men
and patterning their 'intellectual production'. To see the
actual relation between the two, we would need to elaborate
Marx's ideas on cognition and consciousness, on class struggle
and revolution, in the same detail as Marx developed the
socio-economic analysis of capitalism.)

Istvån Mészåros[12] has demonstrated the aesthetic aspects
of Marx's concept of alienation, as elaborated in the *Economic
and Philosophical Manuscripts of 1844*.[13] In the latter we
find the first extended presentation of Marx's ideas at the
time of his break from Hegel and revolutionary—democratic
ideals. He follows the idealists in seeing the 'abstractness' and
'rationality' of bourgeois relations as negating the concreteness and particularity demanded of art, but he already defines
the proletariat as not only a victim of alienation but also a
force impelled to revolutionise society. Marx begins in 1844
to discuss the character of labour when it assumes the 'estranged' form required by capitalism, but his critique remains
somewhat abstract. It cannot yet demonstrate the laws of
development of this labour, but all the same Marx even at
this stage insists on certain characteristics of human labour
which are central to his concerns in *Capital*[14] more than 20
years later. Truly, says Marx in the *1844 Manuscripts,* man is
that natural being whose 'life-activity' is *'productive life'* or
'life-engendering life'. This production is 'free, conscious
activity', i.e., it is distinguished from the activity of other
animals by virtue of its flowing from his decision, purpose
and plan, rather than from his physical nature—he has physical needs, but these are always mediated by a man-made
world in terms of which he makes decisions and plans and

utilises implements fashioned from nature—and it is 'free' in the sense of the same absence of direct dependence on physical need and inborn capacity to satisfy it.

In the condition of alienation—estranged labour—men are compelled to work, to produce, in order to survive physically, to perpetuate their animal existence. Consumption becomes an animal, de-socialised appropriation, instead of an act which is expressive of the historically gained ('educated') needs of men, in a dialectical unity with planned, co-operative, and at the same time richly individualised, production. Men can perceive, reflect upon, understand and act upon, and change their mode of being as a species, which is their mode of productive labour. In the animal the individual is one with its species, in unbroken identity with it. The individual's character as a member of the species is genetically determined, not subject in any way to conscious control or change or development in the life of the member of the species. Should the physical character of the animal be capable of acquiring new characteristics, these cannot be transmitted to the next generation, cannot become properties of the species. If there are animals which in a certain sense may be said to 'produce', this does not change the essentials:

> . . . an animal only produces what it immediately needs for itself and its young. It produces one-sidedly, whilst man produces *universally*. It produces only under the dominion of immediate physical need, whilst man produces even when he is free from physical need and only truly produces in freedom therefrom. An animal produces only itself, whilst man reproduces the whole of nature. An animal's product belongs immediately to its physical body, whilst man freely confronts his product. An animal forms things in accordance with the standard and the need of the species to which it belongs, whilst man knows how to produce in accordance with the standard of every species, and knows how to apply everywhere the inherent standard to the object. Man therefore also forms things in accordance with the laws of beauty.[15]

Consequently, a society based on estranged labour must be

totally hostile to the 'forming of things in accordance with the laws of beauty'. In such a society alienation ensures that man's productive activity is grasped by his consciousness, and is consciously pursued, and the product appropriated and consumed, as *means* only—means to the end of individual physical survival or satisfaction. Here men are denied the birthright they won in their advance from the animal.

Elsewhere in his book Mészáros shows that Marx's later work on political economy was a more concrete development and not a rejection of the early concept of alienation, but in considering the aesthetic implications of the theory of alienation he confines himself, strictly in accordance with the task he has undertaken, to the *1844 Manuscripts.* In these essays Marx tends still to write in terms of 'man', his natural being and his 'needs', rather than the 'men in definite historical relations', the individual as 'the totality of his social relations', as a member of a definite class, etc., which predominate after the critique of Feuerbach is completed.[16] In 1844 it had hardly begun. (It must at the same time be accepted that Mészáros and others are right to point out that even within much of the terminology of Feuerbach, which he retains in the *Manuscripts,* Marx already goes beyond many of Feuerbach's conceptions: his viewpoint is already historical; his concept of alienation is primarily that of the alienation of the labourer in a specific society and economy, as against Feuerbach's alienation of the 'generic' human individual; he sees that only a real revolution can put an end to alienation; and this latter conclusion is characteristic of the centrality of practice throughout this work, in contrast to Feuerbach's 'contemplative' materialism.)

The continuity between these early writings and *Capital* is illuminated by a consideration of the notes and rough drafts which Marx made in preparation for his major work.[17] If the *1844 Manuscripts* showed how the individual in capitalist society was cut off from fulfilling his true nature as producer, these notes of 1857—8, together with the three volumes of *Capital,* remove any basis which had been left in 1844 for a speculative view of 'human nature': 'human beings become individuals only through the process of history . . .'[18] In every historical form of society a particular type of individuality develops, and only in the most primitive societies was man a 'species being' *(Gattungswesen).* This latter term, taken from Feuerbach and used in 1844 to represent something like the essence of man as a socially producing animal, is now firmly placed historically:

> He [man] appears originally as a species-being [*Gattungswesen*] ,clan being, herd animal—although in no way whatever as a *zoon politikon* in the political sense. Exchange itself is a chief means of this individuation [*Vereinzelung*]. It makes the herd-like existence superfluous and dissolves it. Soon the matter [has] turned in such a way that as an individual he relates himself only to himself, while the means with which he posits himself as individual have become the making of his generality and commonness. In this community, the objective being of the individual as proprietor, say proprietor of land, is presupposed, and presupposed moreover under certain conditions which chain him to the community, or rather form a link in his chain. In bourgeois society, the worker e.g. stands there purely without objectivity, subjectively; but the thing which stands opposite him has now become the true community [*Gemeinwesen*], which he tries to make a meal of, and which makes a meal of him.[19]

It seems clear that, in discussing the human needs of real individuals as part of the consideration of aesthetic value, Marxists should proceed from these historically particular individualities, and that the only general concepts of aesthetic meaning would have to be abstracted and generalised from the contradictory development of these forms, and not deduced, in the manner of Lukács, from the general nature of man as producer.[20] This historically concrete concept of human individuality is not simply a notion for analysing past social formations. If it corresponds to reality, it provides a starting point (a considerable step forward from the *1844 Manuscripts)* for a conception of the conditions for going beyond the destructiveness of capitalism in relation to art.

Thus:

> It has been said and may be said that this is precisely the
> beauty and the greatness of it: this spontaneous intercon-
> nection, this material and mental metabolism which is
> independent of the knowing and willing of individuals,
> and which presupposes their reciprocal independence and
> indifference. And, certainly, this objective connection is
> preferable to the lack of any connection, or to a merely
> local connection resting on blood ties, or on primeval,
> natural or master-servant relations. Equally certain is it
> that individuals cannot gain mastery over their own social
> interconnections before they have created them. But it
> is an insipid notion to conceive of this merely objective
> bond as a spontaneous, natural attribute inherent in indi-
> viduals and inseparable from their nature (in antithesis to
> their conscious knowing and willing). This bond is their
> product. It is a historic product. It belongs to a specific
> phase of their development. The alien and independent
> character in which it presently exists vis-à-vis individuals
> proves only that the latter are still engaged in the creation
> of the conditions of their social life, and that they have
> not yet begun, on the basis of these conditions, to live it.
> It is the bond natural to individuals within specific and
> limited relations of production. Universally developed
> individuals, whose social relations, as their own communal
> [gemeinschaftlich] relations, are hence also subordinated
> to their own communal control, are no product of nature,
> but of history. The degree and the universality of the
> development of wealth where this individuality becomes
> possible supposes production on the basis of exchange
> values as a prior condition, whose universality produces
> not only the alienation of the individual from himself and
> from others, but also the universality and the compre-
> hensiveness of his relations and capacities.[21]

The hostile environment which capitalism provided for art
and literature was not a matter of particular institutions in
capitalist societies, which after all might be reformed in accordance with moral or aesthetic standards. Nor was it neces-

sary to rest content only with the kind of 'cultural criticism' which saw the rational and calculating spirit of capitalism as the source of the unfavourable climate for art. What produced and sustained these 'negative' features of capitalism in relation to art? If Schiller and Goethe were right in seeing that society no longer provided the kind of relation between artist and people that existed in the Greek *polis*, why was that so? Marx proposed that the *political economy* of capitalism provided the key:

> The reciprocal and all-sided dependence of individuals who are indifferent to one another forms their social connection. This social bond is expressed in exchange value, by means of which alone each individual's own activity or his product becomes an activity and a product for him; he must produce a general product—exchange value, or, the latter isolated for itself and individualized, money. On the other side, the power which each individual exercises over the activity of others or over social wealth exists in him as the owner of exchange values, of money. The individual carries his social power, as well as his bond with society, in his pocket. Activity, regardless of its individual manifestation, and the product of activity, regardless of its particular make-up, are always exchange value, and exchange value is a generality, in which all individuality and peculiarity are negated and extinguished.[22]

It becomes clear that the social order, the world of his own products which is and appears totally alien to the individual, is *at the same time* the accumulation of all the conditions for men's collective appropriation and conscious control of the means of production and the product. In the desperate and culturally impoverished situation of the individual vis-à-vis the 'community' is concentrated and expressed in inverted form the fundamental contradiction of capitalist society: between socialised production and individual ownership and •appropriation. What Marx called the accumulation of misery at one pole of society is the condemnation of the vast majority to the position of propertyless labourers subjected to the 'abstract' requirements of capital and its augmentation. And yet the same capital—'dead labour dominating living labour'—is, when transformed into machines, supply of energy, raw materials, and human labour-power itself in the expenditure of wages, the very form in which the conditions for the next decisive step in men's control of the world (with all that that implies for human freedom and the development of art) must develop:

> Nature builds no machines, no locomotives, railways, electric telegraphs, self-acting mules etc. These are products of human industry; natural material transformed into organs of the human will over nature, or of human participation in nature. They are organs of the human brain, created by the human hand; the power of knowledge, objectified. The development of fixed capital indicates to what degree general social knowledge has become a direct force of production, and to what degree, hence, the conditions of the process of social life itself have come under the control of the general intellect and been transformed in accordance with it. To what degree the powers of social production have been produced, not only in the form of knowledge, but also as immediate organs of social practice, of the real life process.[23]

From Marx's scientific and historical analysis it emerges that the dehumanisation wrought by capitalist development is at the same time a by-product of the hidden process of accumulation of just those conditions which must eventually allow for the victory of human freedom. This contradictory historical process in the economic foundations of society is not apparent in the everyday reflection ideologically of capitalist social relations. Indeed, entirely opposite conclusions suggest themselves. Their form may be an ignorant optimism, a naive reforming criticism, or a pessimistic despair which finds itself more and more confirmed by experience. The individual's relation to society is obscured by the objective from that relation assumes: 'Labour on the basis of exchange values presupposes, precisely, that neither the labour of the individual nor his product are *directly* general; that the product attains this form only by passing through an *objective mediation*, by means of a form of *money* distinct from itself.'[24]

This objective mediator and its powers are the developed form of value, the form which every product assumes. Having shown in the *Grundrisse* that 'labour on the basis of exchange values' produced a specific type of individuality, Marx proceeded in *Capital* with a method about which he was later very explicit. He started with the elementary form taken by the product of labour in the specific society: the commodity, the economic cell-form of bourgeois society.[25] In dissecting the value form Marx was setting out to expose in its essentials the 'germ' of the development of capitalism, its functioning and its demise. If Marx was right, that the value form must abstract from all qualitative and concrete considerations in order to establish the comparability, the relations, and the mutual transformations of all products, and of humans themselves as repositories of the commodity labour-power, then all the consequences for art need to be posed. The ideological conceptions necessitated by such a mode of production must clash with any true objectivity, let alone any independent aesthetic evaluation or consumption of objects. What 'value' will be placed on the independent struggle of the artist to master the reality he sees? Who will pay him, and on what basis? Time? Volume of production? Demand and supply of the product? Will not perception itself (that of the artist and of the audience) be altered? And, perhaps most important, if works of art are deemed possible, must they not rise to the height of inventiveness in finding ways to represent not only what the eye sees but also the necessity of a struggle against the prison of the value form (i.e. of bourgeois society)?

In the absence of laboratory conditions and equipment, says Marx in his foreword to *Capital*, Volume I, it is necessary to resort to abstractions in the analysis of economic forms. By such an 'abstract' analysis of the commodity and its value form Marx was able to expose the *necessary* character of the actual forms of appearance of the social relations and forms of objectivity of capitalism. (The artist must work through and against these forms if he is to produce artistic forms adequate to the contradictory content.) Here we sum-

marise some of the most important steps in Marx's argument
and the conclusions which emerged.[26]

The commodity, one of millions produced every minute
as the only form the product of labour can take under
capitalism, is in reality not the simple thing it appears but a
unity of opposites. It is at the same time object of use (use-
value) and bearer of exchange-value. This exchange-value (the
commodity's interchangeability in definite proportions with
all others, regardless of their physical nature) is shown to be
a 'form of appearance' of the common substance of all
commodities, viz., their 'value'. The value of the commodity
means quantity of socially necessary labour (measured in
time) required for its production. The labour producing commodities also has a dual character, two mutually contradictory sides: it is at the same time a concrete labour (tail-
oring, coalmining, etc.) directed at the making of a particular
use-value (coat, coal, etc.), and abstract labour, by which is
meant labour considered as the expenditure of human labour-
power as such.

The value form develops to the point where the commodity's value appears in the form of another commodity considered only as use-value. That is to say, the value of a piece
of cloth cannot be expressed in cloth. For its value to be
represented there must be another use-value whose purpose
at this point is simply to represent the value of the first
commodity. A definite quantum of the total social labour
is thus transmuted into a property of a piece of metal or of a
yard of cloth. Value, which appears in every exchange
throughout social life, is actually a relation between producers—a social relation of production—but enters consciousness
as a property of things. This is why Marx calls it fetishism.
At the same time, the mutual relations and interdependence
of the producers are achieved only 'after the fact', in the
exchange of products. Here is a world in which things, commodities, have the capacity to demand behaviour of each
other which has nothing to do with their physical nature,
similarities, interdependences; and men and women themselves are drawn into just such relations with these same
commodities and with each other through them. The deter-
minant of these relations is value. The value relations are

historically determinate relations between producers whose separate and qualitatively distinct labours have been equalised, so that time can measure them against each other. But, again, the labours thus equated appear in social life only as a 'social—natural property' of material things, of products in exchange. 'As exchange-values, all commodities are but definite measures of *congealed labour-time*.'[27]

Capitalist social life must have its particular effects on perception, and this can hardly be outside the concern of the artist or writer. Within 'the phantasmagoric form of a relationship of things' is the content of a 'historically determined social relationship of men'. The human hand produces things which then 'appear like independent structures endowed with their own life and standing in relationship to one another and to men'. If religious belief and ritual, with the attendant fetishism and conferment of mystical powers on material objects, produced a characteristic art, what will capitalism's 'fetishism' bring forth? Is it not necessary to rethink the definition of the 'capitalist spirit' as essentially rationalist? And if capitalist rationality is cast aside as the explanation for the decline of great art, what replaces it? May it not be that it is the irrationalism, the peculiar abstractness of capitalist social relations, of which rationality and accounting of time, money and energy are only the macabre completion, which creates such difficulties for the artist's pursuit of beauty and truth? How, after all, shall a man find his place in this society and in relation to nature? He would have to penetrate that actually existing shell of social relations where, for every product, 'it is as commodity that it is a citizen of the world' (i.e., it relates to the social world not by virtue of its qualities but as value, excluding thereby the 'universal standards' and 'laws of beauty' suggested by Marx). The same goes for the commodity labour-power; and for the man who is reduced to a unit of labour-power, it is as commodity (and not as a man) that he is a citizen of this world.

When Marx uncovered this truth did he say any less than all those theorists of the novel who see it as the expression of the individual's search for authentic values in a world of degraded values? This is only one of the questions suggested by this small though fundamental part of *Capital*. One should hold fast to the essential development made by Marx in comparison with the *1844 Manuscripts*. There Marx had described the way in which capital accumulated to oppress the worker, who was reduced to a commodity but at the same time provoked to revolt. Now Marx proceeds, beginning with the analysis of the commodity and the value form, to demonstrate the necessity of the development of capitalism and of the revolution to overthrow it. There are Marxist interpreters of literature and art who find the structure of commodity exchange very exciting but are singularly uninterested in this achievement of Marx, which surely has even wider and deeper implications for art, as for humanity's whole future, than the structure of the value form taken as a thing in itself.

We refer only briefly to the precision which Marx was now able to give in *Capital* to the dialectic of the ideological reflection of capitalist economy. From the analysis of the value form, money, abstract and concrete labour, the production of surplus value, and the wages system, Marx could demonstrate clearly the basis in social relations of production of those characteristics of the state and civil society with which he had been centrally concerned in his transition from revolutionary democracy to communism ('The relations between capital and labour, the axis on which our entire present system of society turns' [Engels]). All the illusions of freedom and citizenship in politics, law and ideology in general could now be seen as derived from one objective relation. The wage-worker appears on the market as a free agent, selling his labour-power, the only commodity he has for sale, at its value, as one might sell any other commodity. He is paid as if for his labour:

> Hence, we may understand the decisive importance of the transformation of value and price of labour-power into the form of wages, or into the value and price of labour itself. This phenomenal form, which makes the actual relation invisible, and, indeed, shows the direct opposite of that relation, forms the basis of all the juridical notions of both labourer and capitalist, of all the mystifications of the capitalist mode of production, of all its illusions as

to liberty, of all the apologetic shifts of the vulgar economists.[28]

The reality concealed by the transformation of value and price of labour-power into the form of value and price of labour is that the monopoly of ownership in the capitalist class creates a situation of compulsion, exploitation, oppression. The appropriation of the value produced by the worker's labour, which includes the element of surplus value (i.e. that value produced in excess of the value required to replace what was expended in wages), is hidden by the formal equality of the exchange relationship in which labour itself appears to be bought and sold. Here lay the secret of the division between public (state) and private (social–economic) life. It cannot be healed by moral or intellectual efforts, nor can it be repaired by political reform. Only the self-movement of the economic contradiction from which it derives, through the class struggle it inevitably produces, can abolish the division.

The first volume of *Capital* is concerned only with the process of capitalist production. It is in the unfinished Volume III that Marx approaches the characterisation of the capitalist system as a whole, a unity within whose contradictory development the explanation of everyday phenomena, including the phenomena of consciousness, might be explicated. The developed forms of capital and capitalist exploitation result in a 'perfected' ideological inversion of reality to justify them. A Marxist would hardly know where to begin in discussing with, say, Talcott Parsons, who looked on the role of the artist[29] in such a way as to consider the means of 'rewarding' him as a datum, somehow part of the *modus operandi* of the 'central value system', which is the principal means of societies' continuing as systems and defining themselves one against another.[30] What Marx showed was that a definite series of social and ideological relationships was involved before the specific mode of either the 'orientation' or the 'reward' of the artist or writer could be understood. Should these original relations and mediations be obscured from view, as in an analysis of the Parsons type, then what results is an ideological reflection and defence of the basic relations rather than their scientific explanation. The revenues of the classes in capitalist society, and, at a secondary level, the subsequent distribution of incomes, appear to be straightforward 'functional' rewards for particular roles which have resulted from what sociologists call 'differentiation'. The functions of these roles are ultimately in terms of perpetuation of some 'central value system' or normative structure. Marx showed how the main classes (capitalists, wage-labourers and landlords) had been produced by a particular historical development from the break-up of feudalism. In the resulting situation, the form of appearance is that,

> . . . capital attracts to the capitalist, in the form of profit, a portion of the surplus-value extracted by him from labour, . . . monopoly in land attracts for the landlord another portion in the form of rent; and . . . labour grants the labourer the remaining portion of value in the form of wages.[31]

All this, together with the way that the rate of surplus value is transformed into a 'rate of profit' on business investment, make more definite and pronounced the inversion which was already inherent in the basic production relations, where 'the subjective productive forces of labour appear as productive forces of capital'.[32] The results of production must be realised in the sphere of circulation:

> But in reality this sphere is the sphere of competition, which, considered in each individual case, is dominated by chance; where, then, the inner law, which prevails in these accidents and regulates them, is only visible when these accidents are grouped together in large numbers, where it remains, therefore, invisible and unintelligible to the individual agents in production. But furthermore: the actual process of production, as a unity of the direct production process and the circulation process, gives rise to new formations, in which the vein of internal connections is increasingly lost, the production relations are rendered independent of one another, and the component

values become ossified into forms independent of one another.[33]

The sociologists' explanation of the structure of modern society is not one whit different in character from the work of the vulgar economists of the last century, doing no more than repeat the everyday ideological illusions of consciousness and 'arranging them in a certain rational order' which 'simultaneously corresponds to the interests of the ruling classes by proclaiming the physical necessity and eternal justification of their sources of revenue and elevating them to a dogma'.[34]

If Marx was right in his concretisation of the notion that the capitalist order of society and artistic production were mutually antagonistic and in his verdict on the 'apologetic' character of bourgeois social science, then it is clear that sociology is not merely unable to develop a theory of the social relations of art and literature, but is actually a self-justification of those social conditions which militate against art and literature. 'Sociology' can only defend and rationalise those very components of the novel which for the novelist are only starting points to be shattered if his work is to move from mere repetitive mirroring of the forms of appearance to the contradictory whole constituted by essence *and* its necessary and obscuring appearance.

Those interpreters of Marx who explicitly view literature as ideology (or as a production which works on and enables us to see ideology), including those who do not go beyond the structure of class consciousness in defining the 'world' of creative works, have as one of their sources a rejection of Marx's materialism: they tend to sever social relations (and ideology) from the active relation between men and the rest of nature. The meaning of Marx's demonstration of the inversion of the subject—object relation in capitalism is not that the subject finds himself in no position to get a correct conception of the actual relations. One might be forgiven for thinking that that was all that was involved, after listening to the advocates of 'demystification' of ideology, 'as though it were a question of the dialectical reconciliation of concepts and not of the resolution of actually existing conditions', as

Marx put it in a slightly different context. Marx's target is not the self-consciousness of the spirit, or of actual men for that matter, but the self-creation of the individual in his social relations, in all its dimensions, with the individual able to educate and develop his humanity, refine his needs and his manner of fulfilling them, not in the narrow 'individual' sense taught by capitalist society, but with the historically developed needs and satisfactions of the 'universal' individual. For Marx the 'aesthetic education' of men is at the core of this real and continuous transformation, and of the revolution men must make to initiate 'the realm of freedom'. It goes without saying that for this conception to have any objective meaning it must emerge from the social reality in which men suffer the exploitation and material and ideological oppression of capitalism, and not simply be ideally counterposed to it. At the most basic level Marx can conceive of the class of 'direct producers' making this revolution because he does not separate social relations of production from production itself, which is the actual relation between men and nature.

Sartre leaps back over Hegel as well as Marx, and returns to Kant and his elemental 'scarcity', when he proposes to restore the rights of the irreducible human, the agent of praxis, with his 'project'. This is Sartre's answer to what he considers to be Marxism's lapse into mechanical determinism. He himself appears to accept unquestioningly the objectivist view that the dogmatic degeneration of Marxist theory in the Stalinist-dominated period was actually a development of Marxism itself, and that to strike a blow for freedom one must find some ground for asserting individuality. The contradiction between freedom and history, which was made to seem inescapable by Stalinism, was accepted as an objective contradiction by Sartre and the existentialists. In their own way, therefore, they accept the verdict of the Stalinist bureaucracy that the Marxist theory and practice of historical materialism and proletarian revolution are not the path of struggle for the liberation of mankind, but, on the contrary, a process which involves the negation of freedom. To this perversion of Marxism, and to the bureaucracy which perpetrates it, they counterpose not the defence and development of Marxism itself, as dialectical materialism and as revolutionary practice in the working class, but the impotent project and will of an individual who is not 'the totality of his social relations' but the lonely, irreducible, historically powerless, fragmented atom reproduced by capitalist oppression.

It is evident that for Marx there is no abstract 'human nature' or irreducible man with his 'project' (in the end, the latter seems little different from the 'problem-solving' animal of Dewey's instrumentalism, a refinement of the crude pragmatism of James, the worldly origins of which are not difficult to grasp). Men distinguish themselves from the rest of nature by producing, by their purposive activity, and this production is always social:

> These distinctive social characters are, therefore, by no means due to individual human nature as such, but to the exchange relations of persons who produce their goods in the specific form of commodities. So little does the relation of buyer and seller represent a purely individual relationship that they enter into it only in so far as their individual labour is negated, that is to say, turned into money as non-individual labour. It is therefore as absurd to regard buyer and seller, these bourgeois economic types, as eternal social forms of human individuality, as it is preposterous to weep over them as signifying the abolition of individuality. They are an essential expression of individuality arising at a particular state of the social process of production.[35]

Eighteenth century social and economic theory had been unable to go beyond the framework of accepting the necessity or 'naturalness' of the social relations of private property, married to a hope of overcoming their effects by some sort of moral education. Marx, in his insistence that men produced not only the material means of their life but also their own social relations, considered the necessity of these relations, however oppressive, to be historical in character. They had a dialectical character in that they were transformed into their opposite in history. And the source of this development was that they were 'socio-historically necessary forms of expression of a fundamental ontological relationship'.[36] This ontological relationship is not something metaphysical, something inhering in each individual man and his relation to the cosmos, but the 'nature-imposed necessity' (Marx) of labour. The 'standpoint of the proletariat' or of 'socialised humanity', as against that of 'the isolated individual in bourgeois society', is the conscious theory and practice which corresponds to the recognition of this 'ontological relationship'. A closed system like Hegel's in which the end is written into the premises could not rise to the level of a concept of this 'open-ended' relationship, in which men make their own history.

As we have seen, Marx characterised the social relations of capitalist production as leading to abstraction from the material qualities of products, their use-value, and from the concrete character of labour. The socialisation of labour, which is the precondition of a future freedom, develops only at the same time as an increasing separation of the individual from the qualitative relation with nature and from human relations with other men:

> All production is an objectification [*Vergegenständlichung*] of the individual. In money (exchange-value), however, the individual is not objectified in his natural quality, but in a social quality (relation) which is, at the same time, external to him.[37]

Money had existed in pre-capitalist societies, but only in capitalism did its function 'as the general representative of wealth and as individualised exchange-value' come to dissolve all other relationships. The full development of the capital— labour relation, and the progress of the productive forces which it facilitated, could, at the same time, take place only through the universalisation of the function of money. Money is a kind of 'community' (*Gemeinwesen*) of men and goods which subverts all ancient communities, but capitalism has no 'community' other than this:

> It is the elementary precondition of bourgeois society that labour should directly produce exchange value, i.e. money;

and, similarly, that money should directly purchase labour, and therefore the labourer, but only in so far as he alienates [*veräussert*] his activity in the exchange. Wage labour on one side, capital on the other, are therefore only other forms of developed exchange value and of money (as the incarnation of exchange value). Money thereby directly and simultaneously becomes the real community [*Gemein-wesen*], since it is the general substance of survival for all, and at the same time the social product of all. But as we have seen, in money the community [*Gemeinwesen*] is at the same time a mere abstraction, a mere external, accidental thing for the individual, and at the same time merely a means for his satisfaction as an isolated individual.[38]

All the characteristics of human labour which suggest the productive creativity manifested in art are here devalued, obscured from view, and actually eliminated for the most part. Labour in its concrete aspect, the means of satisfying human needs, is placed in subjection to the organising of labour as abstract labour, the means of fulfilling capital's need for 'abstract' value, individualised as money. (And here lies the root of all the inverted and dehumanised false 'fulfilment' of capitalism's supposed consumer society as the answer to revolution.) This community of money relates men to one another in a new way. It is as remote as it could possibly be from the community in which epic poetry or classical sculpture flourished. It subjects individual men to a mystified view of nature, of their own nature, of their own productive activity, which no true art could fail to challenge rather than merely reflect:

Since it is an individuated, tangible object, money may be randomly searched for, found, stolen, discovered; and thus general wealth may be tangibly brought into the possession of a particular individual. From its servile role, in which it appears as mere medium of circulation, it suddenly changes into the lord and god of the world of commodities. It represents the divine existence of commodities, while they represent its earthly form. Before it is replaced by exchange value, every form of natural wealth pre-supposes an essential relation between the individual and the objects, in which the individual in one of his aspects objectifies [*vergegenständlicht*] himself in the thing, so that his possession of the thing appears at the same time as a certain development of his individuality: wealth in sheep, the development of the individual as shepherd, wealth in grain, his development as agriculturist, etc. Money, however, as the individual of general wealth, as something emerging from circulation and representing a general quality, as a merely social result, does not at all presuppose an individual relation to its owner; possession of it is not the development of any particular essential aspect of his individuality; but rather possession of what lacks individuality, since this social [relation] exists at the same time as a sensuous, external object which can be mechanically seized, and lost in the same manner. Its relation to the individual thus appears as a purely accidental one; while this relation to a thing having no connection with his individuality gives him, at the same time, by virtue of the thing's character, a general power over society, over the whole world of gratifications, labours, etc.[39]

And yet, again, it is this very domination over men by their products that makes possible the historical progress necessary for the 'leap' to freedom:

But it is inherent in the attribute in which it here becomes developed that the illusion about its nature, i.e. the fixed insistence on one of its aspects, in the abstract, and the blindness towards the contradictions contained within it, gives it a really magical significance behind the backs of individuals. In fact, it is because of this self-contradictory and hence illusory aspect, because of this abstraction, that it becomes such an enormous instrument in the real development of the forces of social production.[40]

Now one of the consequences for whatever art and literature is produced in capitalism is very obvious. How can the artist or writer relate to the other individuals in society in any way other than through the 'community' of money? What a price must be paid for the artist's 'freedom' and independence of the ties of communal requirements or patronage or any other kind of visible restraint or personal dependence! Where will he find the necessary confidence that his choice of subject matter, artistic materials, or technique will lead him any nearer to the truth or will find any response? How will he receive and measure response, except by the market? If the commodity which is the 'individualisation' of abstract value, of congealed labour time in general (money), is the only token of the relation between the writer and his work on the one hand and his audience on the other, what remains of the essentially concrete, particular, individual nature of artistic production? ('. . . art, instead of smoothing and flattening its content out into polished generalities, particularises it rather into living individuality'.[41]) What real 'aesthetic education' of either producer or consumer can take place? On this score, Mészáros is right[42] to draw attention to Marx's emphasis on the dialectical interaction between production and consumption. The product — and this goes for the artist's product — is shaped by the consumer as well as by the producer. If an artist thinks he can simply 'use' the existing media to transmit his art to the masses, and simple appropriate the financial proceeds to keep alive while he produces more purely individual works expressive of himself, then he does so at his peril as artist. However convenient is a notion of art as nothing more than self-expression, for those needing a rationalisation of such an existence, it contributes in reality to a destruction of the conditions of art. In a society where there is no 'aesthetic education', there can be no receptivity for art, and very soon the artist's acquiescence in commercialism will result in his subjection to the criteria of 'public demand'. This is only one of the ways in which aestheticism is destructive of art itself.

Now it is held by Althusser and his followers that the writer or artist communicates to his audience a view of ideology 'from within'. Furthermore, every society is said to 'secrete' ideology. It follows that capitalist society will present no more fundamental problems for art than does any other social formation, including socialism for that matter.

It is difficult to reconcile this with Marx's view. He considered that the artist communicated through artistic forms the unity and conflict of subject and object, the constant struggle to transform and control nature, and not only the ideological forms arising on this basis. One recent critic has welcomed Althusser's reputed discovery of 'a new theoretical domain' in which one may 'break with the problematic of subject (cogito) and object'. Certainly, if, for Marx, the subject, in relation to object, was cogito (I think), then such a break would be necessary and possible (though it provokes an 'abstract' nightmare of the mind jumping out of its own nature as mind in order to accomplish the feat). But it is nearly a century and a half since Marx arrived at the philosophical, and thenceforth the practical, standpoint of 'revolutionising practice', breaking from Feuerbach and all 'contemplative' (cogito?) philosophy, materialist as well as idealist. For Marx the relation between subject and object is one of social labour to transform the object. The subject comes out of the object, is in a contradictory unity with it. This idea was already present in the *1844 Manuscripts:* 'Industry is the actual historical relation of nature, and therefore of the natural sciences, to man.'[43] It was the understanding of this 'actual historical relation' which led Marx to characterise industry as 'an open book of the human faculties'. This insistence on the social—historical production relation with nature as the essential content of anything that could be called human nature is not contradicted but is on the contrary confirmed and given definition by his attacks on the way in which particular social forms, and especially capitalism, reduce labour to alienated functions.

The specifically capitalist forms of abstraction, commodity fetishism, and the inversion of the relation between subject (the living producers) and object (nature, and accumulated past labour), so inimical to creative art, are forms which reach their full development, as we have seen, with the total predominance of the relation between capitalist owner and propertyless wage-labourer. This very lack of property, the workers' own brutal separation from the instruments of production, has its own direct influence, through the labour process, on the possibilities of art under capitalism, as Marx indicates — by contrast — in one of his summary notes in the *Grundrisse*:

> Dissolution of the relations in which he appears as proprietor of the instrument. Just as the above form of landed property presupposes a real community, so does this property of the worker in the instrument presuppose a particular form of the development of manufactures, namely craft, artisan work; bound up with it, the guild—corporation system etc. (The manufacture system of the ancient Orient can be examined under [1] already.) Here labour itself still half artistic, half end-in-itself etc. Mastery. Capitalist himself still master-journeyman. Attainment of particular skill in the work also secures possession of instrument etc. etc. Inheritability then to a certain extent of the mode of work together with the organization of work and the instrument of work. Medieval cities. Labour still as his own; definite self-sufficient development of one-sided abilities etc.[44]

Doubtless Marx was here referring back to the unpublished text of *The German Ideology,* in the section dealing with Feuerbach:

> In the towns, the division of labour between the individual guilds was as yet very little developed and, in the guilds themselves, it did not exist at all between the individual workers. Every workman had to be versed in a whole round of tasks, had to be able to make everything that was to be made with his tools. The limited intercourse and the weak ties between the individual towns, the lack of population and the narrow needs did not allow of a more advanced division of labour, and therefore every man who wished to become a master had to be proficient in the whole of his craft. Medieval craftsmen therefore had an interest in their special work and in proficiency in it, which was capable of rising to a limited artistic sense. For this very reason, however, every medieval craftsman was completely absorbed in his work, to which he had a complacent servile relationship, and in which he was

involved to a far greater extent than the modern worker, whose work is a matter of indifference to him.[45]

It is clear from these remarks that Marx did not look for some restoration of past social conditions in order that art might flourish, any more than he thought it possible or necessary to restore earlier forms of labour. The separation of labour (of the labourer, the direct producer) from the means of production implies, Marx points out, that in capitalism labour is 'separated from all means and objects of labour, from its entire objectivity'. ('This living labour, existing as an *abstraction* from these moments of its actual reality (also not-value); this complete denudation, purely subjective existence of labour, stripped of all objectivity . . . ')

This abstract character of labour, 'the secret of the whole critical conception' (Marx), is the secret also of the hostility of capitalism to art. The worker brings labour, 'not as itself *value,* but as the *living source* of value', into relation with 'money posited as capital', and what he brings 'is not this or another labour but *labour pure and simple,* abstract labour; absolutely indifferent to its particular specifity, but capable of all specificities'. It is because of this that his economic character is not that of coalminer against coalowner, or weaver against textile magnate, but that of a worker against a capitalist. Furthermore:

This economic relation — the character which capitalist and worker have as the extremes of a single relation of production — therefore develops more purely and adequately in proportion as labour loses all the characteristics of art; as its particular skill becomes something more and more abstract and irrelevant, and as it becomes more and more a *purely abstract activity*, a purely mechanical activity, hence indifferent to its particular form; a merely *formal* activity, or, what is the same, a merely *material* [*stöf-flich*] activity, activity pure and simple, regardless of its form.[46]

All considerations of form, of 'creating things according to the laws of beauty', as Marx had expressed it in the

1844 Manuscripts, are suppressed. No longer do men mature as craftsmen, taught to bring the best out of natural materials by masters who convey to them the tested knowledge and skills of all past generations that have worked at the same problems. Artistic form is entirely dissociated from the content of labour. At the same time as debasing the worker, however, this abstractness of labour makes of the ex-craftsman and his descendants workers along with all those others whose worlds were once sealed off one from another. They are brought into a single relation with capital, and so in a contradictory way with the entirety of productive forces. So is the ground prepared, not only in the shape of advanced means of production but also of the class struggle and revolution, for the restoration of the producers' control over their own labour and its product, this time as 'the associated producers'.

For Marx the creation by man of his own nature, a self-creation possible only through his action in transforming nature according to his needs, is the single historical process, in which labour, science and art live and must be understood. If this unity is to be any clue to the understanding of art and literature, it is necessary to go beyond a mere comparison or juxtaposition of the labour process and artistic creation, and not to rest content with asserting the non-contradiction of artistic and scientific modes of cognition. If in art and literature men educate their feelings, and in so doing their personalities as wholes, then that 'education' demands that all the social contradictions and historical struggles arising out of the social relations in which the labour process takes place (and these contradictions and struggles are just as much men's creation as are the material products of labour) must be faced, comprehended, and their transcendence prefigured.

In every case the specific historical character of the labour process and the social relations of production must be the starting point. Under capitalism, that which appears in social life to be fixed, 'reified' ('external to the individual and exercising constraint on him', as Durkheim had it, only declaring this external character of 'social facts' to be common to all human life and not specific to capitalism), is in fact the product of the same men who come up against it in life as its victims. Cannot art have an essential role in preparing man for the practice in which he needs to engage to break the rigid institutional and ideological framework? A work of art is successful if it takes us beyond its finished appearance to a feeling of how the artist was able to mobilise and unify all the necessary subjective and objective means to bring out the final result (for fine detailed analytic examples of this characteristic of painting, of Max Raphael, *The Demands of Art*). Then we understand, through the experience of the work of art, how to see the essence which is concealed as well as expressed by its appearance forms, and we are led to share the essentially human experience of the labour of cognition which reveals this. How is the truth of cognition 'proved'? By the artist's success in representing the whole, but in such a way as to bring out how conscious and purposive human effort discovers nature's secrets, and yet must pierce the veil of social and ideological relations in doing so. The explicit subject matter of a work of art may not be the class struggle or the condition of society in some aspect. The vital question is not simply, What does he include or exclude? We must ask, rather, Does his work help to equip the reader, the onlooker, the listener, as a whole man endowed with passion, will, thought and the capacity for action, to confront, or in some cases simple to accomplish the feat of not succumbing to, those human creations which have assumed independence of his control and have taken on the appearance of unalterable obstacles?

If as Marx suggested, real objectivity comes not from detached contemplation but from engagement in the struggle to transform the world, then the relation between art and cognition might be viewed in a new light. One of the vital dimensions of the struggle to change the real conditions of social life is that the fixity and externality of the social forms of class society be challenged, not in the manner of a protest or revolt in the name of some abstract freedom, but out of a knowledge of the process by which they were formed and by which they will be abolished. That means comprehending the specific character of the given social—economic forms. For this it is necessary to penetrate beyond appearance to the productive labour of men themselves, who first confront these 'external' forces as 'object' and discover themselves to be 'subject'. The relation between the form attained by the work of art, on the one hand, and the active struggle through which it was formed, on the other, is one which becomes clear and inspiring to the responsive and aesthetically (musically, or whatever) educated consumer. This success, this experience induced by the artist's work, changes the living man or woman in such a way as to refresh, replenish, develop, perhaps at the same time recall from repressed experience and recognise in himself, the necessary resources to respond to life in a way analogous to the artist's creativity: in the unceasing struggle to make reality correspond to our needs, we must learn both the laws of nature, making them work 'for us', and the special character of social 'laws', whose externality must be dissolved in consciousness into their true element, our own labour, so that the objective possibility of overcoming them can be envisaged and willed. In this way art goes beyond the imitation of nature, and beyond the labour process as such. Here again we may see developed in Hegel, in 'abstract' form, what Marx called 'the active side' neglected by previous materialist philosophy:

> Man may not pass his life in such an idyllic poverty of spirit; he must work. What he has an urge for, he must struggle to obtain by his own activity. In this sense even physical needs stir up a broad and variegated range of activities and give to man a feeling of inner power, and, out of this feeling, deeper interests and powers can then also be developed. [47]

Marx's draft Introduction to *Critique of Political Economy,* published posthumously, ends with the following:

> As regards art, it is well known that some of its peaks by no means correspond to the general development of society; nor do they therefore to the material substructure, the skeleton as it were of its organisation. For example the Greeks compared with modern [nations], or else Shakespeare. It is even acknowledged that certain branches of art, e.g., the epos, can no longer be produced in their epoch-

making classic form after artistic production as such has begun; in other words that certain important creations within the compass of art are only possible at an early stage in the development of art. If this is the case with regard to different branches of art within the sphere of art itself, it is not so remarkable that this should also be the case with regard to the entire sphere of art and its relation to the general development of society. The difficulty lies only in the general formulation of these contradictions. As soon as they are reduced to specific questions they are already explained.

Let us take, for example, the relation of Greek art, and that of Shakespeare, to the present time. We know that Greek mythology is not only the arsenal of Greek art, but also its basis. Is the conception of nature and of social relations which underlies Greek imagination and therefore Greek [art] possible when there are self-acting mules, railways, locomotives and electric telegraphs? What is a Vulcan compared with Roberts and Co., Jupiter compared with the lightning conductor, and Hermes compared with the *Crédit mobilier*? All mythology subdues, controls and fashions the forces of nature in the imagination and through imagination; it disappears therefore when real control over these forces is established. What becomes of Fama side by side with Printing House Square? Greek art presupposes Greek mythology, in other words that natural and social phenomena are already assimilated in an unintentionally artistic manner by the imagination of the people. This is the material of Greek art, not just any mythology, i.e., not every unconsciously artistic assimilation of nature (here the term comprises all physical phenomena, including society); Egyptian mythology could never become the basis of or give rise to Greek art. But at any rate [it presupposes] a mythology; on no account however a social development which precludes a mythological attitude towards nature, i.e. any attitude to nature which might give rise to myth; a society therefore demanding from the artist an imagination independent of mythology.

Regarded from another aspect: is Achilles possible when powder and shot have been invented? And is the Iliad possible at all when the printing press and even printing machines exist? Is it not inevitable that with the emergence of the press bar the singing and the telling and the muse cease, that is the conditions necessary for epic poetry disappear?

The difficulty we are confronted with is not, however, that of understanding how Greek art and epic poetry are associated with certain forms of social development. The difficulty is that they still give us aesthetic pleasure and are in certain respects regarded as a standard and unattainable ideal.

An adult cannot become a child again, or he becomes childish. But does the naivete of the child not give him pleasure, and does not he himself endeavour to reproduce the child's veracity on a higher level? Does not the child in every epoch represent the character of the period in its natural veracity? Why should not the historical childhood of humanity, where it attained its most beautiful form, exert an eternal charm because it is a stage that will never recur? There are rude children and precocious children. Many of the ancient peoples belong to this category. The Greeks were normal children. The charm their art has for us does not conflict with the immature stage of the society in which it originated. On the contrary its charm is a consequence of this and is inseparably linked with the fact that the immature social conditions which gave rise, and which alone could give rise, to this art cannot recur.[48]

None of Marx's references to art and literature have been the subject of more commentary than this. It appears not in one of his major published works, but as part of an unfinished and uncorrected manuscript. It is a note by Marx to himself for future reference. We find it at the end of a more or less random series of points which Marx reminds himself 'have to be mentioned in this context and should not be forgotten', and is prompted by one of the headings thereunder, which reads as follows:

6. *The unequal development of material production and, e.g. that of art.* The concept of progress is on the whole

not to be understood in the usual abstract form, Modern
art, etc. This disproportion is not as important and difficult
to grasp as within concrete social relations, *e.g.*, in education. Relation of the United States to Europe. However,
the really difficult point to be discussed here is how the
relations of production as legal relations take part in this
uneven development. For example the relation of Roman
civil law (this applies in smaller measure to criminal and
constitutional law) to modern production.[49]

This 'unequal development', then, is manifested in the fact
that certain periods of the flowering of the arts 'by no means
correspond to the general development of society; nor do
they therefore to the material substructure, the skeleton as it
were of its organisation'. In Marx's words this unevenness
itself presents no great difficulty: it is only a matter of the
specific conditions of production which favour or do not
favour artistic production, or perhaps favour a particular
form of art. If the level of productive forces is low, then the
mythological imagination dominates thinking, so that 'natural
and social phenomena are already assimilated in an unintentionally artistic manner by the imagination of the people'.
This imaginatively transmuted reality is the immediate subject
matter of Greek art. It is not to be expected that where
modern science and technology have rationally mastered these
previously mythologically understood things, the same epic
form will be possible. Now the artist's imagination, to comprehend the modern world and to communicate with the minds
of his fellow men, must be 'independent of mythology'. As
part of the same development of productive forces, the conditions for invention and transmission of epic poetry have
disappeared. The printing press appears.

So much is straightforward enough, and, as Marx says, our
path to the understanding of this unevenness between the
development of art and that of economy and productive
forces is made easier by the recognition, at another level, that
within art itself a particular form (e.g., epic) achieves its
highest development at an early stage of the development of
art as a whole. Now for the difficulty. Whence comes the
ability of Greek art and epic to give us aesthetic pleasure and to

constitute still 'in certain respects . . . a standard and un-attainable ideal'?

What follows only suggests one aspect of the answer to these questions, by way of an analogy, which is as limited, necessarily, as any other analogy. In comparing our reception of the artistic products of Greek civilisation with the view of childhood of the adult individual (and, note, this is the comparison he makes; he is not comparing Greek civilisation in social evolution with childhood in the life of man) Marx seems to make two points: first, that the innocence or naivety of the child is a source of pleasure, and, second, that the adult 'must strive to reproduce its truth at a higher level' (here we take Nicolaus's translation). Accordingly, we can say that the openness and the unburdened pursuit of freedom by the world's first citizens are a natural source of pleasure to men in a society which has left behind all possibility of so simple a life. This in itself does not explain anything about how the epic poet fashioned his material in such a way as to strike this chord so surely — that is a matter for the study of poetic tech-nique — but it does give an answer to the question Marx himself had formulated: what, in the artistic products of men of an entirely different epoch, can provide a source of aesthetic pleasure for us?

To the second question — why these achievements are still a 'norm', an 'unattainable model' — Marx replies with the analogy of the adult's compulsion to develop the truth of the naivety of the child but at a higher level. Just as the adult man cannot return to childhood, so society cannot revert to the classical city—states or the Heroic Age. Nevertheless the adult seeks to recover the innocence of childhood, which takes nature and humanity unguardedly, as they present themselves, but now with the openness of eyes and heart which can anticipate and prepare for the difficulties and dis-appointments involved, yet without bending under them. Similarly, mankind finds in the Greeks the going out of free men on to the earth as they found it. For good historical reasons which have nothing mysterious about them the Greeks emerged to break the umbilical cord of the primitive commune under conditions favourable to the exercise of this freedom (they could be 'normal' children), and so they impressed their bold and free manner of life on the matter of nature and history, mediated through mythological heroes, in a 'beautiful unfolding which cannot be repeated'. (Marx seems to be recalling notes he had made in 1842: 'If we consider the gods and heroes of Greek art *without religious or aesthetic prejudices*, we find in them nothing that could not exist in the pulsations of nature. Indeed, these images are artistic only as they portray 'beautiful human mores' in a splendid from.'[50]) In this way Marx seeks only to show that the 'charm' of Greek art is the natural result of the fact that its social matrix was a life free and organic yet unrepeatable, something we cannot recover. The undeveloped nature of social contradictions facilitated the flourishing of art, and there is no return to that simplicity. But we have the fruits, and the enjoyment of them enters into the creation of those men who are now driven by the developed contradictions of class society to create once again a form of society where men confront nature and their own destiny as free agents, but at a higher level, as collective subject and on the basis of the 2000-year development of productive forces.[51] If someone wants to ask more of this passage, wondering why Marx did not offer some secret of how poetic discourse or the play of light and shade brought forth by a sculptor's chisel are suited to provoking particular emotional responses, then he is looking for answers to a question which Marx did not ask.

It is probable that Schiller's distinction between 'naive' and 'sentimental' poetry was one of the sources of Marx's use here of the analogy of the naivety of childhood. The naive poet has an unproblematical unity with nature. Such a unity does not exist for the sentimental poet, who only strives for it. Schiller, along with Herder, Goethe, Lessing and Hegel, criticised modern literature by measuring it against the standard of the classical or epic ideal, the standard to which Marx refers. In so doing they were raising a question which could not be answered within the limits of the bourgeois world outlook: precisely, how to recover the truth of classical simplicity and purity of form but on a higher level. Schiller and the other great critics knew that epic poetry was the literature proper to a mode of human life which was gone for ever, but they could not yet pose in social—historical terms the 'negation of the negation', the transcending of those social conditions which had begun their career by replacing antique civilisation. Given these limitations, their literary—historical criticism was an aspect of the political idea modelled on classical antiquity which the revolutionary bourgeoisie developed in order to arm itself for the assault on absolutism. In the light of this we can come closer to a full understanding of the comprehensive effort that was necessary theoretically, stretching even to the field of aesthetics, for Marx to carry through the transition from revolutionary democracy to communism, from the left wing of the bourgeois revolution to the proletarian revolution. Schiller saw that only the naive poets of antiquity could portray reality. The modern poet must 'represent the ideal', in opposition to the empirically given. As Lukács has pointed out,[52] this conclusion should not be dismissed as nothing more than a manifestation of idealism, but must be seen as at the same time a recognition in its own way of the fact that capitalist social relations and ideology place formidable barriers in the way of any concrete representation of the reality of life. This positive element can be recovered and developed once it is freed from its idealist form, in the same way as Marx 'rescued' Hegel's dialectical method.

Among all the philosophical precursors of Marx in these matters, it was Hegel who came closest to a concrete historical characterisation of the conditions in which 'ideal' art could flower:

> Therefore what is most fitted for ideal art proves to be a third situation which stands midway between the idyllic and golden ages and the perfectly developed universal mediations of civil society. This is a state of society which we have already learnt to recognize as the Heroic or, preferably, the ideal Age. The Heroic Ages are no longer restricted to that idyllic poverty in spiritual interests; they go beyond it to deeper passions and aims; but the nearest environment of individuals, the satisfaction of their immediate needs, is still their own doing. Their food is still simple and therefore more ideal, as for instance honey, milk, wine; while coffee, brandy, etc., at once call to our

mind the thousand intermediaries which their preparation requires. So too the heroes kill and roast their own food; they break in the horse they wish to ride; the utensils they need they more or less make for themselves; plough, weapons for defence, shield, helmet, breastplate, sword, spear, are their own work, or they are familiar with their fabrication. In such a mode of life man has the feeling, in everything he uses and everything he surrounds himself with, that he has produced it from his own resources, and therefore in external things has to do with what is his own and not with alienated objects lying outside his own sphere wherein he is master. In that event of course the activity of collecting and forming his material must not appear as painful drudgery but as easy, satisfying work which puts no hindrance and no failure in his way.

Such a form of life we find, e.g., in Homer. Agamemnon's sceptre is a family staff, hewn by his ancestor himself, and inherited by his descendants (Iliad, ii). Odysseus carpentered himself his huge marriage bed (Odyssey, xxiii); and ·even if the famous armour of Achilles was not his own work, still here too the manifold complexity of activities is cut short because it is Hephaestus who made it at the request of Thetis (Iliad, xviii). In brief, everywhere there pccps out a new joy in fresh discoveries, the exuberance of possession, the capture of delight; everything is domestic, in everything the man has present before his eyes the power of his arm, the skill of his hand, the cleverness of his own spirit, or a result of his courage and bravery. In this way alone have the means of satisfaction not been degraded to a purely external matter; we see their living origin itself and the living consciousness of the value which man puts on them because in them he has things not dead or killed by custom, but his own closest productions.[53]

Hegel was by no means the only antecedent of Marx who had sought to characterise the type of historical culture in which epic art developed. But when Marx discusses the recovery of that culture's naivety 'at a higher level' he is almost certainly working in the spirit of 'reading Hegel materialistically'. For Hegel a consciousness which works in mytho-logical-religious and artistic images (the imagination of the Greek people, to which Marx refers) is using these images to express necessities of cognition (and through cognition, of the world) *before* mankind yet has the equipment to concep-tualise these same necessities in the appropriate abstractions. In Hegel's terms the reason for our inability to return to the culture of the Greeks is clearly defined. We now look back and see a perfection in their art by reason of its correspondence to our knowledge of the ideal, our perfected 'universality'. But the images in which the Greeks incorporated truth were not deduced from such concepts; rather the artists and poets 'could work what fermented in them into external expression only in this form of art and poetry'.[54]

That it was indeed Hegel who inspired Marx's preliminary note on the 'unequal development' of art and society is con-firmed by the suggestion that mythologies other than the Greek did not and could not inspire art in the same way. We have seen that in a very early manuscript Marx stressed the 'beautiful human mores' characteristic of the doings of the Greek gods (see above, p.63). It was Hegel who had contrasted Greek mythology with its Egyptian and other predecessors.[55] Already in his doctoral thesis Marx, taking up many of these themes, had suggested that *early* Greek art had suffered under Egyptian influence. Where Egyptian mythology centres on an inscrutable living force, the Greeks came to imagine the divine in human form. What Hegel saw here was a grasping in the form of images – in the imagination – of the fact that 'sub-stance is subject', that truth which could not yet be concep-tualised. Only at this stage of development of the Absolute Spirit did self-consciousness express itself in the 'particula-rising' mode of art rather than in some other. Just as the growth of self-consciousness in the individual must rediscover and in that sense recapitulate the progress of the history of consciousness as a whole, so men will take pleasure in the unique form of self-discovery irretrievably expressed by Greek epic and sculpture. If this past is truly irretrievable, what of the works which actually remain? Hegel, once again 'abstractly', provided the groundwork from which Marx began to ponder the question of their 'eternal charm'. In the *Phenomenology* he writes:

> So too it is not their living world that Fate preserves and
> gives us with these works of ancient art, not the spring
> and summer of that ethical life in which they bloomed
> and ripened, but the veiled remembrance alone of all this
> reality . . . so too the spirit of the fate which presents us
> with those works of art, is more than the ethical life realized
> in that nation. For it is the inwardizing in us, in the form
> of conscious memory [Er-Innerung] of the spirit which in
> them was manifested in a still external way . . .

And again:

> But recollection [Er-Innerung] has conserved that experi-
> ence, and is the inner being, and, in fact, the higher form
> of the substance. While, then, this phase of spirit begins all
> over again its formative development [i.e. the Phenomeno-
> logy is succeeded by the Logic], apparently starting solely
> from itself, yet at the same time it commences at a higher
> level. The realm of spirits developed in this way, and as-
> suming definite shape in existence, constitutes a succession
> where one detaches and sets loose the other, and each
> takes over from its predecessor the empire of the spiritual
> world.[56]

There seems little doubt that the fragment from Marx's
Introduction to the *Critique of Political Economy* is no more
than a preliminary note in which Marx proposes to himself,
in outline, to attempt to bring together Hegel's insights into
classical art and certain problems arising, and still unresolved,
in his own 'rough draft' (*Rohentwurf*, the *Grundrisse*). The
draft Introduction itself had been concerned up to this point,
where it breaks off with notes for future reference, with the
methodological problems arising from those categories of
political economy (e.g. money) which have a secondary role
in developed capitalism but show more perfected forms in
earlier stages of economic development. It is this unevenness
and its implications for historical and logical methods of analysis and presentation with which Marx is here occupied in the

first place, and which he tentatively projects into the following: '6. The unequal development of material production and, *for example*, that of art . . . ' [my emphasis, C. S.] (Nicolaus translates: 'The uneven development of material production relative to, e.g., artistic development . . . ')

It is in another well-known passage in the same *Grundrisse* that Marx is most explicit concerning the historical relation of modern society to classical antiquity. Characteristically we also have here the clearest indication of his 'materialistic reading' of Hegel. We find the following passage in that section of the *Grundrisse* entitled 'Forms which precede capitalist production':[57]

> . . . the old view, in which the human being appears as the aim of production, regardless of his limited national, religious, political character, seems to be very lofty when contrasted to the modern world, where production appears as the aim of mankind and wealth as the aim of production. In fact, however, when the limited bourgeois form is stripped away, what is wealth other than the universality of individual needs, capacities, pleasures, productive forces etc., created through universal exchange? The full development of human mastery over the forces of nature, those of so-called nature as well as of humanity's own nature? The absolute working-out of his creative potentialities, with no presupposition other than the previous historic development, which makes this totality of development, i.e. the development of all human powers as such the end in itself, not as measured on a predetermined yardstick? Where he does not reproduce himself in one specificity, but produces his totality? Strives not to remain something he has become, but is in the absolute movement of becoming? In bourgeois economics — and in the epoch of production to which it corresponds — this complete working-out of the human content appears as a complete emptying-out, this universal objectification as total alienation, and the tearing-down of all limited, one-sided aims as sacrifice of the human end-in-itself to an entirely external end. This is why the childish world of antiquity appears on one side as loftier. On the other side, it really is loftier in all matters where closed

shapes, forms and given limits are sought for. It is satisfaction from a limited standpoint; while the modern gives
no satisfaction; or, where it appears satisfied with itself, it
is vulgar.[58]

It is unnecessary now to return in detail to the fragment
on the 'eternal charm' of Greek art. Marx's own words here
leave no room for ambiguity on the contradictory but necessary character of the development of mankind's powers in
alienated forms. The concreteness of these contradictions is
the content of Marx's entire economic and historical analysis,
from which we know the material content of the negation
(return to a 'higher level') of those conditions which had
negated the appealing 'wholeness' of antiquity. (Nevertheless
one Marxist critic could arrive at the verdict that this passage
is 'a Marxian *cri de coeur* for social harmony' spiced with
a 'revolutionary' protest against the vulgarity of 'the modern
world'.[59]) The art of the period, as of any period in which
there was effected a profound change in life with implications
for all future generations, is endowed with a lasting power of
inspiration. The practice of art as an independent, creative,
non-utilitarian activity was part of and not just a portrayal of
the historical progress contained in Greek civilisation, and for
this reason has its 'eternal charm' for those who must effect
their own revolutionary changes. As Arnold Hauser concluded,
the freedom of expression achieved by the Greeks was 'the
most tremendous change that has ever occurred in the history
of art',[60] and this is enough to explain its stature as an 'unattainable model'. The following passage from Max Raphael,
while it oversimplifies the properties which made Greek
society and culture unique, gives some indication of the richness still to be derived, in the history of art, from Marx's insight:

[The palaeolithic paintings] date from a period when man
had just emerged from a purely zoological existence, when
instead of being dominated by animals, he began to dominate them. This emancipation from the animal state found
an artistic expression as great and universally human as later

found by the Greeks to express their emancipation from agriculture, when they broke with an existence bound exclusively to the soil and took up navigation and maritime trade and began to live the social—political life of the polis. The palaeolithic paintings remind us that our present subjection to forces other than nature is purely transitory; these works are a symbol of our future freedom. Today, mankind, amidst enormous sacrifices and suffering is, with imperfect awareness, striving for a future in the eyes of which all our history will sink to the level of 'prehistory'. Palaeolithic man was carrying on a comparable struggle. Thus the art most distant from us becomes the nearest; the art most alien to us becomes the closest.[61]

Marx knew that his bourgeois precursors could not rise above contemplation of the contrast between modern alienation and the ancient 'wholeness', and that the descent into romanticist reaction was the necessary consequence:

In earlier stages of development the single individual seems to be developed more fully, because he has not yet worked out his relationships in their fullness, or erected them as independent social powers and relations opposite himself. It is as ridiculous to yearn for a return to that original fullness as it is to believe that with this complete emptiness history has come to a standstill. The bourgeois viewpoint has never advanced beyond this antithesis between itself and this romantic viewpoint, and therefore the latter will accompany it as legitimate antithesis up to its blessed end.[62]

Marx, in sharp contrast, devotes his work to the scientific exposition of that developing contradiction between productive forces and production relations which makes the restoration of 'wholeness' an objective necessity. It is only by ignoring this work that one might draw the facile conclusion that his remarks about the 'lofty' conception of the ancients are 'a Marxist *cri de coeur* for social harmony'. The *Grundrisse's* rough draft shows that Marx, far from indulging in dreams or protests, was proceeding strictly from his scientific method and results (which later took finished form in *Capital*):

> The exchange of living labour for objectified labour — i.e. the positing of social labour in the form of the contradiction of capital and wage labour — is the ultimate development of the value-relation and of production resting on value. Its presupposition is — and remains — the mass of direct labour time, the quantity of labour employed, as the determinant factor in the production of wealth. But to the degree that large industry develops, the creation of real wealth comes to depend less on labour time and on the amount of labour employed than on the power of the agencies set in motion during labour time, whose 'powerful effectiveness' is itself in turn out of all proportion to the direct labour time spent on their production, but depends rather on the general state of science and on the progress of technology, or the application of this science to production . . . Real wealth manifests itself, rather — and large industry reveals this — in the monstrous disproportion between the labour time applied, and its product, as well as in the qualitative imbalance between labour, reduced to a pure abstraction, and the power of the production process it superintends. Labour no longer appears so much to be included with the production process; rather, the human being comes to relate more as watchman and regulator to the production process itself. (What holds for machinery holds likewise for the combination of human activities and the development of human intercourse.) No longer does the worker insert a modified natural thing [*Naturgegenstand*] as middle link between the object [*Objekt*] and himself — rather, he inserts the process of nature, transformed into an industrial process, as a means between himself and inorganic nature, mastering it. He steps to the side of the production process instead of being its chief actor. In this transformation, it is neither the direct human labour he himself performs, nor the time during which he works, but rather the appropriation of his own general productive power, his understanding of nature and his mastery over it by virtue of his presence as a social body — it is, in a word,

the development of the social individual which appears as the great foundation-stone of production and wealth.[63]

From the highly abstract analysis of the value relation, necessitated by Marx's starting point, the commodity as the form taken by the product in capitalist society, we are brought to its 'ultimate development'. Here capital continues to depend absolutely on labour as producer of surplus *value*, but in the actual development of industrial capitalism the production of 'real wealth' comes to depend less and less on the direct application of labour time, which is the source of surplus value and the life-blood of capital, and 'rather on the general state of science and on the progress of technology'. This 'monstrous disproportion between the labour time applied, and its product, as well as . . . the qualitative imbalance between labour, reduced to a pure abstraction, and the power of the production process it superintends' opens up the true history of man. Still imprisoned within capitalist forms, there develops 'the social individual'; within his grasp is 'the appropriation of his own general productive power, his understanding of nature and his mastery over it by virtue of his presence as a social body'.

It is from this material contradiction, and the struggles to which it gives rise, that comes the real possibility of men's finding those 'authentic values' against the 'degraded' values of the real world which Lukács and others had defined as the essence of the novel:[64]

The theft of alien labour time, on which the present wealth is based, appears a miserable foundation in face of this new one, created by large-scale industry itself. As soon as labour in the direct form has ceased to be the great wellspring of wealth, labour time ceases and must cease to be its measure, and hence exchange value [must cease to be the measure] of use value. The surplus labour of the mass has ceased to be the condition for the development of general wealth, just as the non-labour of the few, for the development of the general powers of the human head. With that, production based on exchange value breaks down, and the direct, material production process is stripped of

the form of penury and antithesis. The free development
of individualities, and hence not the reduction of necessary
labour time so as to posit surplus labour, but rather the
general reduction of the necessary labour of society to a
minimum, which then corresponds to the artistic, scientific
etc. development of the individuals in the time set free,
and with the means created, for all of them.[65]

Here is the real starting point of understanding the relevance of Marxist theory to literature and art. It is the result
of Marx's pursuit of the discovery that 'the anatomy of civil
society must be sought in political economy'. From 'anatomy'
Marx proceeded to the 'law of motion' of capitalist economy
— its negating, overcoming, surpassing, sublating (all those
words which are used to translate the German *aufheben*).
What Marx states in this passage in the *Grundrisse* about the
freedom prepared but obstructed by capitalism presents us
with a very direct and simple conclusion (though it is one
which is almost universally ignored by Marx's self-styled disciples as well as his critics): the historical materialist understanding of literary production cannot be deduced from the
general principles of historical materialism (the model of base-
superstructure, the determining character of economy in the
long run, the *caveat* of 'relative autonomy' etc.) but must be
won in a dialectical analysis of the given social—economic
formation which can demonstrate not the ideal of free artistic
creation frustrated by a hostile environment but the necessary
laws of the production of the actual conditions for that
artistic creation:

As the system of bourgeois economy has developed for us
only by degrees, so too its negation, which is its ultimate
result. We are still concerned now with the direct production process. When we consider bourgeois society in the
long view and as a whole, then the final result of the process of social production always appears as the society
itself, i.e. the human being itself in its social relations.
Everything that has a fixed form, such as the product etc.,
appears as merely a moment, a vanishing moment, in this
movement. The direct production process itself here ap-

pears only as a moment. The conditions and objectifications of the process are themselves equally moments of it, and its only subjects are the individuals, but individuals in mutual relationships, which they equaliy reproduce and produce anew. The constant process of their own movement, in which they renew themselves even as they renew the world of wealth they create.[66]

In the *1844 Manuscripts*, Marx had made an onslaught on the utilitarian ethic of a capitalist society in which culturally developed, specifically human needs are suppressed and replaced by the ego-centred need to appropriate objects in the first place as value and then purely as a source of animal gratification. To this he compares and counterposes man as essentially the producer of his own life, who must overthrow this present condition. When man can recover control of his (unconsciously) self-created destiny, then the development of the individual in an all-round way, the senses 'educated' through the application of all the historically developed forces at man's command, can flourish. In 1857–8 (*Grundrisse*) Marx has not by any means abandoned his notion of the future individual who enters production as 'a different subject . . . who has become, and in whose head exists the accumulated knowledge of society'. The difference now is that Marx has carried out his 'critique of political economy' and feels able to posit the real process of capitalist economy and its negation. There is thus a continuity and a development from 1844, and by the time *Capital* is completed (1865) Marx can claim to have provided a scientific basis for the concepts of alienation and freedom he had first put forward in 1844:

> The realm of freedom actually begins only where labour which is determined by necessity and mundane considerations ceases; thus in the very nature of things it lies beyond the sphere of actual material production. Just as the savage must wrestle with Nature to satisfy his wants, to maintain and reproduce life, so must civilized man, and he must do so in all social formations and under all possible modes of production. With his developments this realm of physical

necessity expands as a result of his wants; but, at the same time, the forces of production which satisfy these wants also increase. Freedom in this field can only consist in socialized man, the associated producers, rationally regulating their interchange with Nature, bringing it under their common control, instead of being ruled by it as by the blind forces of Nature; and achieving this with the least expenditure of energy and under conditions most favourable to, and worthy of, their human nature. But it nonetheless still remains a realm of necessity. Beyond it begins that development of human energy which is an end in itself, the true realm of freedom, which, however, can blossom forth only with this realm of necessity as its basis. The shortening of the working-day is its basic prerequisite.[67]

MARX AND 'REALISM'

If Marx considered capitalism as unfavourable ground for art and literature, in comparison with earlier epochs and in particular with the Heroic and Classical periods in Greece, as well as with 'the realm of freedom' which would succeed it, this certainly did not mean that he thought creative works were not produced in capitalist societies. The fact that the social conditions would undoubtedly affect the nature of the artistic product, by their direct effect on the artist and by their indirect effect on him through the crushing out of aesthetic sensibilities in the audience, could not but pose particular problems which the artist must confront. Marx and Engels, we must emphasise yet again, did not themselves elaborate any theory of these relations and their results.

Whatever later critics may have deduced from Marx's theories, he himself certainly nowhere draws the conclusion that the inroads of reification or fetishism, by their suppression of the qualitative, the concrete, the particular, made the representation of reality by artists and writers impossible. Perhaps the implication of Marx's theory for this question is that artistic creation becomes difficult and demanding in the extreme, because the artist must produce a work which penetrates not only the appearances of natural objects but also the screen which separates men from the true appropriation of nature and their own products. Since Marx accepted what was common ground for many philosophers and critics, that works of art cannot be designed on the basis of a theoretical or analytical ground plan of the social reality — 'The totality as a conceptual entity seen by the intellect is a product of the thinking intellect which assimilates the world in the only way open to it, a way which differs from the artistic, religious and practically intelligent assimilation of this world'[68] — the question arises of how the artist shall imagine and portray the contradiction at the heart of production and consumption, and therefore also in perception itself.

This problem, which is the root of all the controversies about 'realism', cannot be satisfactorily answered, or even posed, if we seek a direct connection between the economic structure with its direct ideological effects (value form, abstract labour, money, surplus value, capital, etc.; commodity fetishism, illusion of equality and freedom, inversion of subject and object) on the one hand, and works of literature on the other. This was the path taken by Lucien Goldmann in his works on nineteenth- and twentieth-century literature. On such a basis it seems impossible to break out of the closed circle — economic determinism in the formation of all social and ideological relations; literary reflection of the ideology; 'realism' therefore restricted to a sharper definition of the ideology, which is itself a screen obscuring reality—which is a modern version of the cave, but with something more opaque than darkness to contend with.

Such an impasse cannot be avoided if historical materialism is interpreted as a kind of economic reductionism, in which individual consciousness is said to be determined by the economy and then to proceed to contemplate the rest of social life in terms of the resultant ideological forms. Men in capitalist society do not apprehend reality by receiving an imprint on their brains from the economic structure and then proceeding to interpret society and nature accordingly. The living whole of society grows every day out of the economic foundations, but it is not freshly hatched out in accordance with the latest changes in production and economy. As a whole, and in each of its many interconnected parts, this social life develops with relative autonomy and with laws of motion which only 'in the long run' correspond to or are limited by the laws of motion of the economy (most fundamentally, the contradictory relation between forces of production and social relations of production). The purpose of these remarks is not so much to say that literature itself is one of these elements of social life with 'relative autonomy' and its own particular set of relations with other such elements in a given society, relations which do not pass at every stage of their development through a reworking of their ultimate derivation from the economic base; it is, rather, to suggest that the reality from which the content of a literary work is taken is more than the 'mode of production of material life', the 'anatomy of civil society'. Just as the men and women of capitalist society, divided into classes, may or may not find themselves in a given period driven by their experience to a comprehension of 'the historical process as a whole', so the writer may or may not be driven in various ways to seize on a particular development in life the grasping of whose inner contradictions and interconnections leads to an illumination of the whole.

It is the task of a theory of aesthetics to discover in what ways the accumulated craftsmanship, technique, mastery of particular forms and their relation to content, etc., have or have not proved fruitful, or proved capable of modification and development, in responding to the new needs pressing forward in each historical situation. In the tension between the traditional forms of their craft and the impulses in social life demanding representation, committed artists and writers experience an inner compulsion to find adequate forms to express a content which is as yet not fully formed, or takes forms which restrict man's mastery of the content. In his work the artist strives to give form to the struggle for consciousness of that unity of action, feeling and thought which is necessary to live, to work, to be human or to become human, in the society in which he finds himself. 'Realism' may find the subject matter of this struggle in unexpected places; it may discover that in the most 'personal' of experiences this struggle is engaged. Whatever the difficulties of such discovery and representation in the given epoch, say that of capitalism, they do not, *a priori,* add up to impossibility, but only to an ever-heightened contradiction between forms of appearance and essential content in social life. Within this contradiction, and only there, presses forward the negation of the present, a negation which is indispensable for humanity. This contradiction is not merely an ideological straitjacket, within which the artist may only give sharper definition; it is a living reality within which exists and must be discovered and nourished the seed of life, of a new society. Struggling with every resource he can muster, the artist aids men in the battle to hold fast to this reality.

Marx could not have had a theory of the revolutionary role of the proletariat if he had conceived of consciousness as only a reflection of economic categories. Economic structure does not exhaust the 'social being' which determines consciousness. Far from being paralysed by the ideological reflections of capitalist economy, the working class (one almost feels it necessary to apologise for introducing the working class into the current discussion on ideology, science, theoretical practice, etc.) is thrown, in real life, into conflict with those reflections:

> Were Criticism better acquainted with the movement of the lower classes of the people it would know that the extreme resistance that they have suffered from practical life is changing them every day. Modern prose and poetry emanating in England and France from the lower classes of the people would show it that the lower classes of the people know how to raise themselves spiritually even without being directly overshadowed by the Holy Ghost of Critical Criticism.[69]

And, again:

> The criticism of the French and English is not an abstract, preternatural personality outside mankind: it is the real human activity of individuals who are active members of society and who suffer, feel, think and act as human beings. That is why their criticism is at the same time practical, their communism a socialism which gives practical, concrete measures and in which they do not just think but act even more, it is the living real criticism of existing society, the discovery of the causes of 'the decay'.[70]

The reflection of social being in consciousness is therefore active and not passive; it is part of the self-transformation in which men engage when they confront the necessity of producing their means of life and of shaping the conditions in which that production can take place. If a writer presents us only with faithful details of the immediate experiences of men, but fails to bring to us in any way a feeling of the necessity and possibility of men's transformation of these experiences and their source, then his 'realism' is a dead conformism with the given. A writer who does not challenge the prevailing techniques and modes of presentation in his craft will tend to trivialise, i.e., reduce to the level of an unquestioned and opaque 'fact of life' every element of experience which he tries to represent. The life of the artist or writer in our society cannot avoid having at its centre the conflict between such a conformism, on the one hand, and, on the other, a search for those forms and techniques which will enable men to find the inner resources, the will, to break through the old forms of life and thought.

It is suggested therefore that those 'Marxist' theories of literature which give the main emphasis to 'reification' and the structure of the 'vision of the world of a class' fail to achieve a Marxist theory of realism, because they make an unwarranted abstraction of the ideological reflection of economy, separating it entirely from the totality of which it is part. Without this totality the element of negation of the structure of ideology cannot be grasped. Men live and fight in the whole which grows up on the base of economic relations, and come to their understanding of the world in that life and that fight. The working class is much more 'interesting' than the 'Marxist' pundits of a 'science' of literature dream. The real process is exceedingly difficult for the isolated intellectual (or the artist) to understand, for in his own life he *does* encounter and approach the social whole primarily *as an object of thought*. (To all the neo-Lukácsians in the theory of class consciousness, reification, etc., it is necessary to say that it is in the class struggle, with all its complexities and reflections, that men learn to comprehend, negate, go beyond the existing reality, discovering in a conflict that their immediate and unpostponable interests cannot be met without the development of new practices whose elaboration demands a comprehension not only of their own experience as a class but also of the relations between classes, between class and state, between states, and the social relations of production and forces of production underlying this whole. It is in this way that a transformed class consciousness comes about, and not through receiving (and, hopefully, decoding — though with what?) demystifying messages from a radical intelligentsia which has settled in its collective mind the true 'potential consciousness' of the working class. The *reductio ad absurdum* of the kind of political attitudes nourished by this modern 'cultural criticism' is that rejection of the idea of the revolutionary role of the working class when the workers are judged to be unwilling to break away from their television sets, deepfreezes and automatic washers in order to listen and get the message, thus making it necessary for the intellectuals and their students to resort to demonstrative protests and gestures, intended to provoke somehow a shock of recognition. By this devious route the highly complex theorising of the left intellectuals brings them to the more simple-minded anarchist recipe of 'propaganda by deed', which is, after all, not very new.)

In what sense then could the novel, the typical literary form of bourgeois society, be realistic, be art? Whatever its resemblance at first sight to epic, it lacked the foundations in experience to become epic, which had that 'underlying community of objective life and action'. For epic to be the predominant literary form, 'man must not yet appear cut adrift from a living connection with nature'.[71] In a long struggle against the religious ideology of the feudal Middle Ages, artists and writers — from the Florentine painters who humanised religious themes, to the eighteenth-century French philosophers — had sought to restore the 'rights' of the human being as a natural entity. Without this humanist tradition the realistic mode developed by the novel could not have reached the point which it achieved by the end of the eighteenth century. But there was a crucial weakness in that tradition. Although the French Enlightenment philosophers did to a certain extent put flesh and blood on the abstract materialism of Hobbes and Locke, they did not go beyond the basic idea already put forward by their English predecessors, in being unable to conceive of human behaviour except in terms of the pursuit and realisation of self-interest.

In this way the search for a materialist outlook on life was restricted within definite limits. The material reality of society and history was thought of as the aggregate product of the natural self-interest of the individuals comprising society. These same limits bounded the explicit outlook on social and political matters of the nineteenth-century novelists. The possibility of realism, even given this restriction (the clash between a writer's explicit philosophy and the meaning of his creative work is a commonplace), is opened up by the fact that this philosophical advance on the old religious world view did challenge the writer to leave aside Christian illustrative literature and strive to grasp and portray the actual conditions of life. By so doing he must encounter something central to the existing reality: that the promised freedom (the condition of epic, had it been fulfilled) had proved to be in a way 'freedom from existence, and not freedom in existence' (Schiller). This is the famous discovery of the 'prose' of bourgeois existence which follows the poetry and heroism of the French Revolution. It was the source of Stendhal's agonising question: why, in a world promised by the removal of the absolutism of state and church, does the quest for happiness produce only frustration and failure? Anticipating the fruits of the bourgeois revolution — the liberty, equality and fraternity consequent on the abolition of the feudal estates, the oppression of the *ancien régime,* and the obscurantist control of the Church — the eighteenth century Enlightenment felt a living sympathy with classical antiquity and the epic. But now, having broken the bonds of the *ancien régime,* men found themselves separated from each other, from nature, and from their own products, as though by a screen which was semi-transparent and yet impenetrable. These were bitter fruits indeed. By adding equality before the law to equality in the eyes of God men had but exposed a much more fundamental inequality. The new order brought its citizens face to face with the necessity of recognising that it was 'inequality' in the hitherto hidden depths of social production which kept men enslaved, and that the very pursuit of the new freedom (the freedom equally to buy and sell commodities) deepened this enslavement. If the 'realism' of the epic of antiquity was nourished by the soil in which it grew, the novel could attain realism only by grasping and re-presenting a contradiction which the ancient world did not yet know.

The individuality of bourgeois society is victim of the illusion that its motives, achievements and disappointments are matters of a direct relationship between the free individual and the environment as it immediately presents itself. Romanticism in the novel, as René Girard[72] has shown, does not go further than a representation of experience within these terms. The problem of realism is whether there are novelists who have been able to show in some way the reality underneath these forms of appearance: the reality of a 'socialised' individuality which discovers itself and its unrealised powers in and through these same forms of appearance. In the few places where Marx and Engels expressed their views on the representation of reality in literature, they showed clearly their debt to Hegel in the criticism of this romantic view of individuality. For Hegel the 'heroes' of history were those whose own aims,

> ... involve those large issues which are the will of the World-Spirit. They may be called Heroes, inasmuch as they have derived their purposes and their vocation, not from the calm, regular course of things, sanctioned by the existing order; but from a concealed fount — one which has not attained to phenomenal, present existence — from that inner Spirit, still hidden beneath the surface, which, impinging on the outer world as on a shell, bursts it in pieces, because it is another kernel than that which belonged to the shell in question. They are men, therefore, who appear to draw the impulse of their life from themselves; and whose deeds have produced a condition of things and a complex of historical relations which appear to be only their interest, and their work.
>
> Such individuals had no consciousness of the general Idea they were unfolding, while prosecuting those aims of theirs; on the contrary, they were practical, political men.

But at the same time they were thinking men, who had an insight into the requirements of the time — what was ripe for development. This was the very Truth for their age, for their world; the species next in order, so to speak, and which was already formed in the womb of time.[73]

What is 'inner Spirit' in Hegel is the productive work of mankind itself, as yet beyond men's consciousness and control. It was a materialist inversion of this 'inner Spirit' that Marx and Engels had in mind when they discussed the extent to which characters in literature were 'representative'. As Engels explained in his oft-quoted letter to Lassalle, in criticism of the latter's historical drama *Sickingen,* a truly living character with convincing individuality consisted not of ingeniously contrived idiosyncrasies but of a genuine concentration of the specific social—historical forces at work and the possibilities that these opened or did not open for men. To this end, Marx and Engels suggested to Lassalle that the drama would have been more realistic, the tragedy more profound, and the individuality of the noble heroes more pronounced, had Lassalle included, in the manner of Shakespeare rather then Schiller, the plebeian world created by the disintegration of feudalism. Interestingly, there is here not just a 'materialistic reading' of Hegel in the general sense, but also in particulars. Marx's and Engels' comments (1859) recall Hegel's remarks on 'the representative' in Goethe's play on the same subject (*Götz von Berlichingen*):

The time of Götz and Franz von Sickingen is the interesting period in which chivalry with the independence of noble individuals was passing away before a newly arising objective order and legal system. Goethe's great insight is revealed by his choosing as his first subject this contact and collision between the medieval heroic age and the legality of modern life. For Götz and Sickingen are still heroes who, with their personality, their courage, and their upright, straightforward good sense, propose to regulate the states of affairs in their narrower or wider scope by their own independent efforts; but the new order of things brings Götz himself into wrong and destroys him. For chivalry and the feudal system in the Middle Ages are the only proper ground for this sort of independence. Now, however, the legal order has been more completely developed in its prosaic form and has become the predominant authority, and thus the adventurous independence of knights-errant is out of relation to the modern world and if it still proposes to maintain itself as the sole legitimacy and as the righter of wrong and helper of the oppressed in the sense that chivalry did, then it falls into the ridiculousness of which Cervantes gave us such a spectacle in his Don Quixote.[74]

For Marx and Engels realism required that the meaning of the drama must emerge from the action and development of the play and the characters. The whole reality which the writer presents must be able to convince the audience, without the necessity of any resort to making individual characters the mouthpieces of whatever conclusions the author may have reached about the central questions. Engels wrote elsewhere that, while there certainly could be no quarrel with 'tendentiousness' in literature,

> I think that the bias should flow by itself from the situation and action, without particular indications, and that the writer is not obliged to obtrude on the reader the future historical solutions of the social conflicts pictured. And especially in our conditions the novel appeals mostly to readers of bourgeois circles, that is, not directly related to us, and therefore a socialist-biased novel fully achieves its purpose, in my view, if by conscientiously describing the real mutual relations, breaking down conventional illusions about them, it shatters the optimism of the bourgeois world, instils doubt as to the eternal character of the existing order, although the author does not offer any definite solution or does not even line up openly on any particular side.[75]

*   *   *

If art does not merely describe, but also penetrates beneath the surface in such a way as to reveal the necessity of a unity of action, feeling and thought for the purpose of changing reality, does that mean that art will somehow achieve a more nearly complete representation of reality than does science, as some idealist theories claim? There is a grain of truth here. Art discovers and develops aspects of reality which are not the direct concern of science and cannot be comprehended by its methods. The necessary productive disposition of mankind, through which men conquer this same necessity, is symbolised and represented in works of art, and this productive disposition must *include* science, or else it lapses into illusion, subjectivism, and impotence. And yet this scientific component of man's necessary development to freedom requires for some centuries the career of 'the consciousness of the theoretical man who is alien to Nature'.[76] This is a historical phase absolutely necessary in the growth of mankind's productive forces, abstracted and poor though it appear in contrast to the rich and contradictory whole of the ancient philosophers of nature. In the period of the Renaissance and of the first years of the Industrial Revolution artists and writers celebrated the unity of art and science, but they conceived of both as elements in the growth of a humanity able to develop without the alienation and social division of labour which capitalism was to impose.[77] For Marx only the full development of the capitalist system and its superseding by social revolution can create the conditions for the 'total man', the conception of which, 'contains within it the highest values of the past, especially art, as being a productive form of labour freed from the characteristics of alienation, and as being a unity of the product and the producer, of the individual and the social, of natural Being and the human being.'[78]

This is the sense in which art constitutes a reality which is not mere ideology. To be realistic, art and literature do not merely describe the immediate data of experience, and certainly not only the ideological categories with which they are comprehended. What is essential is that the meaning of the human struggle to transcend this experience and this ideology is wrested *from* the forms of appearance, *from* ideology, and presented to men and women in such a way that they prepare, in whatever way their lives demand and make possible, to survive and overcome them.

3
Literature and Revolution: Trotsky

More than once Georg Lukács gave a purported summary of his own place in the history of Marxist work on literature and aesthetics. These accounts refer from time to time to the writings of Plekhanov and Franz Mehring in the period of the Second International, in which they had repulsed idealist attacks on historical materialism, and in the course of so doing had demonstrated the social and historical roots of literary works and tendencies,[1] usually in opposition to neo-Kantian critics. However, Lukács (for reasons which are well-known, and to which we refer in our next chapter) took the greatest care to avoid any treatment of the one Marxist, Trotsky, whose work on literature was carried out after Lukács' own entry into the communist movement, that is to say in the revolutionary wave which followed the Russian Revolution of 1917 and overwhelmed the reformist Second International.

Trotsky's *Literature and Revolution*,[2] together with a number of other articles and speeches of the 1920s, was concerned primarily to lay the basis for a Marxist response to the cultural problems raised by the Russian Revolution, and in particular to answer those who advocated a programme of 'proletarian culture'. Here, in the turmoil of unprecedented social changes, Marxist theory and practice were put to the decisive test. Unless 'Marxists' in the field of literature and literary criticism see Marxism as an abstract, general doctrine, developing independently of history and purely through scholarly research and speculation, they surely cannot separate themselves and their work from the development of Marxism itself. Lukács is one of those many Marxists who are not slow to comment on the effects of Stalinism on literature and criticism, as well as the effects of the developments in capitalism which have matured alongside it. From the standpoint of Marxist theory, it is surely unlikely that there could be any rediscovery and development of Marxism[3] against the Stalinist distortions, independently of the actual struggle which Marxists (and in particular Trotsky) carried out against Stalinism, including the proletarian culture myth which accompanied its early development. We shall suggest in later chapters that Lukács, along with Goldmann and others, rejecting any consideration of Trotsky's work, and at the same time claiming to disavow Stalinism, was fundamentally at one with Stalin's positions on political and historical questions, and that this is intimately connected with his writings on literature. In the most simple terms, those who, in one way or another, came to defend the bureaucratic *realpolitik*, even if they did not like the look of some of its obvious theoretical and practical consequences (which they characterised abstractly and inadequately as 'dogmatic sectarianism'), could not avoid the danger of thereby turning away from the historical and methodological principles of Marxism. Trotsky defended and developed those principles in the whole struggle against Stalinism, and in *Literature and Revolution*.

The First World War and the October Revolution put an end to the period in which the development of Marxism could be seen as primarily the defence and extension of a body of knowledge against its opponents in philosophy, political economy, historiography and political theory. Now the relation between theory and practice comes to the fore. There is the appearance of literary schools and tendencies which do not content themselves with an implicit or even explicit attitude towards Marxist theory, but take up a definite position in relation to the Revolution itself. The world war has a shattering effect on the relation between capitalism and its literary and artistic world, an effect then compounded by the October Revolution and the revolutions and counter-revolutions of post-war Europe. Marxists, on their side, feel called upon now to understand and develop their theory as 'a guide to action', and this means dealing with questions of 'culture

and revolution' concretely, practically, and not merely abstractly and in general. It means finding answers in strategy
and tactics—with 'cultural policy' as a part of such strategy
and tactics—to the problems of actual development of organisation and consciousness in the working class in its relation
with other classes and strata, including the literary intelligentsia. This did not mean that questions of the nature of
culture were reducible to tactical considerations. Questions
of the evaluation of literary tendencies, of the quality of
literature and art produced under the immediate impact of
the Revolution, of state and party policy towards literature
and art, all became inextricably and inevitably intertwined
with the 'question of questions': what were the consequences
of the fact that socialist revolution made its first break in a
backward country, where those preconditions for socialism
which Marx took to be the product of capitalist development
were absent? This is of course a 'cultural' question of the first
order. Around this issue the crucial historical struggle un-
folded.

No sooner had the international working-class movement
been split between communism and social democracy than
communism itself faced a split no less profound: 'socialism
in a single country', banking on the internal resources of
Russia and stability in external relations, as Stalin proposed
in the Autumn of 1924 (thus reviving an old theme of social
democracy); or the strategy of world socialist revolution,
continuing what had been taken as read by communists before
Stalin's innovation, i.e., that while Tsarist Russia was the
'weakest link in the chain of imperialism', thus providing
the conditions for a successful proletarian overturn, the conditions for 'the victory of socialism' did not exist within
Russia but only on a world scale, so that the future of the
workers' state in Russia depended on the extension of the
revolution at least to the advanced countries of Western
Europe. It is only in the context of the opening up of the
struggle between these two perspectives, with all the associated
questions of the cultural backwardness of Russia, that
Trotsky's attack in *Literature and Revolution* on the concept
and programme of a proletarian culture can be understood.
In this controversy Trotsky was compelled to return many

times from questions of immediate policy to fundamental matters of the historical role of productive forces and technique and of the nature of cognition. This was hardly surprising, in view of the fateful issues involved. 'Proletarian culture' was essentially a narrow pragmatic conception of a new culture constructed on the foundations of the perceived characteristics of the working class and its revolution. It soon became the instrument of policy for those who, following Stalin and Bukharin, presented the 'building of socialism' in a national framework in similar pragmatic terms, disregarding the absence of any of the necessary cultural and productive conditions for socialism. Instead of a new culture eventually emerging from the acquisition and reworking of all past culture, the bureaucratic conception would soon require a 'culture' which could be summoned by order of state in order to confirm and support the lie that socialism could be achieved by a forced march which ignored the absence of the cultural preconditions for socialism. The enthusiasts of proletarian culture in the years immediately following the Revolution would have been horrified to know that they prepared the ground for the 'illustrative literature' of the 'final victory of socialism' in 1936.

Trotsky's introduction to *Literature and Revolution* states his main point very clearly:

> It is fundamentally incorrect to contrast bourgeois culture and bourgeois art with proletarian culture and proletarian art. The latter will never exist, because the proletarian regime is temporary and transient. The historic significance and moral grandeur of the proletarian revolution consist in the fact that it is laying the foundations of a culture which is above classes and which will be the first culture which is truly human.[4]

As for 'proletarian culture' under capitalism, Trotsky restates Marx's position, that the proletariat is in the first place an exploited class, separated by exploitation and oppression from the historical gains made by humanity in its struggle with nature. The proletariat develops class consciousness, concentrated into political strategy, tactics and organisation, together with the theoretical conquests which must enrich and develop through them. Only by abolishing itself as a class (by abolishing the property foundations of capitalist society) will the proletariat put itself in a position to acquire and develop culture. The bourgeoisie, before it comes to rule society, growing up in the pores of the feudal order, builds up its own type of private ownership, and along with this its schools, churches and academies, and trains its own corps of administrators, philosophers, architects, dramatists and poets; but the proletariat grows up in a capitalist society whose very condition of existence is that the proletariat shall have no property. With this lack of property and of any life relatively independent of the mode of exploitation carried out by the ruling class, the proletariat is deprived of culture in a way in which the nascent bourgeoisie was not. It can become conscious of its historical role and its aims only by becoming conscious of its lack of culture. Consequently, to proceed in cultural policy from the idea of an art and literature which correspond to the nature of this class is to court disaster, to fly in the face of reality:

> The proletarian has to have in art the expression of the new spiritual point of view which is just beginning to be formulated within him, and to which art must help him give form. This is not a state order, but an historic demand. Its strength lies in the objectivity of historic necessity. You cannot pass this by, nor escape its force.[5]

The policy considerations which follow from this are not matters of whether to be more or less liberal in dealing with writers:

> The Marxian method affords an opportunity to estimate the development of the new art, to trace all its sources, to help the most progressive tendencies by a critical illumination of the road, but it does not do more than that. Art must make its own way and by its own means. The Marxian methods are not the same as the artistic. The Party leads the proletariat but not the historic processes of history. There are domains in which the Party leads, directly and imperatively.

There are domains in which it only cooperates. There are, finally, domains in which it only orientates itself. The domain of art is not one in which the Party is called upon to command. It can and must protect and help it, but it can only lead it indirectly. It can and must give the additional credit of its confidence to various art groups, which are striving sincerely to approach the revolution and so help an artistic formulation of the Revolution. And at any rate, the Party cannot and will not take the position of a literary circle which is struggling and merely competing with other literary circles. The Party stands guard over the historic interests of the working class in its entirety. Because it prepares consciously and step by step the ground for a new culture and therefore for a new art, it regards the literary fellow-travellers not as the competitors of the writers of the working-class, but as the real or potential helpers of the working-class in the big work of reconstruction. The Party understands the episodic character of the literary groups of a transition period and estimates them, not from the point of view of the class passports of the individual gentlemen literati, but from the point of view of the place which these groups occupy and can occupy in preparing a Socialist culture. If it is not possible to determine the place of any given group today, then the Party as a party will wait patiently and gracefully.[6]

(It is interesting to note the way in which the issues in this historic controversy are distorted in the extreme if they are viewed in an abstract 'literary' manner. For example, it is surely a travesty of the truth to suggest, as Raymond Williams does when discussing Lenin and Trotsky's rejection of any policy of cultural directives, that it was 'from the reservations' [i.e. their reservations on complete liberty of expression] that the Stalinist 'version of commitment' [striking euphemism!] 'became powerful'! At a stroke, by substituting the succession of concepts for the struggle of real forces, Williams erases the actual political and physical destruction of Lenin's and Trotsky's followers, a destruction which was the prerequisite for Stalin's 'version of commitment'. Williams writes as if there was a single continuous process 'from the

cause of humanity to the cause of the people to the revolution to the party to the [shifting] party line.'[7] What we have
here is, as so often, not an objective account of the sources,
content and consequences of a particular theoretical and practical struggle [Trotsky's battle with the advocates of proletarian culture, which merged in part with the battle against
the bureaucracy's 'socialism in a single country'] but a deduction from the received truth that Stalinism found its source
in elements already existing in the communism of Lenin and
Trotsky.)

For all his opposition to any policy of 'creation of literary
schools by decree', Trotsky was certainly not inclined to discuss literary tendencies solely in the terms they decided. His
clash with the Russian Formalists, for example, is well known;
and when some of the Futurists claimed that their work
'freed art of its thousand-year-old bonds of bourgeoisdom',
Trotsky warned them of the dangers of sterility:

> The call of the Futurists to break with the past, to do away
> with Pushkin, to liquidate tradition, etc., has a meaning
> in so far as it is addressed to the old literary caste, to the
> closed-in circle of the intelligentsia. In other words, it has
> a meaning only in so far as the Futurists are busy cutting
> the cord which binds them to the priests of bourgeois lite-
> rary tradition.
>
> But the meaninglessness of this call becomes evident as
> soon as it is addressed to the proletariat. The working class
> does not have to, and cannot break with literary tradition,
> because the working class is not in the grip of such tradition,
> The working class does not know the old literature, it still
> has to commune with it, it still has to master Pushkin, to
> absorb him, and so overcome him. The Futurist break with
> the past is, after all, a tempest in the closed-in world of the
> intelligentsia which grew up on Pushkin, Fet, Tiutschev,
> Briusov, Balmont and Blok, and who are passive, not be-
> cause they are infected with a superstitious veneration for
> the forms of the past, but because they have nothing in
> their soul which calls for new forms. They simply have
> nothing to say. They sing the old feelings over again with
> slightly new words. The Futurists have done well to push

away from them. But it is not necessary to make a universal law of development out of the act of pushing away.[8]

Estimating the prospects of these 'revolutionary innovators of form', Trotsky first took account of the concrete class relations within which their development took place. One should not draw mechanical conclusions from the fact that Marinetti and the Italian Futurists, seeking social equivalents for their 'revolutionary' formal experiments, embraced Mussolini's brand of political originality. In Russia the Futurists' demonstrative rebellion had coincided with the overthrow by the proletarian revolution of the conditions they despised. There was no time for their experimental forms and style to be incorporated by the old circles, as so often happens, 'because these circles do not exist any longer'. In 1924 Trotsky could therefore envisage for Futurism 'the possibility of a rebirth, of entering into the new art, not as an all-determining current, but as an important component part'.[9]

Trotsky's comments on Futurism make clear that his insistence on judging art 'by the standards of art' and on appropriating the artistic traditions of the past did not imply a rejection in this field of the precepts of historical materialism. Against those who considered the work of art such a uniquely individual product that it could not be amenable to a historical materialist analysis, Trotsky replies along the line marked out by the writings of Marx on society and individuality:

Individuality is a welding together of tribal, national, class, temporary and institutional elements and, in fact, it is in the uniqueness of this welding together, in the proportions of this psycho-chemical mixture, that individuality is expressed. One of the most important tasks of criticism is to analyze the individuality of the artist (that is, his art) into its component elements, and to show their correlations. In this way, criticism brings the artist closer to the reader, who also has more or less of a 'unique soul', 'artistically' unexpressed, 'unchosen', but none the less representing a union of the same elements as does the soul of a poet. So it can be seen that what serves as a bridge from soul to soul is not the unique, but the common. Only through the common is the unique known; the common is determined in man by the deepest and most persistent conditions which make up his 'soul', by the social conditions of education, of existence, of work, and of associations. The social conditions in historic human society are, first of all, the conditions of class affiliation. That is why a class standard is so fruitful in all fields of ideology, including art, and especially in art, because the latter often expresses the deepest and most hidden social aspirations.[10]

Without equating art and ideology, Trotsky can still draw the conclusion that art serves ideological purposes. The producers of ideology in other fields, such as philosophy or historiography or law, do their work from the given starting point in scholarship within the discipline and with unquestioning acceptance of the material life upon which rest their assumptions and their very existence as specialists. The artist may well find it possible to work within the framework of traditional forms, continuing to find these a vehicle for his inspiration, only to find himself one day faced with the results of revolutionary changes in the material on which he works, the consequence of imperceptible accumulated changes to which he had been blind. Perhaps the greatest artists, as Hegel suggested, are those who are able to raise their art, through original formal developments, to the level of comprehension in imagination of the implications of these tendencies beneath the appearances. In Trotsky's view the October Revolution had clearly revealed this relation between art-forms and the content of social life:

To speak of the bourgeois character of that literature which we call non-October, does not therefore necessarily mean to slander the poets who are supposedly serving art and not the bourgeoisie. For where is it written that it is impossible to serve the bourgeoisie by means of art? Just as geologic landslides reveal the deposits of earth layers, so do social landslides reveal the class character of art. Non-October art is struck by a deathly impotence for the very reason that death has struck those classes to which it was tied by its whole past. Without the bourgeois land-holding system and its customs, without the subtle suggestions of the estate and of the salon, this art sees no meaning in life, withers, becomes moribund and is reduced to nothing.[11]

In his controversy with the Formalists Trotsky refused to accept Shklovsky's notion of an aesthetic or artistic reality totally independent of social conditions (Shklovsky had drawn this conclusion from the striking resemblances in both content and treatment of narrative in cultures quite separate one from another). Besides systematic analysis of the formal structure of works of literature, art, architecture, etc., a knowledge of the historical sources of the artist's inspiration is necessary:

> The methods of formal analysis are necessary, but insufficient. The architectural scheme of the Cologne cathedral can be established by measuring the base and the height of its arches, by determining the three dimensions of its naves, the dimensions and the placement of the columns, etc. But without knowing what a mediaeval city was like, what a guild was, or what was the Catholic Church of the Middle Ages, the Cologne cathedral will never be understood. The effort to set art free from life, to declare it a craft self-sufficient unto itself, devitalizes and kills art. The very need of such an operation is an unmistakable symptom of intellectual decline.[12]

Trotsky felt no contradiction, then, between the recognition of art's unique methods, its own standards, 'its own laws of development',[13] on the one hand, and the recognition of the determination of its content by 'social being', the history of which is the history of class struggles on definite production foundations, on the other:

> A work of art should, in the first place, be judged by its own law, that is, by the law of art. But Marxism alone can explain why and how a given tendency in art has originated in a given period of history; in other words, who it was who made a demand for such an artistic form and not for

another, and why . . . It [art] is not a disembodied element feeding on itself, but a function of social man indissolubly tied to his life and environment.[14]

Trotsky goes on to make an analogy with the vital but nonetheless relative importance of form in the historical development of law. By its nature law demands formal consistency, internal coherence, and a certain rigidity. However,

> Its moving force lies in economics—in class contradictions. The law gives only a formal and an internally harmonized expression of these phenomena, not of their individual peculiarities, but of their general character, that is, of the elements that are repetitive and permanent in them. We can see now with a clarity which is rare in history how new law is made. It is not done by logical deduction, but by empirical measurement and by adjustment to the economic needs of the new ruling class.[15]

*   *   *

It is useful to dwell briefly on Trotsky's views on individuality and individualism, since he needs to consider these questions rather more concretely, i.e., in terms of the whole social formation and its development, than could Marx in his more abstract analysis of basic economic forms (though to the latter should be added his brief characterisation of bourgeois individualism—in *The German Ideology*—as a 'historically justified illusion'). Just as the Revolution could provoke a shock of recognition of the social interconnections of law and of art, so, Trotsky suggested, did the revolutionary epoch throw a brutally clear light on the reality of bourgeois individualism. Individual enterprise could no longer provide the necessary framework to develop mankind's productive forces; the emancipation of men from the social order based on individual capitalist appropriation was now a question of socialising the ownership and control of the means of production; individual freedom could in no way be achieved in opposition to that collective force which must expropriate the bourgeoisie, nor any longer in pursuit of a self-interest which by some 'hidden hand' could be thought to produce universal good. The social order which sustained the bourgeois idea of individual autonomy and freedom had reached the point of its imminent negation. But it was a fact that art and literature, throughout the era of capitalism's challenge to feudal absolutism and then of its ascendancy, had, with whatever variations, fed upon that same individualist idea:

> Having broken up human relations into atoms, bourgeois society, during the period of its rise, had a great aim for itself. Personal emancipation was its name. Out of it grew the dramas of Shakespeare and Goethe's 'Faust'. Man placed himself in the centre of the universe, and therefore in the centre of art also. This theme sufficed for centuries. In reality, all modern literature has been nothing but an enlargement of this theme.
>
> But to the degree in which the internal bankruptcy of bourgeois society was revealed as a result of its unbearable contradictions, the original purpose, the emancipation and qualification of the individual, faded away and was relegated more and more into the sphere of a new mythology, without soul or spirit.[16]

The great literature of the whole period of the rise and domination of the bourgeoisie is thus one of the permanent gains of culture, representing and celebrating as it does the first step to breaking the chains formed by the conviction of direct dependence on God and the unchallengeable character of the coercive force of hereditary authority. In the art and literature inspired by this historical advance men find the beginnings of the confidence needed to measure their world and experience by a human standard. Work, love, life and death, age and youth, can be faced as problems of human need, problems to be faced and resolved in the realm of the human and not accepted as visitations of blind fate or divine providence. Such was the promise. Even though poets and novelists glimpsed the anti-human and anti-artistic tendencies of capitalism, they were able to express their criticisms in terms of the humanist and individualist tradition, i.e., in terms of the conditions for individual fulfilment and not by appeal to some mystical authority. But then comes the time when the gains of the bourgeois era can be preserved and developed only by the surpassing of this framework, by ending bourgeois relations and the bourgeois class as such. An individuality which appeals to the humanist tradition and asserts itself against rather than through the collective actions necessary for human emancipation will end in impotence and mysticism:

> Our age is an age of great aims. This is what stamps it. But the grandeur of these aims lies in man's effort to free himself from mystic and from every other intellectual vagueness and in his effort to reconstruct society and himself in accord with his own plan. This, of course, is much bigger than the child's play of the ancients which was becoming to their childish age, or the mediaeval ravings of monks, or the arrogance of individualism which tears personality away from the collectivity, and then, draining it to the very bottom, pushes it off into the abyss of pessimism, or sets it on all fours before the remounted bull Apis.[17]

The 'great aims' of the twentieth century, however, could not be achieved except by the class of proletarians, who had yet to appropriate the indispensable gains made by bourgeois individualism. And this appropriation was a condition of the elaboration of any post-revolutionary culture. Against those who set up bourgeois individualism in art and literature as an abstract opposite, Trotsky wrote:

> The trouble is that the average proletarian is lacking in this very quality. In the mass, proletarian individuality has not been sufficiently formed and differentiated. It is just such heightening of the objective quality and the subjective consciousness of individuality that is the most valuable contribution of the cultural advance at the threshold of which we stand today.[18]

The last phrase has now a ring of bitter irony. Beyond that threshold on which the Soviet working class stood in 1924 was not at all a path of cultural advance on which they could form and develop individuality, but one upon which that individuality was sacrificed on the altar of a bureaucracy whose 'culture' became more and more a mixture of ideological distortion and manipulation, with the old 'Great Russian' coarseness, swaggering and bullying, now arming itself with modern techniques of terror. Half a century later, it is now well known that, despite the previous Stalinist success in suppressing the historical record, Trotsky's struggle against Stalin and his faction (representing the interests of the bureaucracy with which it merged more and more) began in alliance with Lenin on Lenin's proposal (see especially, M. Lewin's *Lenin's Last Struggle*). One of the memoranda written by Lenin in the course of this fight, and acknowledged officially to exist only in 1956, brings out particularly clearly the cultural implications of this fight:

> But now, we must, in conscience, admit the contrary; we call ours an apparatus which, in fact, is still quite alien to us; which is bourgeois and tsarist mishmash, and which it was in no way possible to get rid of in five years without the help of other countries as we were 'busy' most of the time with military engagements and the fight against famine.
>
> It is quite natural in such circumstances that the 'freedom to withdraw from the union' by which we justify ourselves will be a mere scrap of paper unable to defend the non-Russians from the onslaught of that really Russian man, the Great Russian, the chauvinist, in substance a rascal and a lover of violence, as the typical Russian bureaucrat is. There is no doubt that the infinitesimal percentage of Soviet and sovietized workers will drown in that sea of chauvinistic, Great-Russian riff-raff like a fly in milk.[19]

This was only one of a series of notes and letters, dictated by Lenin during his final illness, aimed at Stalin and his group in the apparatus. The dreadful backwardness in production, the exhaustion of the masses in revolution and civil war, which as always produced its reaction, and the isolation following the defeat of the German revolution in 1923—these were the conditions which favoured the dominance of that faction that rested on the personnel of the old state machine and on the better-off peasants and small entrepreneurs given a new lease of life by the unavoidable New Economic Policy of 1921. The programme of 'socialism in a single country', announced nine months after Lenin's death and four months after the appearance of *Literature and Revolution*, was a succinct expression of the cultural as well as the political horizons of the bureaucracy and its allies. Had the next generations of Russian workers been able to see *Literature and Revolution* (as they certainly still are not), it is doubtful if they would have shared the 'anti-humanism' of some of our latter-day 'Marxists', given such passages as:

> What the worker will take from Shakespeare, Goethe, Pushkin, or Dostoievsky, will be a more complex idea of human personality, of its passions and feelings, a deeper and profounder understanding of its psychic forces and of the role of the subconscious, etc. In the final analysis, the worker will become richer.[20]

Trotsky refused to ignore the fact that because of its position as an oppressed class, the proletariat after conquering power remained 'uneducated aesthetically', however 'spiritually and therefore, artistically . . . sensitive'.[21] For this reason, as we have seen, he took issue with the Futurists on their dismissal of individualism. They took from the Revolution what corresponded to their own feelings, seeing in the abstraction of the 'collectivist nature' of the proletariat the equivalent of their own rejection of a jaded individualism in literary and artistic circles. In this way, said Trotsky, they themselves fell into an 'egocentrism . . . extreme individualism', ignoring the cultural needs of the masses, who must absorb and transcend the old culture. *Literature and Revolution* is the clearest statement of this necessity, and there Trotsky achieves a noble and inspiring vision of the 'truly human' culture of the future. But more than this was needed, as Trotsky well knew. For the mass of workers to become 'aesthetically educated', to 'absorb and assimilate the elements of the old cultures', was not a matter of repeating the history of those cultures but rather of a 'free and conscious' plan and choice based upon them. The condition of this freedom was a material one: the productive foundation for socialism laid by capitalist development itself. Marx had written in 1845:

> ... this development of productive forces (which at the same time implies the actual empirical existence of men in their *world—historical,* instead of local, being) is an absolutely necessary practical premise, because without it privation, *want* is merely made general, and with *want* the struggle for necessities would begin again, and all the old filthy business ('all the old crap') would necessarily be restored ... [22]

Revolution in backward Russia confirmed this cryptic formula. It was entirely consistent for the bureaucracy, which rejected the strategy of world revolution necessary to transform that situation, to reject also the cultural policy conclusions drawn by Trotsky:

> The proletariat also needs a continuity of creative tradition. At the present time the proletariat realizes this continuity not directly, but indirectly, through the creative bourgeois intelligentsia which gravitates towards the proletariat and which wants to keep warm under its wing. The proletariat tolerates a part of this intelligentsia, supports another part, half-adopts a third, and entirely assimilates a fourth. The policy of the Communist Party towards art is determined by the complexity of this process, by its internal many-sidedness. It is impossible to reduce this policy to one formula, to something short like a bird's bill. Nor is it necessary to do this.[23]

In later years Trotsky returned to the question of the relation between the artist's individuality and the Revolution. In the period of his exile, when the Stalinist betrayal and terror were at their height, the immediate question was no longer one of the policy of the young Soviet state and the principles which should guide it. The victorious 'Thermidorean bureaucracy', as Trotsky termed it, had now successfully transformed the world communist movement into its instrument. Its use of the 'weapon of culture' within the USSR, and internationally, demanded a literature which was above all acquiescent in the vast lie machine and brutal terror with which all opposition was being liquidated. In a situation where Fascism had triumphed in Italy, Germany and Spain and a world war had become inevitable, and in which the revolutionary movement was in danger of total destruction at the hands of the Stalinist leadership, Trotsky saw a world—historical crisis of all mankind, in which the relation between political commitment and freedom of artistic creation was thrown into the sharpest possible relief, particularly in contrast to the conformist literature required by Stalinism. It is for this reason that 'Towards a Free Revolutionary Art',[24] published over the names of André Breton and Diego Rivera in the autumn of 1938 and drafted in collaboration with Trotsky, constitutes more than a propaganda manifesto (though in the latter aspect it has inestimable importance). It bears the same relation to the theory and practice of a Lukács of those years as did Trotsky's mortal combat with Stalinism to Khrushchev's 'if we had opened our mouths, we would have lost our heads' in the 'secret speech' at the Twentieth Congress:

> In the contemporary world we must recognise the ever more widespread destruction of those conditions under which intellectual creation is possible. From this follows of necessity an increasingly manifest degradation not only of the work of art but also of the specifically 'artistic' personality.[25]

At the historical limit of the development of capitalist society, then, the inimicality of capitalism to artistic production reaches its own extreme. Again, how shall the artist defend his individuality and respond to the need to create, unless he identifies with those forces which can remove the social order, which was built on individual appropriation?

> Only naturally, he turns to the Stalinist organisations which hold out the possibility of escaping from his isolation. But if he is to avoid complete demoralisation, he cannot remain there, because of the impossibility of delivering his own

message and the degrading servility which these organisa-
tions exact from him in exchange for certain material
advantages.[26]

Breton and Rivera called upon artists and writers to turn to
'those who with unshaken fidelity bear witness to the revolution . . . [and] who, for this reason, are alone able to bring it
to fruition, and along with it the ultimate free expression of
all forms of human genius'.[27] Two conditions were required,
if art were to play a revolutionary role. And here Trotsky (in
a situation where, as we have noted, the relations are more
starkly revealed) reverted to the positions he had first developed in *Literature and Revolution*. In the first place, there
must be complete opposition to any restriction on artistic
creation, let alone commands from above (whether from the
state in the USSR and its apparatus abroad, or through the
demands of capital):

> In the realm of artistic creation, the imagination must es-
> cape from all constraint and must under no pretext allow
> itself to be placed under bonds. To those who urge us,
> whether for today or for tomorrow, to consent that art
> should submit to a discipline which we hold to be radically
> incompatible with its nature, we give a flat refusal and we
> repeat our deliberate intention of standing by the formula
> *complete freedom for art*.[28]

However, Trotsky and his collaborators affirm that not only
the defence of this freedom but also the production of artistic
works of true stature in our day will in their opinion come
only from participation in the revolutionary struggle to resolve
mankind's mortal crisis:

> It should be clear by now that in defending freedom of
> thought we have no intention of justifying political indif-
> ference, and that it is far from our wish to revive a so-called
> 'pure' art which generally serves the extremely impure
> ends of reaction. No, our conception of the role of art is
> too high to refuse it an influence on the fate of society. We
> believe that the supreme task of art in our epoch is to take

part actively and consciously in the preparation of the revolution. But the artist cannot serve the struggle for freedom unless he subjectively assimilates its social content, unless he feels in his very nerves its meaning and drama and freely seeks to give his own inner world incarnation in his art.[29]

Trotsky found himself at the very centre of the most critical development in Marxist theory and practice, in the Russian Revolution, and it is from the necessity of striving for an all-round development of Marxism to fight through the critical years which followed that the strength of his work on literature derives. All his resources had to be concentrated on the fundamental questions of historical materialism: the relation of intellectual or 'spiritual' culture to the development of productive forces as a whole; the relation between art's own development and the stimulus and demands of the class struggle; the associated problem of the relation between individuality and social forms. These questions were certain to arise in acute form in the period of transition from capitalism; but because the first step in the socialist revolution had been taken in backward Russia, which then remained isolated, they came up for review and development in even sharper form. What is remarkable is that, in the context of those historical events and the political and theoretical battles in which he took the leading role, Trotsky was scrupulously careful to demarcate the specific problems presented by the analysis and understanding of art and literature, in their most fundamental relation to philosophy, to dialectical materialism. From what standpoint? It was not of course only a question of meticulous scholarship and breadth of vision, which characterise all Trotsky's works. Like Marx, he wrote in order that others should learn to accept the same responsibilities as he had for the struggle for human emancipation. Revolutionary practice must proceed always in a struggle to master consciously all sides of the historical totality.

In his efforts to overcome the great problems which were accumulating in the field of cultural policy Trotsky felt compelled to correct all oversimplified and mechanical views of the sources of a new art. And here he expanded on the opinion we have already noted in Marx and many before him, that it is important to distinguish between the artistic and scientific modes of comprehending the world: 'In the field of poetry we deal with the process of feeling the world in images, and not with the process of knowing the world scientifically.' Neither Trotsky nor any other Marxist pretended that this 'feeling the world in images' is an activity of which we have a scientific account. There is great scope for historical, biographical and psychological research on that score, and it is obvious that to think that somehow the secret of the process can be deduced from the general principles of Marxism would be nonsense. The works of artists come to be accepted by us as creative because we experience a transformation of our feelings on the reception and contemplation of images. This response is not totally separated from thinking and analysis (any more than is the work's production) but neither is it the same thing. Why and exactly how it is that we are affected in this way by sensuous, representative images we do not know. But we *can* know from the study of history why it is that certain of these images and certain types of image-making arise and are important at particular times, or even for very long periods.

For example, Trotsky goes into some detail to 'place' the Futurists historically and to trace the effects of their history in a failure to achieve organic unity in their poetry. This analysis illuminates the problem of the specific importance of questions of form:

> Mayakovsky's works have no peak; they are not disciplined internally. The parts refuse to obey the whole. Each part tries to be separate. It develops its own dynamics, without considering the welfare of the whole. That is why it is without entity or dynamics. The Futurists have not yet found a synthetic expression of words and images in their work.[30]

It was particularly in criticising the work of the great Futurist poets that Trotsky found it necessary to emphasise the distinction between abstraction and scientific cognition, on the one hand, and artistic imagination, on the other. When poets embraced the cause of the October Revolution, and produced poetry in which they sought to express their new-found allegiance and enthusiasm, the results were almost always disappointing, to say the least. In rebelling against the pre-revolutionary world of conformist and conventional art these poets had rebelled also against the establishment to which that art-world was attached. They had found in the practice of their own art, with its invention of new styles of life as well as art, a way of taking strength from their profound conviction of the worn-out and debilitating nature of the old society. They were the latest in a long line of great bohemian rebels against bourgeois society, rebels whose social roots had been indicated by Marx in 1848[31]. and later by Plekhanov.[32] These Russian Futurists, however, were in full spate when they unexpectedly encountered a revolution:

> Futurists became Communists. By this very act they entered the sphere of more profound questions and relationships, which far transcended the limits of their own little world, and which were not quite worked out organically in their soul. That is why Futurists, even including Mayakovsky, are weakest artistically at those points where they finish as Communists. This is more the result of their spiritual past than of their social origin. The Futurist poets have not mastered the elements of the Communist point of view and world-attitude sufficiently to find an organic expression for them in words; they have not entered, so to speak, into their blood. That is why they are frequently subject to artistic and psychologic defeats, to stilted forms and to making much noise about nothing. In its most revolutionary and compelling works, Futurism becomes stylization.[33]

These 'stilted forms', which so often gave the impression of a striving for effect ('Mayakovsky shouts too often, where he should merely speak') frustrated by some lack of inner resources, are the result, then, of the separation between the worlds of feeling of the artistic intelligentsia and of the working class, a separation which has profound historical roots and cannot be overcome by an effort of will any more than by decree. On its side the proletariat needs still to assimilate bourgeois culture. The artist, for his part, no matter how much he wishes to change his allegiance completely, cannot jump out of his skin. Again: 'It is one thing to understand something and express it logically, and quite another thing to assimilate it organically, reconstructing the whole system of one's feelings.'[34] Trotsky gave the example of Boris Pilnyak:

> One cannot approach art as one can politics, not because artistic creation is a religious rite or something mystical . . . but because it has its own laws of development, and above all because in artistic creation an enormous role is played by subconscious processes — slower, more idle and less subjected to management and guidance, just because they are subconscious. It has been said that those writings of Pilnyak's which are closer to Communism are feebler than those which are politically further away from us. What is the explanation? Why, just this, that on the rationalistic plane Pilnyak is ahead of himself as an artist . . . [35]

For the artist who proved capable of 'reshaping the world of his feelings . . . by means of a scientific programme . . . the most difficult inner labour . . . ',[36] there arose in any case the question of frankly recognising that the period after the Revolution was a transitional one, in which it would be sheer idealism to anticipate the later period of communism, in which the relations between art and industry, between mental and manual labour, between artist and audience, would be transformed:

> Art is created on the basis of a continual everyday, cultural, ideological interrelationship between a class and its artists. Between the aristocracy or the bourgeoisie and their artists there was no split in daily life. The artists lived, and still live, in a bourgeois milieu, breathing the air of bourgeois salons, they received and are receiving hypodermic inspirations from their class. Does the proletariat of today offer such a cultural—ideological milieu, in which the new artist may obtain, without leaving it in his day-to-day existence, all the inspiration he needs while at the same time mastering the procedures of his craft? No, the working masses are culturally extremely backward; the illiteracy or low level

of literacy of the majority of workers presents in itself a very great obstacle to this. And above all, the proletariat, in so far as it remains a proletariat, is compelled to expend its best forces in political struggle, in restoring the economy, and in meeting elementary cultural needs . . . [37]

*   *   *

The problem of 'realism' in literature is not something separate from the question Marx had raised: how to explain the continued appeal of works of art produced by past cultures? At its simplest the unity of the two problems is posed by reformulating both: what reality do men find in works whose historical subject matter is remote from their own experiences? Just as Marx suggested that modern men found in the forms of Greek art the embodiment of attitudes to the world which coincided with the strivings necessitated and the future promised by their own relationship to nature and history, so Trotsky pointed to a real content in works of art which was not exhausted by the effects of the class structure of the society in which the artist lived. If Pushkin's poetry could still arouse feelings which certainly did not result from any sympathy with the class whose characteristic assumptions and feelings he shared, there must be a reason. Pushkin expressed the standpoint of the nobility: 'But the expression that Pushkin gave his feelings is so saturated with the artistic, and generally with the psychological, experience of centuries, is so crystallised, that it has lasted down to our time.'[38]

In another example in the same work Trotsky suggested that there was a reality about such a thing as the fear of death which persisted even though different forms of it succeeded each other, and that poetry on this theme by Dante, Shakespeare, Byron, Goethe, 'and also by the Psalmist', moves men deeply today. In such works, characters, situations, feelings and actions are pictured or suggested realistically, to the extent that the poet or dramatist works in such a way as to conceal nothing of the essential forces and pressures which men feel and act upon. Only from this can come the attainment of a particularity which is rich in the wealth of its interconnections, a true individuality rather than a striking singularity. To convey in sensuous form such individuality is the secret of the successful artistic image. The way, for example, that these particular men and women, formed by the artist so that their problems are not oversimplified and abstracted, confront the fear of death, is something which can be a vital source of energy for every future generation. To the common element in the experience (what is common, in this example, is not only the fact of the fear of death but also the unrelenting necessity of confronting and overcoming it whatever the particular historical situation) is added something else: the fact that poets have over the centuries accumulated a specialised lore and craftsmanship which has become more or less perfected in its ability to grasp and express these sensuous aspects of the relation between the general and the particular.

This 'artistic . . . experience of centuries . . . crystallised', is no less real than the 'historically specific', which some Marxists make the sole criterion of realism. What is more, it makes room for the central element of practice in human life and cognition; and in this way points to the fundamental flaw in that historical relativism which is so often mistaken for Marxism.

Following the thread suggested by Trotsky's remarks about the clear light shed on innovation in, for example, law and art in times of revolution, we find a highly suggestive indication of the way in which Marxism may tackle the changing relations between form and content in art. Many others before and after Trotsky have shown the importance of avoiding an abstract separation and opposition between form and content, and demonstrated the way in which the artist works to bring out 'the form *of* the content' rather than manipulating the subject matter in order arbitrarily to fill a given preconceived form. What Trotsky is able to suggest (and it does not go beyond a suggestion) is the way in which such considerations of internal structure of the work will articulate with analysis of the changing social—historical reality which structures the world of thought and feeling of the writer and his audience:

[Marxism] does not at all 'incriminate' a poet with the thoughts and feelings which he expresses, but raises questions of a much more profound significance, namely, to which order of feelings does a given artistic work correspond in all its peculiarities? What are the social conditions of these thoughts and feelings? What place do they occupy in the historical development of a society and of a class? And, further, what literary heritage has entered into the elaboration of the new form? Under the influence of what historic impulse have the new complexes of feelings and thoughts broken through the shell which divides them from the sphere of poetic consciousness?[39]

Naturally the degree to which the results of historical changes in social consciousness can find expression without major changes in the forms of literature and art is a matter for empirical research in each case. No doubt we can expect that the approach and the immediate aftermath of revolutions will pose most urgently the problem of the obsolescence of artistic forms and the need for innovation, but again care is necessary. How often have revolutionary classes sought inspiration in past historical achievements, and found their way to this inspiration in an appeal to ancient forms against the modernism of the rulers? And in general terms, literary changes are not different from other changes in social consciousness in this aspect: 'Artistic creation is always a complicated turning inside-out of old forms, under the influence of new stimuli which originate outside the art.'[40] The old forms are developed and transformed, not created completely anew by the new stimuli. They represent not relics of dead civilisations but acquisitions of mankind in the struggle for life, for men's mastery of their own fate. Again: 'Literature, whose methods and processes have their roots far back in the most distant past and represent the accumulated experience of verbal craftsmanship, expresses the thoughts, feelings, points of view and hopes of the new epoch and of its new class.'[41]

It is because literary forms have this character that 'verbal form is not a passive reflection of a preconceived artistic idea, but an active element which influences the idea itself'. However, when the Formalists wished to go beyond this, Trotsky waxed sarcastic:

Reasoning 'formally' one may produce 'Eugene Onegin' in

two ways: either by subordinating the selection of words to a preconceived artistic idea (as Pushkin himself did), or by solving the problem algebraically. From the 'Formal' point of view, the second method is more correct, because it does not depend upon mood, inspiration or other unsteady things, and has besides the advantage that while leading to 'Eugene Onegin' it may bring one to an incalculable number of other great works. All that one needs is infinity in time, called eternity ... But such an active mutual relationship — in which form influences and at times entirely transforms content — is known to us in all fields of social and even biologic life. This is no reason at all for rejecting Darwinism and Marxism and for the creation of a Formalist school either in biology or sociology.[42]

Formalism, just as much as neglect of form, results in inability to see the actual dialectic of development of art:

Each new literary school — if it is really a school and not an arbitrary grafting — is the result of a preceding development, of the craftsmanship of word and colour already in existence, and only pulls away from the shores of what has been attained in order to conquer the elements anew.[43]

What is the relevance of all this to the question of realism, said by Lukács and his followers to be the central category of a Marxist theory of literature? While giving due importance to literary form and technique, and explaining that these had a 'content' in and of themselves, Trotsky certainly did not think that mastery of form and technique would by itself guarantee the production of works which could be called realistic (in the broadest sense). Here all the social and psychological influences which form the consciousness of artist and audience come into play. Trotsky had occasion to take up the ideas of the 'Lef' group in Russia, a group which reacted violently against a realism which it thought too contemplative and acquiescent in the existing reality. Its members proposed an art and architecture which expressed an active, transforming attitude to nature and society. Trotsky saw this as a false distinction, and one which must lead to the throwing away of invaluable artistic and technical acquisitions. If the 'Lef' group wanted art to be 'not a mirror, but a hammer', then they should remember that to the man who wields a hammer, knowledge of how hard to strike, exactly where and when, depends on an accurate knowledge of the object and on practice in the arts of gaining such knowledge.

> Of course no one speaks about an exact mirror. No one even thinks of asking the new literature to have a mirror-like impassivity. The deeper literature is, and the more it is imbued with the desire to shape life, the more significantly and dynamically it will be able to 'picture' life.[44]

This, incidentally, is what Trotsky had in mind when he reminded the Formalists that, whatever the importance of the fact that the 'laws of art' have their own 'peculiarity', it must not be forgotten that what the art works on is natural and social reality. Eagleton[45] has commended Trotsky's phrase, 'Artistic creation is a deflection, a changing and a transformation of reality, in accordance with the peculiar laws of art',[46] and suggests that it was an idea built upon by Macherey,[47] who argues that 'the effect of literature is essentially to *deform* rather than to imitate'.[48] This is another example of the dangers of isolating quotations from their contexts and then fitting them into some imaginary continuity of ideas. Trotsky's point, in this sentence, was that when art proceeds with its (relatively) independent work, it *is* reality that it 'deflects'. And the essential point for Trotsky is that the artistic mode of 'transforming' reality, far from deforming it, as Eagleton and Macherey think, is one of the ways in which men come to grasp the unity of opposites constituted by nature and man's practice of cognition in and of it.

In the most general sense Trotsky's emphasis here makes a link between Marx's *Theses on Feuerbach*, with its emphasis on human practice as objective and at the same time source and criterion of knowledge, and the search of Benjamin and Brecht for a contemporary art which is able to go beyond passive reflection to active transformation of reality. This starting point of necessary practice in the cognition of an independently existing material reality works against any oversimplified and abstract 'construction' of reality according to some conclusion about the working class and its 'revolutionariness'. Rather, the most dynamic and realistic art, that which is able truly to inform human feelings and human practice, is that which works its way through 'that real, true revolution which is developing obstinately and moving from country to country, and which appears, therefore, to some pseudo-revolutionists as a boresome repetititon'.[49] From this single reality writers who come equally well equipped in terms of artistic training and mastery of technique may well produce very different results and degrees of success as realists. Besides their decision to be realistic, besides their technique, besides the breadth of their experience, there is the matter of the 'standard' of their realism. They may be restricted to a naturalistic portrayal of the brute facts of existence (like Pilnyak, for whom 'the disorder of the Revolution' was 'a fundamental fact'). On the other hand, a historical standard can help to take the work beyond 'episodic and sometimes anecdotal subjects':

> The invisible axis (the earth's axis is also invisible) should be the Revolution itself, around which should turn the whole unsettled, chaotic and reconstructing life. But in order that the reader should feel this axis, the author himself must have felt it and at the same time must have thought it through.[50]

4
A Man for all Seasons: Georg Lukács

The intellectual career of Georg Lukács is unique.[1] It runs from the days of the Austro-Hungarian Empire and Wilhelmine Germany, through the First World War and the Russian, German and Hungarian Revolutions of 1917–19, into the inter-war transformation of the Comintern and the victories of Fascism, the Moscow Trials, the Popular Front and the Nazi–Soviet Pact. It spans the 'anti-Fascist' coalitions of the Second World War and its immediate aftermath, the subsequent Cold War, the crisis of Stalinism, the 1956 Hungarian Revolution, the Sino–Soviet split, the invasion of Czechoslovakia in 1968. It closes with Lukács an internationally famous scholar, engaged at the end on monumental general systems of philosophy and aesthetics. Lukács and his admirers have constructed the myth of an independent Marxist thinker who, while making formal concessions to the Stalinist bureaucracy in the form of double-edged formulations, self-criticisms, Aesopian writings on literary rather than directly political matters, and long silences, nonetheless produced a great body of Marxist work, an important and unique contribution to the Marxist theory of literature and art. In particular, Lukács is always anxious to appear as an opponent of the 'dogmatic sectarianism' which he sees as the essential character of Stalinism.[2]

That Lukács was more knowledgeable and sophisticated than the hundreds of official spokesmen for Stalinism on 'cultural' questions may be readily admitted. But the nettle must be grasped. From the beginnings of Stalinism in 1924 until his own death in 1972, Lukács, for all his 'theoretical' work, was at no time an opponent of the Stalinist revisions of Marxist theory. He conducted no fight, even in words, against the bloody consequences of these revisions, in the USSR or internationally. His later writings make many references to the sufferings of Communist intellectuals at the hands of 'dogmatic sectarianism', but he is silent on the horrendous political and physical consequences of Stalinism for millions of workers. Most important, he makes clear that the basic platform of Stalin — that of 'socialism in a single country' — meets with his complete agreement. Given all this, the question must be asked: is it possible that his literary criticism and the attendant philosophy could somehow be a development of Marxism unaffected by this political reality? Is it conceivable that Lukács worked successfully on 'the independence and theoretical originality of Marxist aesthetics'[3] while reconciling himself to the situation in Russia in 1931? Did silence on the Moscow Trials and the rest provide the ideal setting for Lukács's declared aim of 'determining the place of productive and receptive aesthetic conduct and theorising within the real order of human actions'?[4] If scholarly convention decrees that such a framework for considering Lukács's theories is emotive or too partisan, one should draw some conclusions about the function of such conventions. It is not a matter of damning Lukács' literary theories by pointing to his politics. Rather, it is suggested in what follows here that the limitations of Lukács's development of the ideas of Marx on aesthetics and literature are the limitations of that social force to which he reconciled himself in life, i.e. the Soviet bureaucracy. That adaptation did not fundamentally disturb Lukács's initial aspiration: that of a 'progressive' bourgeois intellectual, seeking everywhere the path to the fulfilment of a bourgeois democratic revolution which somehow was lost but which the bourgeoisie's best sons must be persuaded to find again.

All the thousands of words written by Lukács about 'praxis' remain at the level of human practice in general, the labour process as such, so that he is not obliged to discuss the real theoretical implications of his own political practice and its relation to the practice of the proletarian revolution. One way of seeing Lukács is as the extreme example (type?) of the

bourgeois intellectual who shows great sympathy for the proletariat and its struggles so long as these can be contained
within the scope of the bourgeois—democratic ideal and do
not spill over into the realm of political independence of the
working class. It was exactly such a bourgeois—democratic relation to the proletariat that met the requirements of Stalinism.
Within this framework Lukács could blatantly and crudely
ignore the work of Trotsky on literary as on all other questions. And the same basic orientation meant that the philosophical, sociological and aesthetic ideas absorbed by Lukács
in the neo-Kantian circles of pre-1917 Germany were not
negated by revolutionary Marxism when Lukács declared himself a communist, but were adapted (not without initial
clashes) to an 'orthodoxy' which not only did not disturb
the bureaucracy but helped to validate its rule and its 'theoretical' credentials. In reality Marxism could only be developed
in the course of a struggle against Stalinism.

Against this background it is perhaps easier to sense some
of the implications of Brecht's criticism of Lukács in the
1930s — that he remained tied to a canon of realism in literature which was that of the nineteenth-century bourgeoisie.
When it came to questions of history and class struggle, Lukács
did not proceed from the revolutionary role of the proletariat
and the economic contradictions of capitalism, but from the
ideological consequences of the 'totality' of capitalist ideology;
so that reification became the enemy, and 'consciousness' the
solution. The specific developments of the class struggle
under capitalism never receive from him any analysis that
goes beyond the description in his early work of a capitalist
oppression which is essentially defined in terms of its ideological effects. The struggle against capitalism is presented as
above all a struggle against 'false consciousness'.

This basic theoretical position has many implications for
Lukács's literary theories. Before turning to these it is important to note certain striking examples of the way in which his
literary writings were directly affected by his service to the
Soviet bureaucracy. Lukács, like his friend the bourgeois-
liberal Thomas Mann, was very concerned to rescue the progressive traditions of the German bourgeoisie, and one result
was a considerable body of work on the thinkers of the

German Enlightenment and the young Hegel in particular. *Goethe and His Age*[5] contains illuminating accounts of the ideas on aesthetics of Schiller, Goethe and Hegel, in particular of their views of the literature of classical Greece and its relevance for the understanding and development of modern civilisation, including art and literature. Lukács is undoubtedly right to point out the following:

> The affirmation of bourgeois society, even during its ascendant period, remains always an affirmation 'in spite of everything'. This internal contradiction of bourgeois realism, which manifests itself most revealingly precisely in its greatest representatives, at the same time forms for the realist literature of the bourgeoisie the problem of the positive hero; a problem which even the greatest representatives of this literature have been unable to resolve.[6]

Certainly among the qualities of the great novelist is refusal to ignore the impossibility of being at the same time great in any human sense and great or successful in the bourgeois sense. Girard has made the same point in his analysis of the work of Stendhal. Bitterly exposing the destructive consequences of the 'vanity' inherent in bourgeois society, and seeking thereby to discover true self-awareness, Stendhal wished aways to create a hero who could conquer vanity and also be nobly and passionately independent of any belief in God. In not one of his works was this aim achieved. The bourgeois revolution had promised human liberation, but bourgeois society could not provide the real conditions for men to have in real life what he had always aspired to in religion.

It can hardly be said that in his own day Lukács found any quality of honest objectivity within himself, in relation to this very question of the impossibility of a 'positive hero', to equal that of his revered ancestors. While he was writing his essays on Goethe, Schiller and Hölderlin, 'progressive' novelists were turning out positive heroes by the dozen on the recipe of socialist realism. Even some 20 years later,[7] when he criticised openly the disastrous results in literature of the dogmatic sectarianism of Stalin and Zhdanov, he could not ask the obvious questions: do not the conditions of bureaucratic dictatorship over the working class in the economically and culturally backward conditions of countries like Soviet Russia constitute at least as hostile an environment to the achievement in literature of a 'positive hero' as did the emerging capitalism of the late eighteenth and early nineteenth centuries? Lukács did not, indeed could not, pose this question, because even after the death of Stalin, the East German uprising of 1953, the 'great thaw', the 20th Congress and the Hungarian revolution of 1956, he remained firmly in the camp of 'socialism in a single country', and so had no basis for any concrete criticism of the socialist realism which flowed from it (see above, pp. 88ff.). In the period up to 1940, when such works as *Goethe and His Age* and *The Historical Novel* were written, his silence on the Moscow Trials, the Spanish betrayal, and all Stalin's atrocities, including the liquidation of many writers and critics whom he knew, was no doubt motivated by these basic political positions. Lukács himself is thus an example of the destructive affect on culture of the reality of 'socialism in a single country'.

Lukács has 'explained'[8] that his work on realism in the 1930s involved certain 'tactical compromises',[9] such as the required reverential references to Stalin's genius, but that this did not affect 'the real, essential content' of his work. As we have indicated, and propose to show in detail, these small 'tactical' questions are of little importance in view of the fact that in any case there was no disagreement between Lukács and Stalinism on the basic questions. Recalling how the 'actual situation' had developed, Lukács refers to the formation of the union of Soviet writers, which replaced the old RAPP (Union of Proletarian Writers): 'This also meant a struggle against so-called literary Trotskyism, which only recognised the possibility of propagandist literature in the transitional period before the full realisation of Socialism.'[10] Here, when he has the opportunity to take up in detail the fundamental questions of 'proletarian culture' and its critique in relation to the general historical and cultural problems, which would have meant responding to the position of Trotsky and Lenin on these matters, Lukács chooses very consciously to distort the issue in a manner which can only be described as cynical.

Indeed, 'It does not matter how justified friends and enemies are in referring to Trotsky in this matter, such outstanding theoreticians as Mehring unquestionably represented that point of view.'[11]

'It does not matter . . . ', but it does not seem to occur to Lukács that a historical—materialist understanding of why it became politically necessary to defeat 'Trotskyism' on all fronts which in the end could only be done by the physical liquidation of thousands, is the *sine qua non* of the understanding of the literary struggles in which he was so busily engaged. It is only from this rarefied position — which in any other critic he would have characterised as 'ideological', i.e., suffering from the illusion of an ideal autonomous development in a specialised sphere — that he could write:

> I only mention in passing that those leaders of the RAPP who were expressly Trotskyites, especially Averbach, who disappeared finally at the time of the Great Trials, ceased to take part in the management of literature. It is much more important that it was possible to recruit Gorky and a few other famous writers, who were kept out by RAPP, into the union.[12]

In the light of these judgements it is difficult, to say the least, to accept Lukács's 1967 dismissal of his participation in the 'personality cult' of Stalin in the 1930s as 'tactical'. If that were the case, why was it necessary for him gratuitously to make the following comparison in 1963?

> One mark of the poverty of German history common to both bourgeoisie and working class is the fact that Marx and Engels have so far not entered into the national cultural heritage as Lenin and Stalin have in Russia.[13]

There is something distasteful about a criticism of the German 'cultural heritage' for its failure to absorb Marx and Engels, when the Stalin whom he here raises to the level of a Lenin, a Marx or an Engels, was responsible for leadership policies in 1929—33 which had led to the victory of Nazism with all its consequences for Germany's (and not only

Germany's) cultural heritage and the destruction of the heritage in Germany of Marx and Engels. Lukács surely offends the most elementary premises of historical materialism when he separates 'cultural' questions from the actual development of the class struggle. So little was Lukács inclined to re-evaluate the fundamental questions that in the same 1963 preface he wrote, 'for over 30 years socialism has existed and grown strong in the Soviet Union'.[14] Isaac Deutscher was not ungenerous when he concluded: 'His case was one of genuine surrender to Stalinism, a surrender which was difficult and painful, yet voluntary and therefore in a sense irrevocable.'[15]

There is chapter and verse in Lukács himself which leaves no room for doubt: his support for, and not mere tactical adaptation to, 'socialism in a single country' must be understood in order to appraise his literary theories:

> The kind of Stalin criticism which nowadays attempts to justify Trotsky or Bukharin in a theoretical way, gets no nearer to real history than the view which — with fewer or more reservations — apologizes for Stalin.
>
> Naturally this preface cannot contain even an attempt at offering a detailed analysis of this important complex of questions. I have to restrict myself to attempting to indicate briefly those ideological developments without which the historical starting-points of the positions I then assumed would remain incomprehensible. The struggle for power was decided in favour of Stalin, between Lenin's death and 1928. The question: Can socialism survive if it can only be realized in one country? stood at the centre of the ideological struggle. Stalin won and it has to be said that he won — however many administrative measures he took in concrete party struggles — primarily because his viewpoint alone was tenable, it alone provided direction and a perspective for the building of socialism at the end of the world-revolutionary wave. What is involved here is not the theoretical and practical mistakes in the concrete building of socialism but a theoretical foundation for the whole period. The next step, as we now see it, was to ensure that in the new period thus established Stalin should be seen as a worthy successor to Lenin. However, the theoretical pre-

condition was that public opinion should accept Lenin not merely as the great tactician of the revolutionary struggle, but as the man who put back in its rightful place and further developed Marxist theory, overcoming the ideological errors of the Second International.[16]

Lukács completely oversimplifies the issues of 1924 and after. To take but one example: when Stalin first put forward the theory of socialism in a single country, he and his faction were also welcoming a new surge of the 'post-war revolutionary wave' in Canute-like defiance of the October 1923 defeat in Germany, and only later did they resort to the 'stabilisation' thesis. Furthermore, while avoiding any but the most cursory reference to the objective situation which he takes to justify Stalin's 'theory', Lukács resorts to the following sophistry: 'The fact that it [Socialism in a single country] was now taken seriously proved that a world revolution could not be held to be imminent in those years.'[17] If the imminence of revolutions could be measured by the expectations of the participants, history would look different indeed!

In the present context we are concerned only to show that the failure of Lukács to discuss Trotsky's work, and his failure therefore to engage in any way with the actual course which the development of Marxist theory of literature had taken, resulted in the substitution of a sterile and abstract orthodoxy for a Marxist analysis. Theory of literature, for Marxists, would need to be understood as part of the development of Marxism as a whole, and through this as part of the whole historical struggle in which Marxism lives. As Lukács himself notes: 'What is involved is . . . a theoretical foundation for the whole period . . . ' Acceptance of 'socialism in a single country' as this theoretical foundation meant that Lukács resorted to the kind of unprincipled distortions which prevent any of that historical accounting which is so necessary to Marxist analysis. In another reference to the prehistory of socialist realism he devotes one paragraph to the 'proletarian culture' controversy:

Conflicts of allegiance in literature are likely to be more complex than in the practical fields of politics and economics. Curiosity, a delight in novelty for novelty's sake, a romantic anti-capitalism, may lead an extreme modernist to accept socialism. He may believe that his 'revolution of forms' is identical with socialist revolution, even its true expression. Again, sectarian communist intellectuals often fall for the dream of a 'proletarian culture', for the idea that a 'radically new' socialist culture can be produced, by artificial insemination as it were, independent of all traditions [*proletkult*]. During the early years of the dictatorship of the proletariat in Russia such beliefs were rampant. The more level-headed communist theoreticians, Lenin in the lead, saw through these futile and basically anti-socialist ventures. But they could not be overcome before the new experience had been assimilated, before artists had understood the new forces at work in society and discovered how to give them artistic expression.[18]

How convenient to defer to the 'level-headed communist theoreticians, Lenin in the lead' without being obliged to explain that it fell to Trotsky, among these 'level-headed theoreticians', to produce the principal works on this question. To add insult to injury, Lukács virtually plagiarises *Literature and Revolution* when he refers to the impossibility of a proletarian culture 'independent of all traditions' and to the necessity of understanding the new forces at work and discovering how to give them artistic expression. He does this, however, only as an explanation of why it took 17 years — a sort of inevitable and natural period of organic growth — to reach the pinnacle of socialist realism, that consummate artistic expression of entry into those '30 years of socialism' to which he paid his respects in 1963 (above). Because none of his self-criticisms question these fundamental political positions, he remains able to write of '30 years of socialism' and at the same time condemn, with hard words but no explanation, the 'monstrous violations of legality and elementary justice' of the Moscow Trials. They were based, he said, on Stalin's 'grotesque reasoning'.[19]

One link between the politics of 'socialism in a single country' and some of the problems of Lukács's views on literature is provided by another element in his political 'confessions'.

In his reply, after nearly 40 years, to the critics of his last foray into the political life of the Comintern, he makes a statement which is more illuminating than he can have intended, or perhaps known. His preface to a volume of collected writings in Hungarian in 1968, which we have already cited, includes the remark that he looked upon the 'Blum theses' ('Blum' was Lukács's 'party name') of 1929 as 'strategy and not merely tactics'. Writing in the same year, in his 1967 preface to *History and Class Consciousness*, Lukács goes to great pains to explain that the political position he put forward in the 'Blum theses' (a political document written by him in opposition to the leadership of the Hungarian Communist Party) represented a 'basic change in [my] outlook' which 'determined from now on all my theoretical and political activities'. And, in case any room were left for doubt, he quotes by way of corroboration his opponent Josef Revai, who wrote in 1950:

> Everyone familiar with the history of the Hungarian Communist Party knows that the *literary* views held by Comrade Lukács between 1945 and 1949 belong together with *political* views that he had formulated much earlier, in the context of political trends in Hungary and of the strategy of the Communist Party at the end of the twenties.[20]

In the 'Blum theses' Lukács sought to change the programme of the Hungarian Communist Party from one of proletarian revolution to one of collaboration with other democratic forces to replace the Horthy dictatorship by a democratic republic. This brought him into collision not only with Béla Kun and the Hungarian Communist Party leadership, but also with Stalin and the Communist International, which had just veered to ultra-leftism of the 'Third Period', in which even social-democrats were characterised as 'social-fascists'. As Lukács explains:

> Although I was on Stalin's side on the central issue of Russia, I was deeply repelled by his attitude here. However, it did nothing to retard my gradual disenchantment with the ultra-left tendencies of my early revolutionary years as

most of the left-wing groups in the European parties were Trotskyite — a position which I always rejected.[21]

To see the 'democratic' programme of the 'Blum theses' as a strategy and not merely a tactic (leaving aside, here, the question of its incorrectness as a tactic) was to anticipate the orientation which was eventually to dominate the Communist International, once the Third Period had died on Hitler's accession to power in 1933. Henceforward, Stalin and his collaborators felt their way to the strategy of the 'Popular Front', in which the political independence and revolutionary role of the working class was surrendered to the requirements of an alliance with the 'democratic' bourgeoisie against Fascism. By 1935 this policy was fully worked out, and in the later form of 'peaceful, parliamentary roads to socialism', 'peaceful coexistence', 'advanced democracy', and even 'Eurocommunism', the basic orientation has not been changed. Now Lukács could have his agreement with Stalin on 'the central issue of Russia' as well as approving a policy outside Russia which was immediately consistent with it. The later bleatings about some mysterious, uncaused 'personality cult' are of little import. Far from having been an underground anti-Stalinist, Lukács, it now seems clear, was a theoretician who marched a step ahead of Stalin in the necessary revision of Marxist theory. He is quite right, though in an inverted way, to note that his acceptance of a Ministerial post in the government set up in Hungary as a result of the 1956 revolution was not at all inconsistent with his decision in 1929 to retire from active politics:

> Nor is there any inconsistency in the fact that in 1956 I had once again to take on a ministerial post. I declared before accepting it that it was only for the interim, the period of acute crisis, and that as soon as the situation became more settled I would immediately resign.[22]

When Imre Nagy and Lukács's other ministerial colleagues, with the exception of Kadar, had been safely removed from the scene, and the general strike and the workers' councils had been suppressed, 'the situation became more settled',

things 'returned to normal', and Lukács returned to his aesthetics, in the safe knowledge that the 'interim' of the intru-
sion of the working class into the blessed peace guaranteed
by the bureaucracy was over. One is tempted to suggest that
the 'power-protected inwardness' which Lukács diagnosed as
the condition of the German literary intelligentsia, from the
time of the provincial princely courts, through the reaction
after Napoleon, to the centralised Prussianism of the late
nineteenth century, was something with which Lukács easily
'empathised'.

A recent presentation of Adorno's criticism of Lukács, by
New Left Books, has a different interpretation, but this flatly
contradicts Lukács's own statements. The Cold War, it is said,
soon found Lukács's writings under attack for revisionism
(1949), despite 'all their ostensible compliances with Stalinist
etiquette'.[23] This judgement avoids the question of just what
was the relation between Lukács's teachings and Stalinism,
quite apart from problems of etiquette. Between 1953 and
1956 young Hungarian intellectuals turned to Lukács, particularly in the 'Petöfi Circle', in seeking ways to criticise the extreme of bureaucratic terror reached by the Rakosi regime
in those years. When the working class came on the scene in
1956, these intellectuals sympathised and worked with the
workers' councils. How did Lukács serve them? According to
his New Left 'presenters', 'When the Hungarian Revolt erupted
in October 1956, Lukács — while lucidly assessing the probable
chances of success of an essentially spontaneous social explo-
sion — did not hesitate to cast his lot with the cause of the
insurgent workers and students.'[24] This is simply untrue. On
Lukács's own account, he accepted a post in Nagy's government until 'the situation became more settled'.

Nor is Adorno's own version (in his critique of Lukács's
The Meaning of Contemporary Realism) any more convincing.
He makes many correct and obvious points against Lukács's
crude attacks on 'modernism', and permits himself furious
words against Lukács's subservience to Stalinism. Yet once
again the fundamental question, that of Lukács's basic theoretical agreement with Stalinism, is denied, and we read:

For all this, it is impossible to rid oneself of the feeling that here is a man who is desperately tugging at his chains, imagining all the while that their clanking heralds the on-ward march of the world-spirit. He remains dazzled by the power which would never take his insubordinate ideas to heart, even if it tolerated them.[25]

This judgement is based on a superficial (or, as Adorno might say, 'unmediated') view of the formal debates on literary mat-ters in the abstract. We have shown that on fundamental ques-tions the bureaucracy did take very much to heart Lukács's ideas. It is absolutely inadequate for Adorno to condemn his relation to the bureaucracy only on the grounds that 'All the symptoms at which he protests have come into being because the dictators and their hangers-on need to hammer into the masses the very thesis which Lukács implicitly endorses by his use of the term socialist realism . . . '[26] The complicity was built in decades earlier, into the foundations of 'socialism in a single country'.

All the evidence points to the fact that Lukács came to believe that a few years after the Russian Revolution the world situation had changed in such a way that the revolu-tionary role of the working class, so central to Marxist theory, retained no concrete meaning. But Lukács did not say this in so many words. Given the kind of regime he chose to live with, he had to take care to cover his tracks, in case some sharpshooter in another situation might make use of his departure from orthodoxy. He therefore pays lip service to this basic principle; but only to explain immediately that it is such a general consideration that it is always other things which determine the actual reality towards which practice is directed, and on which theoretical analysis must concentrate. The 'struggle between capitalism and socialism', along with the revolutionary role of the working class, is acknowledged and at the same time dismissed in this facile manner in Lukács's introduction *The Meaning of Contemporary Realism*:

The struggle between socialism and capitalism is still — as it has been since the 1848 rising of the Paris proletariat — the fundamental reality of the modern age. We would expect literature and criticism to reflect this reality. But this does not imply that every work of art, every cultural event, is directly determined by it. The formative principle of an age manifests itself in devious ways. In a larger perspective, the struggle between capitalism and socialism may be the formative principle of our age. But to relate day-to-day phenomena, or even longer-term trends, directly to this struggle can well be misleading.

Before the Second World War, for example, it was not this conflict that determined the social and political pattern, but the conflict between Fascism and anti-Fascism.[27]

After the Second World War, following a brief interlude, 'the strategists of the Cold War aimed to divide mankind into two hostile camps and to mobilise all non-socialist forces against socialism'. But the working class was saved again, it seems:

> New forces unexpectedly emerged, which were to assume great importance. These forces were opposed to policies leading to the outbreak of the Third World War. This is not the place to outline the growth of the Peace Movement. It is enough to say that the movement came to comprise hundreds of millions of people — a mass movement without parallel in history.[28]

For Lukács the history of the class struggle since the revolution of 1917 is one in which for various reasons important sections of the bourgeoisie have been forced into an alliance with 'socialist forces'. And so we come directly to what is decisive for Lukács's more 'literary' studies:

> Just as there were workers who were misled by Fascism, so there are workers today who fall for Cold War ideology. For the purposes of this study, however, it is far more significant that both the anti-Fascist cause and the Peace Movement attracted large sections of the bourgeoisie, and particularly of the bourgeois intelligentsia. The struggle between capitalism and socialism was, in fact, not directly relevant to either. Indeed, both movements were characterized by a militant alliance between socialist and bourgeois forces.

This had important consequences for modern bourgeois literature.[29]

What seems to emerge is that his mature political views, like the literary standpoints taken up by him, are a consistent elaboration of the general outlook he developed in the crucial years immediately following the 'Blum theses'. There is a sense (as so often, because of Lukács's sophistication) in which he is more correct in this judgement than have been those critics who have rested content with showing how Lukács's allocation of praise and dismissal in criticising literature was very often little more than a crude application of the current policy requirements of Stalinism (thus in *The Historical Novel*, written in the period of the Popular Front against Fascism, he found all manner of literary virtues in any mediocrity who happened to be an anti-fascist 'fellow-traveller'). The common element in his accommodation to the Soviet bureaucracy and his hankering after the democratic bourgeoisie's fulfilling its historic mission is the rejection in practice and theory of the revolutionary role of the working class and the revolutionary character of the period of capitalist decline. If our presentation of the theories of Marx has been correct in essentials, then Lukács's revision on this basic question will certainly entail a view of Marxism which leads, in cultural questions, to conclusions opposed to those actually implied by dialectical materialism. Bertolt Brecht sensed a 'utopian and idealist element' in the critical writings of Lukács:

> It is the element of capitulation, of withdrawal, of utopian idealism which still lurks in Lukács's essays and which he will undoubtedly overcome, that makes his work, which otherwise contains so much of value, unsatisfactory; for it gives the impression that what concerns him is enjoyment rather than struggle, a way of escape rather than an advance.[30]

Replying to the charge of 'formalism' which Lukács had levelled against his experimental drama, Brecht retorts that there could hardly be any greater formalism than that of a critic who has no other criterion than one borrowed from the nineteenth-century novel, and he caricatures Lukács's advice to writers: 'Be like Tolstoy — but without his weaknesses! Be like Balzac, only up-to-date!'[31] As for Lukács's admiration for Thomas Mann, Brecht is scornful in the extreme, seeing Mann as the epitome of the bourgeois writer who is successful and celebrated because his works are artificial, vain, useless. Lukács's purely formal definition of realism, abstracted from the nineteenth-century novel, made him blind to the real significance of newly developing forms and their relation to actual historical changes: 'In questions of pure form, one must not cast around at random in the name of Marxism; that is not Marxist.'[32]

With hindsight, it is easier now than it was when Brecht wrote these words in the early 1930s to see that these aspects of Lukács's literary theories were the product of his most basic theoretical and political positions, and that Brecht's expression of confidence that they could be corrected was sadly misplaced. Lukács's commitment to the ideal of the great realist novel went much further than the recognition of the positive historical content of these works. He was bent, as Brecht feared, on the completion of the bourgeois—democratic ideal, and the working class was to be that force to which enlightened bourgeois should turn. The notion of socialism painlessly merging with and continuing the stream of bourgeois culture was an idealist formula for the reconciliation of Marxism and the outlook of the progressive or democratic bourgeoisie.

Thomas Mann was without doubt a master-chronicler of the German bourgeoisie. Lukács showed how Mann's repeated treatment of the theme of the role of the artist and the internal decay of a humanism which turns to formal aestheticism (*Death in Venice*, *Tonio Kröger*, *Doctor Faustus*) was an acute and concentrated expression of the historical crisis and dilemma of the German bourgeoisie. Yet Lukács fails to carry through to the end his criticism of Mann, because he will not consider the implication of the revolutionary role of the German working class *against* this bourgeoisie. Instead he only finds Marxist phrases to formulate Mann's own programme: the calling up of working-class forces to make real the German bourgeoisie's impotent dream of democracy. This is what he meant (above) when in 1963 he stated that the conflict between capitalism and socialism is decisive in our epoch but only 'in general'; in reality the question of alliances for democracy, or for peace, is the key question. The struggle for proletarian revolution is not the strategic question; that is the democratic alliance with the bourgeoisie (the 'Blum theses'). History has proved many times that, while there are, certainly, indispensable tactical alliances which must take advantage of shades of difference between political tendencies in the middle classes, there is positively no third road, at the level of principles and strategy, between Marxism and bourgeois ideology. And Lukács cannot avoid providing yet another 'proof' of this. His admiration for Thomas Mann is not tempered by the fact that Mann could say: 'Within the bourgeois world itself lie infinite possibilities, possibilities of boundless self-liberation and self-mastery . . . [It has] a certain transcendental quality by which it transforms itself.'[33]

What then can Lukács mean by describing the work of Mann as 'the summit of bourgeois consciousness' as against the petty day-to-day changes of opinions in the German bourgeoisie?[34] If Mann could express such confidence in the 'bourgeois world' after his arrival in the United States as an exile from Nazi Germany, it was no less clearly a product of time and place than had been his jingoism during the First World War or his advocacy of support for the wretched social democracy in the months preceding Hitler's accession to power. But Lukács must above all have his allies. In 1955 he writes: 'Mann's originality — his buoyancy, serenity and humour — springs from a true self-knowledge of the contemporary bourgeoisie.'[35]

At this point one is inclined even to spring to the defence of Mann against Lukács! In point of fact the demands of reality forced Mann in his work to recognise and represent in imaginary situations and characters the fact that the bourgeoisie is a historically doomed class, in which 'self-knowledge' certainly would not produce 'buoyancy, serenity and humour'. If in his explicitly political statements Mann expressed such confident moods, it is only because — like many another writer, as Lukács well knew — he had not devoted the same struggle, knowledge and concentration to politics and philosophy as to the literary art, and so tended to voice one or another version of the current received wisdom.

Thomas Mann turned again and again to the images of sickness and inner decay which broke through the shining but brittle shell devised by the creative artist who chose to ignore reality for the sake of formal perfection. Even though he could express in the abstract his confidence in the 'infinite possibilities' of the bourgeois order, he did not come remotely near any representation of such hope in his creative work. Nor is there any trace of an internal dialectic, the source of some other hope. Never is there a sense of individuals who must live in and recognise the necessity of one society's decay and yet have the possibility of discovering in the very nearness to extinction brought by that decay the possibility of struggling for a new order of things.

Lukács seems to have considered that the absence of any such dialectic in the world outlook represented in Mann's novels weighed negligibly in the scales against the formal merits of a 'totality' expressing the bourgeoisie's 'true self-knowledge'. This latter characterisation, meriting the description of Mann as a great 'critical realist', according to Lukács, is, as we have seen, conceptually loose and contradictory, and perhaps dependent on Lukács's early commitment to the notions of 'objective possibility', 'ideal type' and 'adjudged' or 'potential' consciousness, borrowed from the sociology of Max Weber. Lukács' welcome to 'critical realism' alongside 'socialist realism' was not merely a tactical extending of the hand to the 'peace-loving' and democratic bourgeois intelligentsia. To be a critical realist required of the writer only that he 'did not oppose socialism'. Lukács's formulation was something like a sigh of relief occasioned by the realisation that he could unequivocally state his real class position (ideologically speaking) with a good 'communist' conscience. The idea of a revolutionary leadership asking the German working class to share Mann's nostalgia for Goethe and the shoots of bourgeois democracy in *Lotte in Weimar* — that was the sort of image which Lukács conjured up in the minds of Brecht and Benjamin, and which they rejected. It was riddled with the outlook which stresses only the continuity of bourgeois culture and socialism, and turns away from the infinitely more difficult theoretical and practical questions of the revolutionary break which is necessary to ensure the possibility of any such continuity from the positive gains of the bourgeois epoch. The literary—critical expression of Lukács' historical outlook is the stress on inner coherence and the category of totality, in which works are appraised for their completeness, and for their resolution and exhaustive treatment of specific historical contradictions. In *History and Class Consciousness*, Lukács refers to that 'all-pervasive supremacy of the whole over the parts which Marx took over from Hegel and brilliantly transformed into the foundation of a wholly new science'.[36] To this Brecht contrasted the project of an open-ended dramatic exposure of contradictions, which did not provide the resolution of these contradictions either by catharsis or any other means, but rather posed the necessity of conflict before such resolution was possible. Lukács's entirely opposite emphasis, and his hostility to all the consequent formal innovations (a hostility made more plausible by his warnings against novelty for its own sake and its class origins), left him in a position on these questions very similar to that taken by Mann himself: 'Form, with the blessing of life, mediates between disintegration and rigidity. Form is moderation, and the measure of value, form is humanity, form is love.'[37]

Unfortunately one cannot say of Lukács what can be said of Mann: that in his own work (particularly *Death in Venice* and *Doctor Faustus*) he demonstrated the glaring limitations of this idea of form, and knew, when he described the form-drunk Aschenbach as 'the poet of all those who labour on the brink of exhaustion', that this made him symbolic of a social form outlived by its human content.[38] Mann's own *Weltanschauung* had horizons which prevented his work from providing any pointer to a historically concrete transcendence of this condition, and this is surely the limitation which should have been crucial to any Marxist evaluation. Mann expressed himself content with Lukács's insight into the historical content of *Death in Venice*: as 'a forerunner of that tendency which signifies the danger of a barbarous underworld within modern German civilisation as its necessary complementary product'. He would have been less pleased had Lukács been able to go beyond a 'cultural criticism' in which the poles of the dialectical opposition constituting the unity of German capitalist society were 'German civilisation' and its 'barbarous underworld'. Ignoring the real dialectic and the revolutionary role of the working class, Lukács thus prepares the ground for the subordination of the fundamental question of revolution to the defence and development of bourgeois 'civilisation', democracy, against the 'barbarous underworld' and its culmination in Nazism.

*   *   *

The 'great realism' of the nineteenth-century French and Russian novelists is characteristic of the periods, respectively, before 'that darkening of the horizon' in France in 1848 and between the Decembrist revolt and the rapid late nineteenth-century development of Russian capitalism. Lukács considers that the appearance of the Parisian proletariat on the streets as an independent force was the cause of a total loss of nerve of the bourgeoisie and its intelligentsia. (In Russia the specific contradictions of semi-Asiatic conditions brought the peasant masses into the picture in a different way from any European development, and posed different questions for the class consciousness of the bourgeoisie, opening the way for a unique development of the novel.) After 1848 the ideological and literary representatives of the bourgeoisie, unable to transcend their own ideological limits and recognise that another revolution was necessary for further human progress, turned away from the concrete—historical understanding of reality, because such an understanding now meant facing up to the necessity of the bourgeoisie's own rule coming to an end. Naturalism began to predominate over realism: a surface description of the quantitative detail of life instead of a penetration of the surface to the essential historical movement. Only where the bourgeoisie had still to confront the problem of its progressive historical tasks was there a chance for great realism (Russia).

Lukács's thesis is an ingenious combination of a number of insights contained in the works of Marx and Engels. Marx noted, in his introductory remarks to *Capital*, that political economy made real contributions to science until the struggle of the proletariat ceased to be sporadic and became general. Engels noted, in his analysis of the 1848 revolution in Germany, that the political collapse of the German bourgeois— democratic movement resulted not so much from its proponents looking over their shoulders at the German workers as from the actions of the more experienced and advanced working class in Paris. Marx analysed, in his *18th Brumaire of Louis Bonaparte*, the changing relations between democracy, the bourgeoisie, and the latter's literary representatives. And Marx and Engels on several occasions declared that, despite his reactionary political opinions, Balzac in his *Comédie Humaine* had given a more accurate and informative picture of Restoration France than had the writings of dozens of historians and political commentators.

Given an understanding of Marx's and Engels's many methodological writings on the necessity to go beyond forms of appearance to essential relations, 'laws of motion', it was not difficult to piece together from these pointers in the historical writings that distinction between realism and naturalism which Lukács saw as characteristic of before 1848 and after 1848. Balzac and Stendhal could create characters and situations in which were concentrated the contradictory forces at work in creating or obstructing the new society. They could expose the way in which the bourgeois order of things created quite new problems — Stendhal's desperate self-questioning about the possibility of happiness and a life of reason in post-revolutionary France; Balzac's recognition of the emptiness created by the world of commerce. Before 1848 the passionate being of writers and artists could represent such contradictions in their work as problems for humanity. But the appearance of an alternative force, whose interest coincided with putting to an end not this or that contradiction but the whole contradictory system, produced a new environment for the artist and his work. Now that the bourgeoisie could not 'afford' realistic art (this new relationship of course developed only with varying degrees of consciousness, on the side of both the bourgeoisie and its literary intelligentsia), the relations between society and its literary producers became more and more problematical. Crude subservience to commercialism and 'art for art's sake' were the extremes of reaction to the new situation.

According to Lukács, much of modern literature (that which he calls 'modernist') is at best a continuation of the naturalist tradition of Flaubert and Zola into the conditions of the twentieth century. It is to be unfavourably contrasted with the 'critical realism' of Thomas Mann, who carries forward the tradition of works centred on historical 'types', combining individuality with representativeness of the principal historical forces at work in reality. Lukács's adept use of Marxist phraseology makes this scheme at first sight persuasive. In fact, however, the terms of the comparison in the two periods have changed. It is somewhat strange that in 1848, when the proletariat was hardly formed outside Britain, its political weight should be thought to produce a qualitative change in literary history, yet in the mid-twentieth century (after '30 years of socialism' in the USSR!), its effect is considered to be extremely muted. For example, Lukács writes in 1957:

> Today, the imminent defeat of Cold War policies, the new perspective of peaceful coexistence among the nations, should allow wider scope for a critical and realistic bourgeois literature. The real dilemma of our age is not the opposition between capitalism and socialism, but the opposition between peace and war. The first duty of the bourgeois intellectual has become the rejection of an all-pervading fatalistic *angst*, implying a rescue operation for humanity rather than any breakthrough to Socialism. Because it is these perspectives that confront him, the bourgeois writer today is in a better position to solve his own dilemma than he was in the past. It is the dilemma of the choice between an aesthetically appealing, but decadent modernism, and a fruitful critical realism. It is the choice between Franz Kafka and Thomas Mann.[39]

The 'first duty of the bourgeois intellectual' is, for a Marxist, a notion no less peculiar that that 'summit of bourgeois consciousness' said to have been reached by Thomas Mann. Marx, in the *Communist Manifesto*, had pointed to the fact that in periods of social revolution bourgeois intellectuals,

successfully struggling to 'comprehend theoretically the process as a whole . . . join the proletariat'. Lukács decided,
though without one word of that thoroughgoing critique of
Marx which might be thought necessary, that there was
another road possible, another 'first duty' for the intelligentsia
on behalf of humanity, 'the rejection of an all-pervading *angst*'.
In the absence of such critique and explanation, the clear
implication of Lukács's position is that the character of the
epoch is no longer revolutionary. The closer he comes to the
present day, the more evident is the untenability of that view,
which separates his political beliefs and actions from a supposedly more positive contribution to literary criticism.
Lukács's agreement with (and even anticipation of) that
abandonment of the revolutionary political independence of
the working class which is at the root of Stalinism defines
also the contours of the world within which he appraises
'contemporary realism'. He characterises the problems dealt
with in Thomas Mann's works as 'the spiritual and moral pros
and cons preceding a particular step forward which history
has taken or is about to take'.[40] This is not very meaningful
unless that 'particular step forward' is specified. Lukács's
The Meaning of Contemporary Realism has the one virtue
that it does tell us how he specifies it: not as the 'epoch of
wars and revolutions', 'imperialism, the last stage of capitalism', or indeed anything of that sort, but an epoch where
'the opposition between capitalism and socialism' gives place
to 'the opposition between peace and war' as 'the real dilemma of our age'.

Lukács was careful from 1929 until his dying day to keep
silent on the questions of the basic economic and political
problems of capitalism and the proletarian revolution, con-
tenting himself with occasional very general declamations
against 'dogmatic sectarianism'. All the same, one is sur-
prised to discover that he takes for granted that it is mean-
ful to refer in 1967 without any definition of theoretical
explanation to something called 'Western manipulated capitalism'. He knew very well that this and very similar concepts
were current in Western Europe and America, and were put
forward with the explicit corollary that the revolutionary
role of the working class was no longer a reality. The strategy

of the communist parties had been redefined at that time as, not the achievement of socialism, but the change from 'state monopoly capitalism' (or 'organised capitalism' or 'neo-capitalism' or 'Western manipulated capitalism'?) to a state of affairs called 'advanced democracy'. No doubt the rejection of *angst* would help, somehow . . .

Here one cannot but recall the criticisms of Lukács by Brecht: the absence of any feeling for struggle, the tendency to be satisfied with formal unity, the stubborn presumption that whatever happened in the twentieth century could be imaginatively grasped and represented by the literary methods of the most successful bourgeois novelists of the nineteenth. There is no evidence to suggest that Brecht, in 1931 or at any later date, reached an understanding of the deep-lying consistency of Lukács's aesthetic views and the historical role of Stalinism, but his own struggle for an 'epic theatre', which started from the cultural problems consequent on the role played by the masses in a revolutionary era, could not fail to bring him into conflict with Lukács. If Lukács is to be criticised by the standards of Marxism, it must be said that when he assigns to the 'critical realist' only the task of 'rejecting an all-pervading *angst*' and 'not opposing socialism', he is acting against the interest not only of revolution but also of art. While Marxism does not prescribe for art (even if Lukács does), it brings forward, theoretically and practically, those revolutionary forces which out of objective necessity must struggle to abolish the present order. If artists and writers are to show the essential in their work, then it must be, with no matter what mediations, a particular concentration of this life-and-death conflict. A 'Marxist' critic who breaks down this quality of the epoch into the small change of cultural criticism, or moods of the intelligentsia, or even 'tactical considerations', is complicit in the cultural decay. And by proposing such inadequate solutions, artistically as well as politically, he turns men away from the fact (a fact which Lukács himself noted many times) that the hostility of capitalism to art is fundamental to capitalism and cannot be ameliorated in piecemeal fashion. How can that fundamental problem be resolved, and how shall literature rise to the level of realism in any meaningful sense, if Lukács is right in saying, 'Acceptance or rejection of *angst*. . . . This dilemma is the key to the assessment of modern literature'?[41]

In *The Meaning of Contemporary Realism* Lukács devotes one or two pages to Brecht, though without returning to the earlier controversy (in one place he refers to 'a local polemic'). His thesis is that Brecht's mature work, beginning after the victory of Hitler in 1933, marked a return to Aristotelian and Shakespearian canons of drama. Henceforth Brecht became 'the greatest realistic playwright of his age'.[42] There is room for a detailed critical study of Brecht's work in order to test this hypothesis; but what is interesting in this context even without such detailed work is that Lukács does not raise the question of the extent to which the change in the objective historical situation, and Brecht's relation to all the forces involved in it, was responsible for any changes in dramatic form and their degree of success in Brecht's later work. Lukács, who constantly warns against a discussion of literature restricted to formal and stylistic considerations, here seems satisfied with just such an interpretation.

The fact is that an extension of the nineteenth-century realism/naturalism opposition into one between socialist and critical realism, on the one hand, and 'modernism', on the other,[43] is inadequate from the Marxist standpoint. The reason for Lukács's weakness here is to be found in his theoretical starting point. He never abandoned his view in *History and Class Consciousness* that 'totality' is the basic category of Marxism. This category he applies to literature, instead of abstracting that specific unity, conflict, interpenetration and transformation of opposites in the actual development of society (in *its* unity and conflict with nature) in which literature lives. 'Totality' is an 'abstraction' of a different kind, denuded of any concrete connection with this real dialectic of history, useful in criticising the striving of nineteenth-century novelists to comprehend as a whole the new and contradictory bourgeois society. But the twentieth century is one not merely of the awful realisation that the new society, capitalism, while carrying humanity forward, is pregnant with new contradictions, new inhumanities. The appearance in history of the force which put an end to the realistic portrayal of those contradictions (1848) is now — with all the attendant difficulties and breaks in continuity — the essential element in social reality. The inevitable weakness of a dialectic which places 'totality' at its centre, making it the criterion of objectivity in consciousness, is now brutally exposed; and literature which has as its most profound content such totality and reconciliation of opposites becomes cut off from life. This, and not only the lapses into subjectivism, the inability to achieve 'concrete particularity', the impotence in the face of social fragmentation, which Lukács dwells upon, is a major source of 'modernism'.

If this is in fact the case, Marxist criticism of 'modernist' works must place at the centre of its concerns the question of to what extent innovations in form may contribute to the development of the means necessary to comprehend the changes in a reality which has surpassed the capacity of the old techniques by themselves to grasp the particular ways in which its laws of motion affect humanity. The changes in techniques of material production and communication change the possibilities for art and literature, especially by opening up a real prospect of crossing the traditional border-lines between the different arts. The modes of perception of both artist and audience are modified. Perhaps it will make sense to speak of the restoration at a higher level of the unity of the arts, and of the artist and his public. The actual development of these technical changes in material production and their effects cannot be comprehended outside of the specific stage reached in the historical contradiction and conflict between productive forces and the social relations of production within which these technical changes occur. For Lukács to suppose that the 'norms' of a realism developed in order to answer different questions, in different material conditions, with different technical means, and for a different class, amounts to dogmatism, which is only more persuasive because it is confused with the correct, but different, point that new literary techniques are not developed afresh from new social conditions and independently of literary traditions. For all his correct words about 'concrete particularity' in realism, and his ideal of truly concrete individualised characters who are simultaneously (and even through their individuality) typical of the specific historical forces at work, he can arrive only at a very abstract 'totality' as the criterion of success in literature: 'the poetry of life lies in life's wholeness and self-sufficiency . . . '; and he notes 'the enduring spell of all works of art that evoke life's inexhaustible dynamism . . . '[44]

It would indeed be remarkable if the means developed by early nineteenth-century novelists to achieve realism in grasping the totality of an emerging bourgeois society could serve equally well for creative literature in the period of decline of that same society. There is an inevitable element of resignation and reconciliation in the great realist ideal suggested by Lukács. For the first half of the nineteenth century it is enough to speak of an 'element', because the very act of facing up to the new contradictions in post-revolutionary society also is expressed in the writings of Balzac and Stendhal, and it is that absolute within the relative (the relative being the unity and continued existence of the new capitalist whole despite the contradictions) which gives their art lasting value. Lukács pointed towards this conclusion, but did not draw it:

> Balzac depicts the last great struggle against the capitalist degradation of man, while his successors paint an already degraded capitalist world. Romanticism — which for Balzac was only one feature of his total conception, a feature which he overcame and developed further — was not overcome by his successors, but lyrically and ironically transmuted into reality which it overgrew, blanketing the great motive forces of evolution and providing only elegiac or ironical moods and impressions instead of an active and objective presentation of things in themselves.[45]

The artistic decline of those who followed Balzac, including the greatest, such as Flaubert, was 'socially and historically unavoidable'.[46] While it is certain that there can be no true understanding of Balzac without placing him historically in this way, this truth is in danger of turning into untruth because of its one-sided emphasis by Lukács. By stressing only that Balzac 'preserved the great heritage of bourgeois humanism and saved what was best in it for the future benefit of mankind',[47] Lukács obscures what Brecht called the element of struggle in the historical 'placing' of Balzac: that men of the future (including, especially, writers) learn above all from Balzac's own battle, against overwhelming odds, to invent or discover the means necessary to penetrate appearances and discover the essential forces which produced those same appearances. The ease with which Lukács applied criteria of realism drawn from one epoch to a very different one is better understood if we take into account one other factor in his outlook: his view of the character of the 'modern' capitalist era. To have concluded that there exists now a 'manipulated capitalism', in which the struggle for socialist revolution no longer determines anything, is of course a widely accepted viewpoint in the socialist and communist parties of today. This is not the place to discuss its distance from a Marxist conception of the contemporary world. For present purposes it suffices to note that, if the revolutionary role of the proletariat and the objective contradictions flowing from the value form and the anarchy of capitalist economy are negated by the ability of the capitalist class to 'manipulate' its society, then little remains of any foundation for a specifically Marxist theory of the relation between society and literature.

Lukács finds no great difficulty in arriving at such a conclusion about modern capitalism (though, as we have noted, he never explains how he does so) because for him capitalism always represents above all a reign of 'reification', of fragmentation of humanity, which then is in danger of being artificially and oppressively integrated (manipulated). Citing Marx, he says in his studies of Schiller[48] that the dilemmas of bourgeois literature are a reflection of the contradiction between bourgeois and citizen, the private and the public: the public, where the 'heroic' must be located, becomes more abstract, ideal, reified; and that everyday private life which the 'naive' poet wants to portray but which becomes sordid and unpoetic in the extreme. But we know that Marx left these characterisations of bourgeois society far behind in his subsequent work. We are left with a yawning gap between these 'dilemmas' and what were shown to be the basic contradictions between capital and labour, between social production and individual appropriation. Not a series of dilemmas, but the relation between classes based on wage-labour and on capital as the 'axis' on which all modern society turns — that was the conception of Marx and Engels. What was the implication for the 'dilemmas' indicated by Lukács and the early Marx of the later Marx's dictum that in the wages relationship is contained the source of all the ideological illusions of both main classes in capitalist society? Lukács never answered this question or the associated one: is the working class an oppressed class, a victim of ideology, of false consciousness, to be sure, but at the same time driven by its life-experience as the principal of the productive forces to revolution; or is it first and foremost the prisoner of reification and alienation? Rather, he never acknowledged the incompatibility of these two viewpoints, and in his work he never went beyond the second, purely ideological, standpoint. Once Marx is seen as carrying over the Hegelian concept of 'totality' without its being negated materialistically, then the revolutionary role of the proletariat is gone, as we see in *History and Class Consciousness*: '. . . when confronted by the overwhelming resources . . . which . . . the bourgeoisie possesses . . . the only effective superiority of the proletariat, its only decisive weapon, is its ability to see the social totality as a concrete historical totality'.[49] This will suffice, since 'the strength of every society is in the last resort a spiritual strength',[50] and 'only ideology stands in the way' of the conscious opposition the proletariat must exercise.

This view of capitalism and of the proletariat was entirely consistent with a theory of class consciousness which amounts to constructing from the outside an 'ideal type' (Max Weber) of what consciousness the class would have, given a rational orientation to all the knowable realities of its life-situation.[51] This abstraction for Lukács, then, constituted the 'essence' of the party (and of the bureaucracy . . . and of our great leader), so that in his work on such questions the actual material struggles of the organised working class, the actual relation between its 'embryo consciousness' in spontaneous struggles and the development of its political consciousness, receive no attention whatsoever. Perhaps his personal situation, together with his greater sophistication, made him more inhibited than his follower Lucien Goldmann, who saw and stated the direct connection between the notion of 'progress of reification' and his conclusion that it was necessary to reject explicitly

Marx's ideas that the proletariat was a revolutionary force and that capitalism could not overcome its contradictions.[52] In Goldmann it is not difficult to see that such conclusions are closely related to his 'genetic structuralism', in which the work of art is tested by the degree to which it is 'homologous' with the 'world-vision of a class'. Lukács's notion of class consciousness has the same inherent logic. All the attempts of Goldmann to give this 'structure' of vision some mobility (destructuration, restructuration, etc) ended with his virtually abandoning the whole scheme, because the real dialectic of movement is outside consciousness, real or adjudged.

Lukács's concentration on alienation and fetishism could be highly suggestive in analysing the problems of consciousness which animated the novelists and philosophers of the late eighteenth and early nineteenth centuries. On Balzac's *Lost Illusions* he writes:

> In *Lost Illusions* the fact that the spirit has become a commodity to be bought and sold is not yet accepted as a matter of course and the spirit is not yet reduced to the dreary greyness of a machine-made article. The spirit turns into a commodity here before our very eyes; it is something just happening, a new event loaded with dramatic tension.[53]

But just as Marx had to go far beyond his early works (*The Jewish Question*, *Critique of Hegel's Philosophy of Right*, etc.), in which he showed the development and the material basis of the political and literary struggles of the whole period from 1789 to the 1840s, so Marxist literary criticism cannot rest at the posing of the problems of realism in the same way that they were posed in Restoration France or in nineteenth century Russia.

In terms of theory the self-criticisms indulged in by Lukács concerning his *History and Class Consciousness* are of no account. The literary work on which he was engaged in the years after that work was published was entirely consistent with the views on capitalism and on consciousness contained in it. Lukács never incorporated into his outlook the great emphasis by the post-1844 Marx on the necessary and progressive nature of capitalism's development of the productive forces and the consequent objective contradictions. Lukács sees science and technology as above all products of reified thinking, 'contemplation at its purest',[54] typical of the separation of thought from praxis. (Contrast this with the opinion of Engels, criticising empiricism, on the content of the concepts used by scientists: 'In any case natural science has now advanced so far that it cannot escape the dialectical synthesis. But it will make this process easier for itself if it does not lose sight of the fact that the results in which its experiences are summarised are concepts; but that the art of working with concepts is not inborn and also is not given with ordinary everyday consciousness, but requires real thought, and that this thought similarly has a long empirical history, not more and not less than empirical natural science.')[55]

If consciousness, whether of the novelist or of anyone else, is an expression of the social whole or of the whole of the possible outlook of a class (Lukács, Goldmann) and not *at the same time* the form in which and against which the growth of human knowledge takes place, then there can be no real revolutionary practice (because then the *objectivity* of consciousness remains always an open question), and art cannot have more than a 'recording' role. Lukács's discussion of revolution, for example, is confined to the moral crisis which must be experienced if ever the old is to give way to the new. *History and Class Consciousness*, with its 'possible' or 'adequate' or 'adjudged' or 'potential' consciousness, all self-criticism notwithstanding, is one of the keys to the form in which Lukács's mature views on literature developed. The creative work in art and literature is that coherent totalisation of all the conceivable problems in social experience — that is Lukács' view. In effect, to see only this ideal coherence is to blind oneself to the relation between art and the real motive forces of men's historical actions. Lukács's aesthetics are all of a piece with his failure ever to recognise the revolutionary role of the working class and the materialist outlook which is necessary for that recognition. For Marx the proletariat is the true heir to the culture of the past, not only because it must learn from art more about the history of past societies, as is implied by Lukács's studies of bourgeois realism. Art and

literature educate for the winning and for the living of that
freedom to which revolution opens the door. For this revolution not only an ideological crisis is required, but knowledge.
That knowledge is not imposed on the working class from
outside by an intellectual elite which has somehow freed itself
from reification. Nor is the great work of art produced by the
imprint on inert material reality of some 'possible consciousness' or 'world vision'. Revolution, like the work of art, is
achieved not by some wondrously efficacious subjective conception (be the subject individual or social) but by a practice
which brings cognition of reality. What Lenin wrote about
the content of philosophy and the crude attempts to interpret
it only as 'ideology' will serve to summarise this stage of the
argument:

> Philosophical idealism is *only* nonsense from the stand-
> point of crude, simple, metaphysical materialism. From
> the standpoint of *dialectical* materialism, on the other
> hand, philosophical idealism is a *one-sided*, exaggerated,
> *überschwengliches* (*Dietzgen*) development (inflation, dis-
> tention) of one of the features, aspects, facets of knowledge
> into an absolute, divorced from matter, from nature, apo-
> theosised. Idealism is clerical obscurantism. True. But
> philosophical idealism is ('*more correctly*' and '*in addition*')
> a road to clerical obscurantism *through one of the shades*
> of the infinitely complex knowledge (dialectical) of man.
>   Human knowledge is not (or does not follow) a straight
> line, but a curve, which endlessly approximates a series of
> circles, a spiral. Any fragment, segment, section of this
> curve can be transformed (transformed one-sidedly) into
> an independent, complete, straight line, which then (if one
> does not see the wood for the trees) leads into the quag-
> mire, into clerical obscurantism (where it is anchored by
> the class interests of the ruling classes). Rectilinearity and
> one-sidedness, woodenness and petrification, subjectivism
> and subjective blindness — voilà the epistemological roots
> of idealism. And clerical obscurantism (= philosophical
> idealism), of course, has *epistemological* roots, it is not
> groundless; it is a *sterile flower* undoubtedly, but a sterile
> flower that grows on the living tree of living, fertile, genuine,

powerful, omnipotent, objective, absolute human knowledge.[56]

I have deliberately refrained from presenting a summary
account of Lukács's writings on realism in the novel, since
these are by now readily available in English translation and
are self-explanatory. They constitute an erudite expansion of
the scattered fragments in which Engels and Marx refer to art
and literature, but in a framework which subordinates the dialectical, revolutionary aspect to the continuity between bourgeois and socialist culture. My concern has been to demonstrate that there is a fatal omission in the critique of Lukács by
even sophisticated critics. It should be added that Frederic
Jameson, for example, writes: 'The fundamental weakness in
Lukács' view of the relationship of art and ideology surely
finds its ultimate explanation in his politics. What is usually
called his 'Stalinism' can on closer examination be separated
into two quite distinct problems.'[57] Jameson has been brought
to the water, but still will not drink. These two distinct problems, it seems, are his complicity in the 'literary terrorism' of
the Stalinist apparatus and his 'Popular Frontism'. Jameson
rejects the 'Stalinism' charge on the first count (because of
his covert 'opposition' and his 'rationality' in keeping his
head on his shoulders — we have already discussed these
claims). On the second, he sees some of the ways in which
Lukács actually anticipated Stalinist policy, but argues that
the idea of 'a progressive bourgeois culture' has become more
'problematic' since Lukács's days in the Soviet Union, thus
undermining his aesthetic. But Jameson, like so many others,
apparently cannot see that the real sense in which it is Lukács's
politics that explains his aesthetics (or rather explains his
failure to develop from neo-Kantian to Marxist theory) is his
acceptance of the historic revision of Marxism: 'socialism in a
single country'.

Interestingly, Jameson himself confirms that this blind
spot is very closely connected with ideas of the way in which
modern capitalism is said to have changed. He uses the obvious
fact that twentieth-century capitalism is not the same as nineteenth-century capitalism in such a way as to support Brecht's
criticism of Lukács's dogmatic definition of realism, but then

tells us what he thinks about the nature of the change. His opinion is remarkably similar to that of Lukács:

> In other words the fundamental difference between our own situation and that of the thirties is the emergence in full-blown and definitive form of that ultimate transformation of late monopoly capitalism variously known as the *société de consommation* or as post-industrial society.[58]

Here once again is Lukács's 'Western manipulated capitalism'. It marks the limits of Jameson's critique of Lukács. Similarly Adorno, despite bitter words about Lukács's use of the concept 'reflection', seemed unable to avoid the very Lukács-like conclusion that the best modern music mirrored the 'total system of late capitalism'. Is it surprising that Jameson, after exhaustive and often highly illuminating studies of contemporary developments in the criticism inspired by Marxism and structuralism,[59] ends up with a project for realism which is a posthumous 'provisional last word' from Lukács? This project, we believe, is a correct deduction from Lukács's positions, all the more telling because Jameson has sympathetically taken into account the many 'critiques' of Lukács's aesthetics and accepted many of them, yet remains baffled by the theoretical implications of Lukács's politics after 1924. For Jameson proposes that the concept of realism be,

> ... rewritten in terms of the categories of *History and Class Consciousness*, in particular those of reification and totality ... [Reification] is a disease of that mapping function whereby the individual subject projects and models his or her insertion into the collectivity. The reification of late capitalism — the transformation of human relations into an appearance of relationships between things — renders society opaque: it is the lived source of the mystifications on which ideology is based and by which domination and exploitation are legitimised. Since the fundamental structure of the social 'totality' is a set of class relationships — an antagonistic structure such that the various social classes define themselves in terms of that

antagonism and by opposition with one another — reification necessarily obscures the class character of that structure, and is accompanied, not only by anomie, but also by that increasing confusion as to the nature and even the existence of social classes which can be abundantly observed in all the 'advanced' capitalist countries today. If the diagnosis is correct, the intensification of class consciousness will be less a matter of a populist or ouvrierist exaltation of a single class by itself, than the forcible reopening of access to a sense of society as a totality, and of the reinvention of possibilities of cognition and perception that allow social phenomena once again to become transparent, as moments of the struggle *between* classes.

Under these circumstances, the function of a new realism would be clear; to resist the power of reification in consumer society and to reinvent that category of totality which, systematically undermined by existential fragmentation on all levels of life and social organisation today, can alone project structural relations between classes as well as class struggles in other countries, in what has increasingly become a world system. Such a conception of realism would incorporate what was always most concrete in the dialectical counter-concept of modernism — its emphasis on violent renewal of perception in a world in which experience has solidified into a mass of habits and automatisms. Yet the habituation which it would be the function of the new aesthetic to disrupt would no longer be thematised in the conventional modernistic terms of desacralised or dehumanising reason, of mass society and the industrial city or technology in general, but rather as a function of the commodity system and the reifying structure of late capitalism.[60]

Without doubt Jameson has comprehended the vicious circle which Lukács's criticism produces, a self-contained world of reified consciousness and protest bent on demystification. There is much talk of 'the reifying structure of late capitalism' but nothing of wage-labour and capital; it seems that not only the awareness of class but also the experience of exploitation and class struggle is blotted out. The category of totality, reinvented or resurrected, is now to project the ('total') world revolution (if that is what Jameson means by 'structural relations between classes as well as class struggles in other countries') and thus bring about a 'violent renewal of perception'. Far from waiting on such 'shock effects' from a reinvented category and its influence on art, the revolution makes its own way, and any counterpart of it in a Marxist theory of literature would have to seek its roots in that real revolution, not in a critique of the contradictions of the outlook of those who, like Georg Lukács, rejected it.

5

The Hidden Structure:
Lucien Goldmann

When Lucien Goldmann, influenced by Kant, by the neo-Kantian Max Adler, and by Piaget, looked to Marxism for intellectual resources, it was in the direction of Georg Lukács that he turned. In this he was at least consistent. Lukács had elaborated a version of Marxism without ever thoroughly reworking and negating his own neo-Kantian past. Raymond Williams has assured us that he was not deterred from embracing one of the main ideas of Goldmann and Lukács by labels like 'left-bourgeois idealism'(?), and declares, 'if you're not in a church you're not worried about heresy; the only real interest is actual theory and practice'.[1] This misses the point by a wide margin. Lukács's reconciliation of Marxism and neo-Kantian idealism was indeed a question of 'actual theory'. And the practice of Lukács, as we have seen (above, Chapter 4) was no mere matter of accident or personal character, but was entirely consistent with an idealist view of 'adequate consciousness' which is disembodied, separated from the working class and personified in a bureaucratic party and leadership standing over the class. If Williams wants only to select pragmatically from a list of concepts those which seem fruitful in literary criticism, that is his affair, but it has little to do with the 'actual theory and practice' of Marxism.

If Goldmann bases himself explicitly on the earlier writings of Lukács (*Soul and Form, Theory of the Novel,* and *History and Class Consciousness*), while Lukács himself renounces a large part of these, it is at first sight surprising that they reach very similar conclusions on certain fundamental questions: not questions of sociology of literature so much as of the social, economic and political characterisation of the post-1945 capitalist world. It is a peculiar kind of Marxism which can dismiss these central questions as irrelevant in considering their ideas on literature.[2] We know that the artist or writer will attain to realism in his creative work only if he finds some way of representing the necessities which make up the most fundamental tendencies for change in his own time. When critics claiming to be Marxists have differences about these tendencies, then of course this must be reflected in their judgements of literature, not merely very generally but directly.

Goldmann's characterisation of contemporary capitalism is one which is consistent with his views of the nature of consciousness and its relation to social being, just as was the case with Lukács. However, Goldmann worked in a different milieu from that of Lukács, not feeling the same immediate political constraints, and gave clearer expression to the direct link between his philosophical revision of Marxism and his politics. Thus:

> But the fundamental problematic of modern capitalist societies is no longer located at the level of poverty — although, I repeat, poverty remains even in the most advanced industrial countries — or even at the level of a freedom directly limited by law or external constraint. Instead, it lies entirely in the contraction of the level of consciousness and in the concomitant tendency to reduce the fundamental human dimension of the possible. As Marcuse says, if social evolution does not change direction, man will live and act increasingly only in the single dimension of adaptation to reality, and not in the other, the dimension of transcendence.[3]

Leaving aside the inadequacy of the formulation that in Marx's view of capitalism 'the fundamental problematic' was 'at the level of poverty', we need only emphasise, in this very clear statement by Goldmann, that he goes out of his way to characterise the dominance of considerations of consciousness as *fundamental*. Since the central concept in his own work in sociology of knowledge and sociology of literature had always been 'potential consciousness'(variously translated 'adequate', 'imputed', 'possible', etc, in order to convey the meaning of 'zugerechnet'), it was surely consistent on his part to see as 'fundamental' a change to a situation in which the impossibility of arriving at consciousness came to predominate. It is remarkable that Goldmann, by a different route, arrives at a result similar to that reached by Althusser and his school. Using the concept of 'overdetermination' adapted from Freud, Althusser 'accepts' historical materialism and the determining of superstructure by base 'in general', but maintains that the economic base has subtle ways of conditioning the pattern of society in such a way that some other factor, such as ideological hegemony in modern capitalism, comes to determine the rest of society. This not only results in a reversal, for all questions of actual practice, of the thesis that social being determines consciousness; it implies as a necessary corollary a revision of the Marxist theory of the state, whose ideological apparatus, and particularly the education system, becomes the major factor in ensuring social cohesion. This resembles very closely the conclusions of Lukács in *History and Class Consciousness* (above, Chapter 4), and it compares with Goldmann's care to give an inferior position to 'the level of a freedom directly limited by law or external constraint'. Is it inconceivable that these Marxists, even though their characterisation of ideology's powers is meant to be critical, will come closer to structural—functionalist sociology of the Talcott Parsons type, with its discovery of a 'central value system' which dominates the functions of every particular society, constituting its distinctive character?

Although he reassures his readers that he considers too pessimistic the conclusions drawn by Marcuse from the effects of 'organised capitalism' on consciousness, Goldmann chooses not to discuss any of the 'tendencies toward overcoming this situation' except 'at the level of literary and cultural creation': the search for new literary forms other than those 'which society has created', and the adoption of the theme of revolt in art and literature. There is nothing in Goldmann's work to suggest that the 'negation' of organised capitalism is in its essentials the product in class struggle of the contradiction between socialisation of production and individual ownership of capital. After all, why should such contradictions be thought to exist, if there is no longer an 'anarchy of capitalist production'? The work of the artist, then, when he sets about uncovering the essential beneath the forms of appearance, is directed at ways of thinking and feeling, as autonomous liberating processes, and not at ways of acting in accordance with objective and understandable necessities. Once again the similarity of the conclusions of the 'humanist' Goldmann to those of the 'anti-humanist' Althusser is striking: literature and art, if Goldmann's logic is pursued to the end, can only draw sharper definitions within ideology.

Marx's whole critique of idealism was centred on the notion that 'criticism' of existing conditions, if it was to cease being impotent protest, must become 'the criticism of weapons' rather than 'the weapon of criticism', i.e., a real transformation of society by that element in it which is forced by existing circumstances into the necessary revolution. To say that Goldmann has returned, in an important sense, to the idealism of the 'critical' Left Hegelians is not to indulge in heresy-hunting, as Williams thinks, but is simply to draw a line between the development of Marxism for working-class revolution and regression to the days when the proletarian revolution was not yet known. The sociology of literature associated with such a view of the relation between consciousness and social reality will be anything but Marxist.

There is no interruption in continuity between these conclusions about the effect on 'possible consciousness' of 'organised capitalism' and the shift in theoretical emphasis which dominates the development of Goldmann's writings on literature, and particularly the novel.[4] He argues that the structure of the novel changes significantly in response to the historical progress of reification. In *The Hidden God*[5] he had demonstrated that the plays of Racine and the philosophy of Pascal developed and were structured in correspondence with the 'tragic vision' contained in the world outlook of a social class (or fraction of a class) at a particular turning point in that class's development. In the course of this work, and in his subsequent first approach to a 'sociology of the novel', Goldmann elaborated his 'genetic structuralism'. In this system the structure of the world vision of a social group was postulated as homologous with the structure of the universe of given literary works. The social groups whose life-situation and historical role necessitated a comprehensive vision would normally be found to be social classes. The form of the literary work would be structured in a manner congruent with the relations between whole and part, history and function, etc., in the world vision of the class. However, the structures of world visions of classes were not conceived as fixed, but rather in a constant process of destructuration and restructuration as the social group found it necessary to confront and adapt to or overcome the new problems constantly thrown up by social life. Hence the structuralism was 'genetic'.

By concentrating on this structural homology rather than the manifest thematic content, as the point at which the 'realism' of works might be assessed, Goldmann considered that he could overcome the errors of a too mechanical sociology of literature, which is unable to raise questions of literary form as such. At the same time, he consistently argues that in the terms of his genetic structuralism the creator of the work is the social class as a collectivity, since it is at the level of the class's relation to society as a whole that the processes of destructing and restructuring must be adequate. The individual writer is exceptionally representative of the class in that he finds ways of expressing a coherence of world vision which in practice is never achieved, never so 'pure'. Evidently we are once again in the familiar realm of 'imputed', 'potential' (*zugerechnet*) consciousness, 'objective possibility' and 'ideal type', the world of Lukács's *History and Class Consciousness* and of Max Weber. For Goldmann, the great writer 'achieves a coherent awareness of what, among the other members of his group, remains vague and confused, and contradicted by innumerable other tendencies'. The historian—sociologist can grasp the relation between the two because he 'can extrapolate the maximum possible consciousness of a group until this consciousness reaches its highest limit of coherence... it is precisely this coherent vision which constitutes the content of the work and thereby the first necessary condition — though by no means always an adequate one — for the existence of either artistic or literary aesthetic values'.[6]

This genetic structuralism, clearly derived from Lukács, is the only developed theoretical foundation put forward by Goldmann for a sociology of literature, yet it has the peculiar property of proving inappropriate as soon as Goldmann puts it to the test in the analysis of the novel form. Its property is peculiar in the sense that the capitalist society on the basis of which the novel develops is the society where the reality of class can at last be discerned (in the light of the necessity of overcoming it), and peculiar also in the sense that the Lukácsian 'imputed consciousness' was invented for the comprehension of just this society. Goldmann's dilemma is an awesome one at this point. On the one hand, he maintains that the structure of exchange relations and reification, independently of any mechanism of class consciousness, structures individual consciousness in modern capitalism. Yet in *The Hidden God* he had located the historical beginnings of the importance of such mechanisms of class consciousness at a historical date almost exactly coinciding with the beginning of the reign of reification!

> ... in the modern world — from the 17th century onwards — artistic, literary and philosophical works have been associated with social classes and closely linked with the consciousness which each class has of itself.[7]

Now, we saw that Lukács's use of the concept of realism grew less coherent and satisfying (from the Marxist standpoint) the closer he came to the contemporary world and its literature, and we tried to establish one source of this inadequacy in his failure ever to negate and develop beyond his early ideas of class consciousness and its relation to the actual development of the class struggle, particularly after the Russian Revolution of 1917. A series of similarly interconnected problems arises in the case of Goldmann. Setting aside for this stage of the argument any evaluation of his interpretation of 'modernist' literature (it was very different from Lukács), we note only that the theoretical edifice for a sociology of literature erected on Lukács's imputed consciousness had to be put aside in order for Goldmann to approach, first the novel in the period of 'organised capitalism', and very soon in the period of the 'crisis capita-lism' (between the two world wars and roughly equivalent to Lenin's 'imperialism, epoch of wars and revolutions', though clearly not 'the last stage of capitalism') which he thought preceded it, and eventually the long era of competitive capita-lism of the nineteenth century and earlier. If Lukács's intellec-tual evolution showed the barrenness of his concept of class consciousness when applied to the proletariat, Goldmann's demonstrates it in the case of its application to the bourge-oisie. He finds that there is only a minor manifestation of the 'explicit values' of bourgeois consciousness in the history of the novel, and that this occurs only at the level of its 'sub-literature'. The exception is said to be Balzac, probably for the reason that his writing coincides with the active period of construction of a new social order. This is a hypothesis which would seem to involve many difficulties, particularly in view of the problematical nature of the 'explicit values' of bourgeois consciousness in a writer whose own explicit values were hardly typically bourgeois or engaged on the con-struction of a new society. Here the argument seems in any case very weak. The idea of a novel's needing to express the explicit values of bourgeois consciousness in order to be open to 'genetic structuralist' analysis is one which in other con-texts Goldmann dismissed as an oversimplification of the concept of the developing structure of a class's world vision and its degree of coherence.

If then there was no period when the bourgeoisie's world vision found expression 'through the link of class con-sciousness',[8] what was left of the ideas of structure and genetic structuralism? It was only Goldmann's introduction, into the original conception, of the actual problems of the class in confronting its real problems which had given hope of bringing life into the notion of structure. What now replaces this developing class consciousness, however general and abstract it was, is something very different. Goldmann finds that the exclusive 'value' of individualism in bourgeois econ-omy destroys any basis for the crucial link of class conscious-ness, the level of the collectivity, in his original theory. In the scheme of genetic structuralism the highest point reached by, or rather attributable to, the consciousness of the class found expression in the most accomplished works of particular writers. Now, however, Goldmann sees capitalism as presenting a reality which cannot be approached with such a hypothesis. There is the level of the market economy with its individualist values, and the level of the production of novels, and 'it is impossible to find a third homologous or similar structure at the level of this [class] consciousness'. This 'absence of intermediating structures in collective consciousness' is 'merely the natural consequence' of the exchange economy and its direct link with the novel.[9]

Criticising those who see reification as the key to understanding only modern works, Goldmann actually concludes that the very 'appearance in literary life of. . . the novel genre or, more precisely, the novel of the problematic hero', is the result of the 'repercussions' of reification from 'the very beginnings of commercial capitalism'. As we have indicated, this statement should be compared with Goldmann's assertion in *The Hidden God* that the importance of class and class consciousness for the interpretation of literature dates from the seventeenth century.

By now we are of course carried beyond *History and Class Consciousness* back to *Theory of the Novel* of 1914. There Lukács defined the world of the novel as the search for authentic values in a degraded world, by an individual who is himself in a state of degradation, though in a different way. (Lukács has explained that this work was written under the direct influence of the neo-Kantians Dilthey, Simmel, Max Weber and others, although he himself was moving from Kant's to Hegel's philosophy at the time.) Goldmann's 'homology' is 'between the reified structure of the liberal market and the [novel] form, whose universe, like the market's, is characterised among other things by the absence of manifest transindividual values'. Yet 'implicitly and through absence, these values structure a universe composed of two elements between which there is a dialectical relation of community and opposition: the degraded world ignorant of these values, and the hero who is himself degraded in a different way'.[10] It seems that the implicit values which structure by their absence are *use-values*.[11]

Here we are at the very crux of the argument of Goldmann.

Lukács's early work delineated three 'ideal-types' of the novel form, based on different orders of adequacy of the spirit to the world in which it is placed.[12] Goldmann found the universe inhabited by these types 'strictly homologous' with the description of liberal market economy given 'by the liberal economists, but above all by Marx (who added to the classical description the analysis of the fetishism of commodities).'[13]

Whatever else it might be, it is not Marxism to say that capitalism is an illusory world of fetishism and exchange-values somehow structured from below or behind, implicitly or explicitly, by use-values. We have already cited Marx and Engels at length (Chapter 2 above) to show that for them the exchange of labour-power at its value for variable capital (wages) was 'the axis on which the whole of modern society turns' and the source of all the basic forms of social consciousness in that society. The million-times repeated reproduction of this relation, in the course of capitalism's necessary drive for surplus value, is what 'structures' social life and consciousness, and in relation to which the significance of every other economic and social category must be estimated. The history of capitalist societies (that real history in which individuals become conscious and in which literature is written and read) is not the history of a world where these forms are elaborated and made coherent in individual brains, but is the history of the class struggle engendered by the capital-labour relation and its development. Marx certainly did not add commodity fetishism to the description given by the classical economists. More than anything else he carried through political economy as a science to the point where it had to be transcended in revolutionary theory and practice, beyond that point of the generalisation of the struggle between bourgeoisie and proletariat which marked the limit of the horizons of the classical economists. Where they saw 'natural — social' laws at work in capitalism as a manifestation of human nature, Marx saw historical 'laws of motion' and the revolutionary role of the working class in abolishing capitalism.

For Goldmann consciousness is 'from the beginnings of commercial capitalism' patterned by the structure of exchange economy, with its tendency to crush out consciousness and qualitative individuality. His qualification — that it is 'never entirely successful' in so doing — does not address itself to the main question. Where Marx saw the material development of exploitation and class struggle changing the social being of the working class and thus creating the conditions for changed consciousness, Goldmann sees something quite different:

> ... the subsistence of a certain number of problematic individuals in this society whose thought and behaviour remain dominated by qualitative values, even though they cannot entirely shield these values from the general action of degrading mediation (in particular, this is the case for creators).[14]

Besides these mysterious problematic creators there is only an equally mysterious

> ... non-conceptualised affective discontent and an affective aspiration aimed directly toward qualitative values, whether this occurs in the entire society or only among the middle strata from which most novelists are recruited [and] the existence in this society of liberal individualist values which, although not transindividual, nonetheless have a universal aim. These values engendered by bourgeois society contradict the important limitations that society brings to bear on possibilities for individual development.[15]

The exceptional individuals orientated towards use-value who (somehow?) escape the determining structure of commodity relations present the same insoluble problem for theory as did the individuals whom the eighteenth-century materialists and their utopian socialist disciples thought would take it into their heads to reform a society which had determined everyone except themselves. The resolution of this contradiction by Marx, through the concept of revolutionary practice (*Theses on Feuerbach*) is here ignored by Goldmann, even though he claims to embrace a 'dialectical' sociology in which 'man is greater than what he is because he is always making himself and making a new world'. The non-conceptualised 'discontent' is brought into the argument from nowhere, like the unexplained 'dysfunctional' and 'affective' elements in modern structural–functionalist sociology or Weber's charismatic leaders. Moreover, this discontent is of relevance, it seems, only in the middle class, from which the novelists are drawn. The final hope is that the liberal individualist values developed by the bourgeoisie itself 'contradict' and presumably will therefore be brought to bear positively on the situation. Here everything is removed to the sphere of values, their mutual contradictoriness, feelings of discontent, and the fortunate existence of individuals capable of remaining orientated towards use-values. This world of make-believe is 'homologous' with nothing, unless perhaps the feelings of impotence and moral outrage of a bourgeois intelligentsia, which, 'disappointed' with a working class that has failed to fulfil the Marxian promise, dares to hope it has not exhausted all the possible combinations of thought and feeling in the bourgeois world outlook and that some of these will perhaps have cheated history. Goldmann wants to say, against experience, that 'the *possible* is the fundamental category for comprehending human history', but, at the same time, 'the fundamental problematic of modern capitalist societies. . . lies entirely in the contraction of the level of consciousness and in the concomitant tendency to reduce the fundamental dimension of the possible'.[16]

*   *   *

Goldmann's evolution to a concept of the structure of the novel as homologous to the structure of market economy, rather than one of the structure of the work as homologous to the world vision of a class, has a confused and confusing aspect. From one point of view it might appear to constitute the correction of a severe one-sidedness and limitation in his earlier view. Interpretations of works as homologous to or expressive and constitutive of the world vision of a class could easily remain restricted to the level of ideological consciousness, so that the issue of how far the work reflected the structure of social reality (and not just a vision of it) was not posed. Essentially the limitation is philosophical, and derives from Kant: there is no doubt a real world beyond what enters sensation and consciousness, but we cannot know it; we know only the world of phenomena on which the mind imposes order. It would represent a step beyond this idealist position if Goldmann had evolved a method of showing how the capitalist economy's reality itself was represented artistically. (One should add that a Marxist theory purporting to show this would have to include the role of class struggle and class consciousness in structuring the experience in which men become able to penetrate the forms of appearance and comprehend them in their necessity.) From the other side, Goldmann's notion of just what reality it is that determines the structure of consciousness and how this determination takes place, is a step backwards even from his genetic structuralism, which had the sole virtue that it directed attention to the most important groupings in society and tried to allow for the changes in consciousness continuously necessitated by changes in social life. In his theory of homology between market economy and the novel Goldmann is thrust back to 'the standpoint of the isolated individual in civil society', by now rationalised and helplessly conscious of his ideological subjection to reification. Some sort of structuralism, with its 'homology', remains, but there is no longer anything genetic about it, any more than there is about other structuralisms. Instead of even the rather crude external 'stimulus-internal response' and 'restructuring' pattern of genetic structuralism, we can only arrive at the self-transforming properties of a structure with which everyone is now familiar, not to say bored. Thus, in reply to Robert Escarpit's comment that the word structure was meaningless, Goldmann replied, as Lévi-Strauss or Piaget might have done: 'Structure means those regularities which condition a totality in such a way that the transformation of one element entails necessarily certain complementary transformations of the other elements in such a way that a global meaning is preserved.'[17] Pressed further, by the question 'structure of what?', Goldmann explained:

. . . the structure of the universe of the novel! For example, in Malraux's novels, erotic or love relations and historico-political action are homologous . . . It is not a matter of a structure of behaviour or of individual character, but. . . of the structure of a totality of interindividual political, erotic, love, etc. relations, which sometimes transform themselves in the course of the narrative.[18]

All this might be interesting, but no one will suggest that there is anything Marxist about it. Goldmann pursued his analysis of Malraux's novels as an example of the collapse of the project of a collective revolutionary hero to 'replace' the quest for a positive individual hero, a quest which had died with the passing of competitive capitalism at the beginning of the twentieth century. Here one can see little more than a sort of auto-sociology of the left intelligentsia, who, shaken by the historical crisis which exploded in August 1914, turned briefly, after the October revolution of 1917, to the working class, but found it wanting. Malraux was a few years ahead of certain others, and his works are certainly amenable to the empathy felt by Goldmann.

In his own comments on the shift from genetic structuralism to the more formal structural homology of exchange economy and the novel Goldmann stumbles across the kernel of the problem, though he picks up his stride too quickly. He notes that the earlier hypothesis worked for 'oppositional groupings' within a given society but not normally for the bourgeoisie in its ascendancy. The reason is that the notion of class consciousness held by Goldmann fails to take into account the fundamental fact that the ideology of the bourgeoisie as ruling class is the ideology of capitalist *society* and not only of one class. Whatever oppositional tendencies grow spontaneously in the working class as a result of its experience, the ideological framework in which it conceives this experience is 'bourgeois consciousness' (Lenin: 'trade union consciousness is bourgeois consciousness'). We have already referred to Marx's statement that the form of wages as price of labour (concealing the reality of purchase of labour-power and extraction of surplus-value) is the source of all the notions of the working class about freedom, justice and so on as well as of the social consciousness of the bourgeoisie. The only 'oppositional' group which, taking Goldmann's own criteria, needs an overall outlook or structured 'world vision' is the proletariat, and Goldmann's writings on modern literature are characterised by a total absence of any treatment of the problems of proletarian class consciousness. To have confronted these problems would have brought him face to face with the vital difference between the proletariat's role and consciousness in capitalist society and the role and consciousness of the bourgeoisie when it was an 'oppositional' class, in feudal society. The bourgeoisie develops capitalist economy *within* feudalism, before its revolution. On this basis the elements of bourgeois culture and values can be developed. The bourgeois have their own schools, universities, academies, even churches and religious doctrines, in the very pores of feudalism, just as they have their businesses. Revolution comes as a necessary political confirmation of the economic, and to a certain extent cultural, developments which have already made the bourgeoisie the strongest class, ready now to establish the political and legal framework for its full development. When the proletariat comes into revolutionary opposition against the capitalist state, it is when capitalism has completed a vast socialisation of the process of production, concentrating the working class into an exploited and oppressed mass, the very opposite of a new and challenging economic and social order with its own forms of appropriation within the old.

These were the questions long ago elaborated by Trotsky (*Literature and Revolution*), and they were an obvious corrective to any theory such as Goldmann's, which sought some *general* structure of class, class consciousness, and their relation to 'cultural creation'. The fact is that, accepting the nostrum that 'organised capitalism' has left no important problems except the narrowing of the possibilities for consciousness, Goldmann cannot even begin to conceive of how the working class can be considered an 'oppositional' group. If it has no revolutionary role necessitated by its role in social production, then there is certainly nothing in its position to make it oppositional. Goldmann says little more than that the workers should be shown that their interests require that to save their dignity they should swim against the stream of reification, and that part of this is to save the great cultural values inherited from the past. Enlightenment by propaganda (demystification) and the fight for values replace revolution necessitated by structural conflict. Goldmann's remedy in the 1960s and 1970s was 'worker-management', which would preserve the values of the market and freedom against the totalitarian threat: ' . . .the necessity of a self-regulation of industrial enterprises and of social institutions which would permit above all *a democratisation of responsibilities*, the only means of meeting the considerable intellectual dangers created by current development.'[19]

The working class is not a mass of stupefied victims of reification awaiting prescriptions from an enlightened intelligentsia which knows the path to authentic values. Willy-nilly, the working class is drawn into great struggles. Within it, profound conflicts develop as the necessary form of the struggle to achieve unity and political independence of the bourgeoisie. There *is* a process of struggle for 'oppositional' class consciousness, Goldmann notwithstanding, and there is much more – a struggle for revolutionary organisation and consciousness. And this struggle is not a process of successive approximations to some 'ideal type' of class consciousness, as Lukács thought. When Raymond Williams writes that Goldmann's work on reification pointed to 'practical work to find, to assert and to establish more human social ends in more human political terms', and also noted that 'the foundation of [Goldmann's] approach is the belief that all human activity is an attempt to make a significant response to a particular objective situation',[20] he does not face up to the fact that the stress on reification eventually crowded out that 'foundation' of genetic structuralism. And when in consequence Goldmann found it possible to ignore completely the dramatic conflicts in the actual struggle for class consciousness in the working class, Williams did not even remark any contradiction between this and Goldmann's earlier precepts. This merely illustrates the fact that there are individuals whose position allows them to accept those aspects of the work of a particular writer which seem useful in elaborating their own abstract scheme on 'Marxism and Literature' while at the same time ignoring the living struggle for Marxism itself.

With a theory of class consciousness of this character Goldmann naturally finds no difficulty in concluding that the Marxist analysis of the proletariat and its revolutionary role has been proved wrong. The working class is now 'integrated'.[21]

With Goldmann's conclusion that the political level reached by the working class at any particular time is nothing but an effect of the degree of integration achieved through reification, we have travelled far from that point at which he posited 'the struggle for the possible' as the fundamental characteristic of human life. The atmosphere is, rather, that of the chill world of Durkheim's social facts 'external to the individual and exercising constraint upon him'. Whatever may have been Goldmann's personal feelings, occasional expressions of hope, and 'corrections' to his pessimism in the aftermath of the general strike of May—June 1968 in France, the fact is that his conclusions about the closing of possibilities for opposition in organised capitalism did not leave any room, theoretically, for the hope of social transformation. For him the structure of modern capitalism is such that it is

> . . . characterised by the appearance of conscious mechanisms of self-regulation. . . capitalism has survived crises which, according to the Marxists, had to be fatal to it; and its theoreticians have become aware of the problems of the overall organisation of society and the economy. . . since the end of the war there have been no more internal crises in Western societies.[22]

The consequences:

> . . . integration of the whole society through a rise in the standard of living. . . and the considerable weakening of traditional oppositional forces. . . and the considerable concentration of decision-making power in the hands of a relatively small group (several thousand people) which I will call *technocrats* . . . [and] the considerable reduction of the psychic life of individuals.[23]

Even without a detailed testing of these sweeping claims against the political and economic developments in France and internationally in the period since these words were written, one is struck above all by the way in which theorists of class consciousness like Lukács and Goldmann are so ready to accept, without critical analysis, descriptions of the supposed ability of capitalism to suppress 'oppositional tendencies' and to produce a situation where the working class is no longer faced with revolutionary responsibilities but must concentrate only on finding allies among critical realists or being demystified by 'exceptional individuals'. It should be noted in passing that Goldmann repeated a familiar pattern by passing through a brief phase of reformist socialism, relying on the gradual and peaceful preparation of the conditions of socialist economy within American capitalism.[24]

*   *   *

Marx noted[25] that the experimental, laboratory methods of the natural sciences are of course not available for political economy, and must be replaced by 'the force of abstraction'. The study of political and intellectual tendencies can hardly be expected to produce exact correlations and conclusions. It cannot exclude or calculate the degree of error due to 'extraneous' factors, relying rather on the proved ability of the investigator to synthesise his material. Even bearing all these reservations in mind, it is difficult to avoid concluding that the picture of Georg Lukács as a brilliant literary critic in the tradition of Marxism (let alone a Marxist philosopher) who was unfortunate to fall among Stalinists is radically false. In Lucien Goldmann we have an almost 'experimental' case-history of what happens to the same philosophical positions when placed in a different environment for their development. On the fundamental historical and political questions of Marxism, on the nature of the epoch and the role of the main classes in it, they come to virtually identical pessimistic conclusions, incapable of pointing to that reality which would provide the basis for an art able to challenge the permanence of the existing capitalist order. The same concepts of reification and possible class consciousness which prepared them for their eventual political conclusions prove internally self-contradictory when they are applied to the present. They have no objective basis for criticism of

literary tendencies, because they reject the objective contradictions and their material result, the proletarian revolution, which is the core of historical materialism. The result
is that their Marxism is little more than a certain skill in
inventing 'Marxist' terms for their subjective and local
preferences (Lukács against modernism, naturalism, subjectivism; Goldmann for the New Novel and Genet; and so on).
Their differences on these matters are thus no more than a
sign of the disintegration of their doctrine in contact with the
real world.

Lukács had never gone farther than his conception (in
History and Class Consciousness) of reification as the structure of knowledge and consciousness, with historical materialism as essentially the analysis and overcoming of this reified
consciousness. The process of defeating capitalism could be
completed in the realm of thought, that realm where the construction of 'possible consciousness' is carried out. The basic
relation of necessary practice in class struggle is lost, and
Lukács can move freely into the orbit of the dictatorship of
the bureaucracy over the working class, and even anticipate
that bureaucracy's own accommodation of bourgeois democracy. Goldmann's rejection of the revolutionary role of the
working class is more explicit, but has the same foundation,
the idea of reification as structure of consciousness separated
from the actual life and practice of the working class and its
struggles, from trade-union defensive battles to revolution.

The truth contained in the theories of reified consciousness
was already in Marx, but without the one-sided exaggeration
of it, leading to idealism, in Lukács and Goldmann. When
Marx showed that in capitalism the labour time incorporated
in every product appeared as a material property inhering in
the product itself, its exchange-value, and traced the ideological illusions flowing from this fetishism, he did not at all
imply that all consciousness in capitalist society consisted of
constructions upon this base. Real history was for him the
history of class struggles, and not the history of individual
men receiving a mental imprint from economy and proceeding to all other aspects of behaviour as if pre-programmed by
that imprint of exchange relations. The working class develops
its struggle in many forms against capital; the ruling class

must resort to many different forms of defence and attack, and by no means relies solely upon the fetishism or reification which is inseparable from commodity production. In all these spheres of conflict consciousness is shaped, and considerable internal differentiation in the working class is necessary for the achievement of revolutionary consciousness. It is an idealist abstraction, leaning on nothing but the immediate forms of appearance in the sphere of ideology, to draw conclusions about the non-revolutionary character of the modern proletariat without historical analysis of these contradictions.

But there is another aspect, to which we have already referred in dealing with the ideas of Marx. The 'universalisation of production on the basis of exchange' (Marx) is not to be seen as exclusively the progress of reification, 'the alienation of the individual from himself and others'. It produces 'also the universality and the comprehensiveness of his relations and capacities'. On this basis Marx says: 'It is as ridiculous to yearn for a return to that original fullness [of earlier stages of history] as it is *to believe that with this complete emptiness history has come to a standstill'*[26] [my emphasis, C. S.]. When Marx adds the remark that the antithesis between this romantic viewpoint of the bourgeoisie, antithetical to the bourgeoisie itself, 'will accompany it as legitimate antithesis up to its blessed end', he can hardly have thought that it would one day be paraded as Marxism. Yet his judgement of the class basis of such ideas remains strictly accurate for the characterisation of the ideas of Goldmann. That these searchers after a Marxist sociology of literature should ignore the continuation of the Marxist tradition in this field by Trotsky's *Literature and Revolution* is less surprising than it might first have appeared. The opportunist political reasons which undoubtedly formed the conscious motives for this choice were only the manifestation of totally opposed tendencies in theory and in practice, an opposition to Marxism with quite definite class implications. Several commentators have noted the connection between the development of the Lukács-Goldmann type of criticism and the failure of revolution to spread in the period after the First World War. Their response to this experience in Central and Western Europe is contrasted to the revolutionary experiences of Trotsky. But

Trotsky and his comrades were not the only ones who, in the field of literature, refused the road taken by Lukács and Goldmann, despite the enormous pressure of the years of counter-revolution, Fascism, the degeneration of the Soviet state, and the approach of the Second World War.

Walter Benjamin sought ways of proceeding precisely from the contradictory essence of the 'universalisation of production on the basis of exchange'. Goldmann (following Pascal) defined man's essential being as self-creative, but saw this unhistorically, and concluded that man now was reduced to fighting a losing battle against reification. Marx had perceived that the labour-process (self-creation) gave rise to specific socio-economic formations with internal contradictions which necessitated their own historical negation and super-session. From the analysis of these contradictions he abstracted the truth of the revolutionary role of the working class. In contrast to Lukács and Goldmann, it was along this path, even if quite separately and from very different social and intellectual origins and initial focus of interest, that, in the field of literature, Walter Benjamin and Trotsky made their contributions.

6

Against the Stream:
Walter Benjamin

... the revolutionary struggle is not fought between capitalism and the mind. It is fought between capitalism and the
proletariat. (Walter Benjamin)[1]

Unlike those leading Marxists who commented on literature
only occasionally, being preoccupied with political, economic
and philosophical theory and practice, and unlike Lukács,
who returned to literary criticism after active communist
politics, Walter Benjamin was a literary critic long before he
became a Marxist, and his work as a Marxist was directed
almost exclusively at problems of literature. He found himself in tragic circumstances. The victory of Nazism forced
him to leave Germany. He had already become convinced
that the proletarian revolution was the only solution to
humanity's crisis, and yet he found the communist parties'
prescriptions to writers and artists to be the very opposite of
revolutionary and thus destructive of any development in
literature and art. Consequently, his life and work in the
1930s suffered from isolation and hostility (he died, by his
own hand, in September 1940, on realising that he was about
to be handed over to the Gestapo by police at the French—
Spanish frontier). Only in Bertolt Brecht did he find any
sympathetic understanding, and that intellectual relationship
was very close.[2] With the exception of the period of intellectual collaboration with Brecht, Benjamin was virtually isolated.
A Marxist in exile, he was at the same time unacceptable
to the Stalinists; and Adorno and Horkheimer, whose paths
crossed his, were going in a different direction. This is shown

by Adorno's profound 'misunderstanding' of Benjamin's work[3] as well as by his and Horkheimer's emergence as leading protagonists of the idea of 'organised capitalism'.

Radical literary critics often refer to Benjamin's rejection of mystifying notions of creativity and genius, notions easily appropriated and used by Fascism. When capitalist society put out of sight the real isolation and deprivation of the artist by perpetrating the myth that his art was a matter of his personal inspiration, that was an operation similar to telling the wage-slave that labour was the source of all wealth, an idea which left absolutely unquestioned the exclusive ownership by non-labourers of the natural sources of wealth and means of production.[4] What is not so well-known, or at least not so well-repeated, is the fact that Benjamin was also passionately hostile to the current wisdom on the left: the doctrines of progress, of 'history is on our side', and of a theoretical attitude of knowing the right answer before analysing and reconstructing the object of thought. He detected and denounced these central themes of the 'Marxism' of German social democracy and Stalinism, locating them at the base of the betrayals which opened the door for Hitler. And his opposition to the cultural policies of the communist parties was inspired by the same understanding. Marx's dictum that the whole ideological superstructure of capitalism was in a process of contradictory transformation, once the contradiction between the social relations of production and the development of productive forces became pronounced, was Benjamin's chosen starting point. He followed Marx also in knowing that these changes in the superstructure could not be studied with the same precision as could the economy. But all the same they must be studied.

Benjamin wrote many things about the commodity, reification, and fetishism, but he did not himself 'fetishise' these phenomena. Like Marx, he saw the universalisation of capitalist production as the contradictory expression of men's historically developed needs and powers. Only in this dialectical framework, he thought, could the dangers of the contradiction be recognised and the necessity of action be understood and felt. His insistence on the importance of technique, means of production and forces of production was not, as critics like Adorno thought, the result of some crudeness in his grasp of historical materialism (seeking to relate artistic phenomena directly to elements of material production). It arose irrepressibly from his conviction that the decay of capitalism, with its world wars, destruction of productive forces, predatory exploitation of nature, and resort to Fascist terror, was the product of the rebellion of the forces of production against the capitalist property relations: 'If the natural utilisation of productive forces is impeded by the property system, the increase in technical devices, in speed, and in the sources of energy will press for unnatural utilisation, and this is found in war.'[5] And how can the capitalist property system be saved from the growing mobilisation of the masses who are themselves the principal 'force of production' and are forced in life to recognise that socialisation of the production process which conflicts with the needs of capital?

> Fascism seeks its [i.e., the property structure's] salvation by giving these masses not their right, but instead a chance to express themselves. The masses have a right to change property relations; Fascism seeks to give them an expression while preserving property. The logical result of Fascism is the introduction of aesthetics into political life. The violation of the masses, whom Fascism, with its Führer cult, forces to their knees, has its counterpart in the violation of an apparatus which is pressed into the production of ritual values.[6]

Faced with Fascism's rendering politics aesthetic, Benjamin suggests that 'communism responds by politicising art'.

This argument constitutes a skeleton outline of the foundations on which Benjamin (and Brecht) criticised those writers and artists who 'supplied' the existing means of artistic and literary production with their products instead of intervening in the actual transformation of those means of production themselves. By accepting the myth of their independent creativity and inspiration as something disembodied, artists would contribute to 'a processing of data in the Fascist sense'. Now that every product of art is reproducible for instant presentation to the masses, it is in danger of being used for producing in the masses that picture of the world and of themselves which the property structure requires for its continued domination of production. These techniques of reproduction, particularly film, are a revolution in perception. Through the revolution in technique, men glimpse the overcoming of the barriers which the division of manual from mental labour and the division of art from science have erected in class society. But the supplying of artistic material to these privately owned means of production and reproduction in a way which does not challenge the character which they have as capital, unified with the capitalist class, is a sacrifice of art, and of all the promise of the new productive forces, to the needs of the capitalists. While the new techniques, as techniques, free art and the reception of art from their esoteric cult-existence in previous history, under decadent capitalism, culminating in Fascism, the apparatus of the arts and their reproduction 'is pressed into the production of ritual values'. In place of the mobilisation of the masses and their development to revolutionary consciousness, we have the totalitarian self-contemplation in the newsreel of the awestruck mass in front of the leader, and the massed worship of the crowd, its real internal divisions obliterated, for the sportsmen who 'represent the race', etc.[7]

In this analysis Benjamin seeks to extend the work of Marx. The latter's revolutionary conclusions from economic analysis should be matched by the work of Marxists on the manifestation in all areas of culture of these developments:

> Only today can it be indicated what form this has taken. Certain prognostic requirements should be met by these statements. However, theses about the art of the proletariat after its assumption of power or about the art of a classless society would have less bearing on these demands than theses about the developmental tendencies of art under present conditions of production.[8]

By this statement, we are forewarned, in a Marxist study of modern literature, against any erecting of criteria from materials to be found in the period of Marx's own lifetime.

'Only today can it be indicated what form this has taken.' To ignore this would be to fall victim to the conception of Marxism as a closed system which contains *a priori* the answers to all questions if only one has the intelligence and will to deduce them. Benjamin directed his polemical writings against all those who drew from Marx's prognoses only the conclusion that writers should 'take the side' of the working class in conceiving their subject matter, demonstrating some automatic 'progressiveness' of the productive forces which must be victorious against the production relations. Before productive forces are employed, before the implements of production come to man's hand, they must first be transformed into capital, an oppressive external force, the domination of dead labour over the living. To imagine that a commonsense adoption of 'progressive' themes within existing literary forms constitutes a revolutionary line in art and literature was considered by Benjamin to be pure nonsense. It was necessary but far from sufficient to appropriate the conquests of the art and literature of the past. In order to understand the present epoch, where forces of production are turned by capitalist property relations and the necessity of controlling the masses into forces of destruction, the artist must use and develop the means of artistic production to penetrate, to understand, to prise out of the changed reality the truth, which he cannot do without developing the means of penetration and presentation themselves. The experience of men, individually exploited and individually consuming, is fitted only to render them overawed and helpless in an environment of destructive terror typified by world war and its results. Left to itself, merely 'supplied' by the writer and artist, the apparatus of the media of reproduction will perpetuate this inadequacy of experience by giving it a false integration and form, while the internal rotting of the social formation continues and threatens descent into barbarism.

Here was a compelling paradox. The great art of the past had a significance for humanity which surpassed the differences between historical stages, having an 'absolute' character in relation to those stages; and yet there was a limit beyond which the appeal to the standards of great art became positively dangerous. Men armed with modern techniques of painting and writing are right to admit themselves inspired and humble in face of the achievements of artistic perfection by artists whose means were much more limited; and they do well to acknowledge that every step made by these earlier generations was necessary for the later advances. These attitudes provoke a definite feeling in response to the works. In them the beauty resides in the invention and development of limited means to achieve the most noble ends which men set themselves in given conditions. But to rest content with this is dangerous: the means at the disposal of the present generation must be used, transformed, in such a way that they serve human ends, and not those ends which are inevitable if their specific form of interconnection with the destructive social system is not recognised and challenged. Thus, if 'the film. . . extends our comprehension of the necessities which rule our lives. . . [and] manages to assure us of an immense and unsuspected field of action'[9] (Trotsky took a similar view of the value of the Formalists' work on language), then it must be developed in the course of driving for such discoveries, not simply used and the products handed to a film industry which incorporates the newly exposed realities in a reworking of the defences of bourgeois ideology. The productive forces do not somehow independently build up the socialist order, as they batter against the walls of private property. The social force to effect the revolutionary change must be formed, and literature and art have a vital role in this. An organised effort to develop techniques is necessary if the work of the artist is to avoid the fate of exploitation by the class enemy; hence Benjamin's 'politicising of art'.

In the conditions of isolation imposed on intellectuals of any independence by Fascism and by the Stalinist bureaucracy, Benjamin did not, any more than the post-war Brecht, find any position of overall political strategy to correspond to his theoretical insights. He reports on conversations with Brecht in 1938 in which they were both strongly critical of the development of Stalinism in the USSR, but can find no way to express this politically. They speak of a 'workers' monarchy' under Stalin, and consider that Trotsky's writings support the necessity of a critical approach to the Soviet Union. But Brecht concludes that the tendencies at work do not yet necessitate a policy such as Trotsky's. Four years earlier Benjamin had read Trotsky's *History of the Russian Revolution* and his autobiography, and stated in a letter at the time that not for years had he experienced such a 'breathless suspense'.[10] In 1934 his speech 'The Author as Producer' contained in first draft the following quotation from Trotsky: 'When enlightened pacifists undertake to abolish War by means of rationalist arguments, they are simply ridiculous. When the armed masses start to take up the arguments of Reason against War, however, this signifies the end of war.'[11] It is perfectly clear from the context that Benjamin did not remove this quotation because he ceased to think it apposite. On the contrary, it accords with the temper of all his thought, particularly after 1933. No doubt the fact that the speech had to be delivered to the Institute for the Study of Fascism in Paris required such censorship.

Brecht's failure to think through to the end the political implications of his criticisms of the Soviet bureaucracy had consequences in post-war years which are well-known; and the relationship between these political experiences and his later work is an important area for research, beyond our scope here. Lukács found the direction of Brecht's later development a positive one. What Benjamin's course would have been is of course a matter of conjecture; but his theoretical work in the 1930s — within the scope of what he attempted, and it was considerable — constitutes a remarkable and unique achievement, in which he consistently holds fast to the revolutionary character of the epoch and the methodology of Marxism, despite all the great historical pressures working against that.

The coming to power of Hitler in 1933 and the unfolding of the full horror of the Nazi dictatorship were the occasion for many intellectuals in Western Europe to fall in with Stalinism and the 'progressive' or 'democratic' orientation which it began to display in 1934 and which was defined clearly at the seventh Congress of the Comintern in 1935. The socialist Soviet Union as the representative of the progress of humanity beyond capitalism and its wars and crises, as well as the only dependable and strong leader of all the democratic forces who must be united against Fascism — this was the outlook with which the work of progressive writers had to correspond. Socialism was the full development of democracy. Fascism was a political victory of unreason trying to hold back the inevitable march to socialism. Benjamin rejected this picture, and insisted on attempting to define the real ideological roots of the collapse of resistance to Nazism, as well as facing up to the reality of Nazism itself: 'Nothing has corrupted the German working class so much as the notion that it was moving with the current.'[12]

Lukács, after many years of silence about Benjamin, refers to him at last as 'one of the finest critics of modernism',[13] but, not surprisingly, does not comment upon this particular text. Great warrior though he was against 'dogmatic sectarianism', it did not occur to him that Benjamin's statement applies no less to the optimistic fatalism of the Marxism of German social democracy, typified by Kautsky, than to the German Communist Party's message of 1931—3: perhaps Hitler will win power, but after him history decrees that it will be our turn. Benjamin's 'Theses on the Philosophy of History'[14] are a ruthless exposure of this outlook, pointing clearly to betrayal, and to the need for a development of Marxist theory and practice to overcome it. To take this lesson among others from the victory of Nazism, as Benjamin did in his last days, is very different indeed from drawing the elitist conclusion we find in Adorno and Horkheimer, who contemplate, sorrowfully, 'the enigmatic readiness of the technologically educated masses to fall under the sway of any despotism. . . '[15] The same Adorno finds Benjamin too crudely materialist. Yet it is Benjamin, in contrast to the mentality expressed in the above quotation, who works to bring alive Marx's stress on the *dialectical* character of his materialism and the component of practice, of changing the world, in cognition and history, refusing any interpretation of the masses as the playthings of ideology or technology. Adorno's 'readiness' of the masses 'to fall under the sway of any depotism' is more reminiscent of Michels's 'desire of the masses to be ruled' as the condition for 'the iron law of oligarchy' than it is of Marx. Benjamin defines his 'Theses' as:

. . . intended to disentangle the political worldlings from

the snares in which the traitors have entrapped them. Our consideration proceeds from the insight that the politicians' stubborn faith in progress, their confidence in their 'mass basis', and, finally, their servile integration in an uncontrollable apparatus have been three aspects of the same thing. It seeks to convey an idea of the high price our accustomed thinking will have to pay for a conception of history that avoids any complicity with the thinking to which these politicians continue to adhere.[16]

This fight against the traitors presents the historical materialist with the task of opposing completely the crass optimism of the 'official' versions of Marxist theory of history. Those Marxists who explained the present — and acted within it — as if it was the inevitable result of the accumulated events of the past and was making its own inevitable and pre-known contribution to the socialist future, are for Benjamin complicit in the betrayal. The past is, on the contrary, seen from the present, and the true lessons of the past are gleaned only by the revolutionary who has engaged in the vital tasks of the present. From the standpoint of the necessity thrust upon him by these tasks (themselves, of course, historical products) he is sensitive to the past, detecting its meaning the more surely through the urgency of grasping what it has become. This sensitivity is acquired in practice and does not result from some special faculty of intuition, and it is not of course a substitute for scientific historical research, rather a spur to it (as Benjamin's own research well illustrates):

To articulate the past historically does not mean to recognize it 'the way it really was' (Ranke). It means to seize hold of a memory as it flashes up at a moment of danger. Historical materialism wishes to retain that image of the past which unexpectedly appears to man singled out by history at a moment of danger. The danger affects both the content of the tradition and its receivers. The same threat hangs over both: that of becoming a tool of the ruling classes. In every era the attempt must be made anew to wrest tradition away from a conformism that is about to overpower it. The Messiah comes not only as the re-

deemer, he comes as the subduer of Antichrist. Only that
historian will have the gift of fanning the spark of hope
in the past who is firmly convinced that even the dead will
not be safe from the enemy if he wins. And this enemy
has not ceased to be victorious. (Thesis VI)[17]

The onward march of Fascism elicited from Lukács a
'strategy and tactics' which were the projection forwards in
time of some democratic and progressive attainments of the
bourgeoisie (above, Chapter 6). Benjamin's 'Theses' of 1940
are the clearest exposé ever written of the connections between this 'Popular Front' political line and aesthetic theories
of the Lukács type. Where Lukács stressed, in a quite unquali-
fied way, not only the appropriation but the continuation of
bourgeois literature, Benjamin demanded 'dissociation'. Even
while understanding very well the cumulative aspect of culture, a Marxist belies Marxism if he thinks that he, and, as
that would imply, the working class, can simply take over
where others left off:

Whoever has emerged victorious participates to this day in
the triumphal procession in which the present rulers step
over those who are lying prostrate. According to traditional
practice, the spoils are carried along in the procession.
They are called cultural treasures, and a historical materialist views them with cautious detachment. For without
exception the cultural treasures he surveys have an origin
which he cannot contemplate without horror. They owe
their existence not only to the efforts of the great minds
and talents who have created them, but also to the anony-
mous toil of their contemporaries. There is no document
of civilization which is not at the same time a document of
barbarism. And just as such a document is not free of barbarism, barbarism taints also the manner in which it was
transmitted from one owner to another. A historical
materialist therefore dissociates himself from it as far as
possible. He regards it as his task to brush history against
the grain. (Thesis VII)[18]

What Benjamin advocates here is not a cool and sceptical
objectivity, but, on the contrary, a rejection of the meaning

given to history by the oppressing class, 'the victors', a rejection in theoretical terms which expresses and at the same time helps to form the struggle by which the working class rejects the ruling class:

> We need history, but not the way a spoiled loafer in the garden of knowledge needs it. (Nietzsche, *Of the Use and Abuse of History*)

Not man or men but the struggling, oppressed class itself is the depository of historical knowledge. In Marx it appears as the last enslaved class, as the avenger that completes the task of liberation in the name of generations of the downtrodden. This conviction, which had a brief resurgence in the Spartacist group, has always been objectionable to Social Democrats. Within three decades they managed virtually to erase the name of Blanqui, though it had been the rallying sound that had reverberated through the preceding century. Social Democracy thought fit to assign to the working class the role of the redeemer of future generations, in this way cutting the sinews of its greatest strength. This training made the working class forget both its hatred and its spirit of sacrifice, for both are nourished by the image of enslaved ancestors rather than that of liberated grandchildren. (Thesis XII)[19]

The 'Theses' are Benjamin's final expression of the considerations which had inspired his lonely battle in the German exiles' circles for a revolutionary attitude to art and letters. He knew, along with Brecht, that the dominance of thinkers in the Lukács mould in Soviet literary circles (and this is how they saw his role, whatever his later protestations about subterranean opposition), reflected a situation in which his own ideas had no chance of prevailing. It was a signal achievement, in this period of great historical defeats for the working class, to have turned all the more determinedly to the proletariat itself as the base from which the intellectual and the artist must decide their roles. Benjamin did this, not with any vulgar idea of 'working-class culture' but from the standpoint of the objective necessity of the socialisation of the means of production and the proletarian revolution. These were the political and theoretical bases of his (and Brecht's) opposition to Lukács's 'in search of bourgeois man' and uncritical identification with the bourgeoisie's cultural treasures. In one of the conversations recorded by Benjamin, Brecht expresses himself in characteristically brusque manner:

> We went on to discuss Russian literary policy. I said, referring to Lukács, Gabor and Kurella: 'These people just aren't anything to write home about' [literally: with these people you can't make state]. Brecht: 'Or rather, a State is all you can make with them, but not a community. They are, to put it bluntly, enemies of production. Production makes them uncomfortable. You never know where you are with production; production is the unforeseeable. You never know what's going to come out. And they themselves don't want to produce. They want to play the *apparatchik* and exercise control over other people. Every one of their criticisms contains a threat.'[20]

Already in 1934, in 'The Author as Producer',[21] Benjamin had dealt roughly with the prophets of the doctrine of 'progressive' literature. The theme of this paper is that the writer's political tendency must be judged not by the progressiveness of his explicit subject matter, but by whether he is technically progressive. And the latter depends on how deeply he has found himself compelled to pose the question of how artists can do their work in the present situation of insoluble conflict between productive forces and property relations. In place of the injunction to the writer to picture everything to which he turns his hand in the spirit of support of the proletariat, Benjamin says bluntly that his reflections 'make only one demand on the writer: the demand to *think*, to reflect upon his position in the production process'.[22] Here, thinking is set against the unthinking use of existing production methods, which will find even the most 'proletarian' writing served up as entertainment. He is not, we repeat, rejecting the gains of past culture, and says he is convinced that this 'thinking' will bring to the side of the proletariat 'the *writers who matter* — that is to say the best

technicians in their particular branches of the trade'.[23] No
doubt he had in mind the many writers who 'did not matter'
and who expressed much solidarity with the proletariat, but
without thinking. He continues by confronting Louis Aragon,
who had recently become the leading literary spokesman of
the Communist Party, and who had offered to 'many of our
friends among writers who are still hesitant. . . the example
of Soviet Russian writers who came from the Russian bourgeoisie and yet became pioneers of socialist construction'.[24]
Benjamin's utterly scornful objection to this facile approach
is that it omits entirely the conflict which is every real writer's
life and work. If this conflict is studied, the conclusions that
emerge are very different from the shining examples held up
by Aragon: 'But how did these writers become pioneers?
Surely not without very bitter struggles and agonising conflicts. What is needed is not examples but to "draw a balance
from these struggles".'[25]

The writer is not a proletarian who writes, and the striking
of proletarian poses will not make the writer a proletarian.
What distinguishes the writer is his craft, the fact that he has
an education, an expertise, a *means of production*, 'which
attaches him to his class, and still more attaches his class to
him'. Can the writer change the actual practice in which his
'educational privilege', his means of production, is manifested?
This, a 'mediated' effectiveness politically speaking, is a
specific contribution to revolution more meaningful than
solidarity which goes along with a continued 'supplying' of
creative work in which high quality only makes it more certain
to be appropriated by the apparatus of reproduction in the
interests of what exists. And Benjamin here suggests a more
positive role than that of weakening the resistance of the
bourgeoisie from within (the viewpoint expressed by René
Maublanc, to whom Aragon had replied). Benjamin goes
farther than Engels, who, noting that in his day the readers
of novels were overwhelmingly middle-class, asked only that
writers bring out the real state of things and thus undermine
the confidence of the readers in the permanence and stability
of existing conditions. The relation between literature and
the masses is, however, completely changed by the transformation in means of production, which makes all cultural

products reproducible in large numbers, and which has brought with it mass literacy. What Benjamin asks is that the bourgeois intellectual face the reality: that he must be a traitor to his class of origin (he takes this phrase from another article by Aragon): 'In a writer this betrayal consists in an attitude which transforms him, from a supplier of the productive apparatus, into an engineer who sees his task in adapting that apparatus to the ends of the proletarian revolution.'[26]

It will not then be asked first of the literary 'fellow-traveller' whether or not he expresses the positive virtues of democracy and Soviet socialism, the heroism of the proletariat, and so on, but:

> Will he succeed in furthering the unification of the means of intellectual production? Does he see ways of organizing the intellectual workers within their actual production process? Has he suggestions for changing the function of the novel, of drama, of poetry? The more completely he can address himself to these tasks, the more correct his thinking will be and, necessarily, the higher will be the technical quality of his work.[27]

Perhaps it is at this point that there is real meaning to the apparently interminable discussion about 'reflection' in theories of realism. For example, Adorno and others have attacked Lukács[28] for using the materialist concept of reflection in an undialectical way. They themselves, however, make generous concessions to idealism by becoming so involved in 'mediations' that they cannot clarify in what way the mediated results in the sphere of ideas remain nonetheless reflections of 'social being'. We must leave that more general philosophical question aside. What Benjamin does is to pose the problem in terms which can take us beyond the sphere of contemplation and towards a unity of theory and practice. The question is not the correspondence between the writer's ideas and the class struggle, but the role of the writer as writer, in the production process, which is not the same as that of the proletarian. It requires specific, rigorous application, study and practice. On this point Brecht was, once again, very lucid bringing out very clearly his and Benjamin's opposition to Lukács's approach: 'they . . . don't want to produce. They want to play the *apparatchik* and exercise control over other people.' The alternatives are the writer who accepts the bureaucrat and the policeman, supported by helpful 'critics', as his ideological guide, and produces with the methods handed down to him; or the writer who thinks and fights to perfect his craft, and also to transform the whole production apparatus of which it is part. These are the alternatives as seen by Benjamin and Brecht in 1938, as they ponder the conflict between the results of 'dictatorship over the proletariat' (Brecht), which must, however, still be supported because in its own way it protects the conquests of the working class in October 1917,[29] and the revolution outside Russia. What they seek are not 'finished works' which glorify democracy and socialism but works which 'possess an organising function besides and before their character as finished works'.[30]

It is not necessary to summarise or describe Benjamin's presentation of Brecht's 'epic theatre', which he took as the best example of the revolutionary literature and drama he was advocating. Brecht strove for untragic heroes and undramatic theatre in a certain sense; he counterposed 'alienation effect' to empathy, identification with the actors, and catharsis or resolution of conflicts. The actor himself must not 'get inside' the role, but exactly the opposite: make plain that he is acting, exposing something which must be seen not in familiar emotional terms but in a non-personal way, representative of social processes rather than exemplifying something already known and accepted. Brecht renovated theatrical techniques of production and stepped right outside the charmed circle of writer, producer, audience and critic, thus disrupting the whole apparatus of theatre. It was in this that Benjamin saw the progressiveness of Brecht's work, especially in contrast with the contemporary writers of the 'New Objectivity' school. So far as the latter were concerned, realism consisted of accurate reporting, and no question of modification of the productive apparatus arose. Benjamin considered this attitude to be not merely inadequate but positively dangerous: 'I maintain that an appreciable part of so-called left-wing literature had no other social function than that of continually extracting new effects or sensations from this situation for the public's entertainment.'[31] And:

> New Objectivity photography has succeeded in turning abject poverty itself, by handling it in a modish, technically perfect way, into an object of enjoyment. For if it is an economic function of photography to supply the masses, by modish processing, with matter which previously eluded mass consumption — Spring, famous people, foreign countries — then one of its political functions is to renovate the world as it is from the inside, i.e. by modish techniques.[32]

The critic of television drama 40 years after will learn a hundred times more from Benjamin's criticism of false objectivity than he will from all the 'progressive' literature and criticism produced by the fellow-travelling and Stalinist circles, from Aragon and Lukács down. Lukács himself was later to write many, many words against 'naturalism', and showered praise at last upon Benjamin (above, p. 177). He did so, however, without ever confronting the real point at issue between him and Benjamin. In the text from which we have just quoted ('The Author as Producer') Benjamin hits at Lukács's ideas without referring to him directly, by showing that Fascism produces very similar formulations to those arrived at by Lukács in his injunction to writers to imitate the great nineteenth-century realists. Gunter Grindel had written, 'the *Wilhelm Meister*, the *Grüne Heinrich* of our generation have not yet been written', and Benjamin comments:

> Nothing will be further from the mind of an author who has carefully thought about the conditions of production today than to expect or even to want such works to be written. He will never be concerned with products alone, but always, at the same time, with the means of production. In other words, his products must possess an organising function besides and before their character as finished works.[33]

Brecht's epic theatre is the example held up as the contrast to documentary-type realism, and to the aim of producing great new works on the model of the old. Its aim is not to reproduce but to uncover or reveal. To reproduce would be to confirm the surface of social life, ideologically perceived and conceptualised as it is. The attempt to uncover reality involves the conviction that the surface is not the whole reality and indeed reflects it in contradictory forms, and that reportage is deceptive. To uncover means having a theatrical technique equivalent to montage in the film: interruption and 'distanciation'. Instead of the spectator's enjoying his feelings being carried along by the action, and the actor's being so far as possible absorbed in his part, there is a sharp break in which the spectator must stop and take up an attitude to the actor and the action, and the actor likewise to the character he plays and to the situation. In this way the epic dramatist 'opposes the dramatic laboratory to the finished work of art'.[34] The technique of interruption — through laughter, through song — is intended to make the audience stop in its tracks and to be amazed and provoked into thought by the sight and sound of those same relations which until now it has accepted as natural and in no way surprising. Men can thus be confronted with their own reality as an object to be studied and changed.

The basic ideas put forward in 'The Author as Producer' were used by Benjamin in the criticism of past as well as contemporary literature. Baudelaire, for example, was, in Benjamin's view a 'secret agent' within his own class. This was not a conclusion which could have been reached with the method Benjamin attacked in 'The Author as Producer' and elsewhere. What was necessary was critical study of Baudelaire's production, which did not proceed independently of the uses to which it had been put, i.e., independently of the tradition into which Baudelaire had been pressed. The real content of Baudelaire's poetry and prose must be carved out of this history: '. . . it is an illusion of vulgar Marxism that the social function of a material or intellectual product can be determined without reference to the circumstances of its tradition.'[35] Any attempt merely to locate, by some normative standard, the 'reactionary' or 'progressive' aspects of Baudelaire's work in its implications for today would be at best a vulgar Marxism of this kind, passing *a priori* judgements on works which have been imperceptibly processed by the dominant ideology. This was the 'first principle' of Benjamin's critical method. Dialectics cannot assume that it knows the concrete definition of its object of study before the study itself: 'Sundering truth from falsehood is the goal of the materialist method, not its point of departure.'[36]

This is the equivalent, for critical methodology, of his suggestion that writers 'only think', instead of applying their already worked-out convictions. The method adopted by Benjamin, as we might expect, produces a type of criticism very different from that of Lucien Goldmann. When Benjamin 'places' Baudelaire historically, it is not by discovering some structure of the universe of Baudelaire's work which is shown to be homologous with the structure of the world vision of a class, or with market relations. Consequently there is no question of Benjamin's being drawn into the discussion of values, which eventually led to Goldmann's theory of genetic structuralism falling apart. In the unfinished methodological note on his Baudelaire study Benjamin proposes to begin the fight to 'sunder truth from falsehood' by examining first the actual relation between bourgeois writers, the press, the state, and the needs of the bourgeoisie itself in its changing relations with other classes, at the vital turning points in Baudelaire's life and work. He is less interested, at the start, in some general change of class outlook resulting from the June days of 1848, which affects the views of writers in different degrees, than he is in the conditions of literary production imposed on the writers of the day. Mallarmé and the theory of *poésie pure* are then seen as the end of a process which began in 1852, when Louis Napoleon, on behalf of a bourgeoisie which had suppressed its own 'democratic left' as well as the proletariat, now suppressed its own 'speaking and writing segment. . . politicians and literati, so that they might confidently pursue their private affairs under the protection of a strong and untrammelled government'. These are the specific conditions for writers under which the bourgeoisie ceased to inspire a literary intelligentsia with the progressive and universal nature of its values. They gave rise to that peculiar situation where, 'the problem of a literature without an object becomes the centre of discussion. This discussion takes place not least in Mallarmé's poems, which revolve about *blanc, absence, silence, vide.*'[37]

By the beginning of the last quarter of the nineteenth century the poetry of Mallarmé and the Parnassiens is set firmly on its course of determined total separation from all non-poetic concerns, seeking no response outside the world of poetry. Baudelaire's work is done in the decisive earlier years of revolution and counter-revolution, the experience of which initiated the development which culminated in Mallarmé. Baudelaire himself lives and expresses the transition from art as utility to art for art's sake. His poetry was the representation of many of the most significant of the new structures of experience and consciousness which were imposed by the emerging industrial capitalism, written at a historical moment which could not be repeated, not least because within only a few years poetry would be driven into its own world, protecting itself by taking its distance from these very experiences. Baudelaire writes *before* poetry has been cut off from its task of making explicit these new forms of experience, in which the socialisation and 'universalisation' created by industry take the contradictory shape of the value form, where men 'empathise' (Benjamin) with commodities. Many times in his work Baudelaire showed that he understood the agonising difficulty of achieving any poetic form for experience in such 'unheroic' circumstances:

> When I hear how a Raphael or a Veronese are glorified with the veiled intention of depreciating what came after them . . .I ask myself whether an achievement which must be rated *at least* equal to theirs. . . is not infinitely *more meritorious*, because it triumphed in a hostile atmosphere and place.[38]

Baudelaire's passionate struggle to create, against these conditions and against the bourgeois who flourished in them (Benjamin stresses the intensely combative style of his life and work), is at the centre of the meaning of his poetry, and it is this which gives to him the possibility, from time to time, of feeling and speaking for those who find themselves challenging the social order because they feel an uncontainable state of inner revolt and are unable to sense anything secure in their future ('The Ragpicker'). Baudelaire's idea of the writer and the dispossessed of Paris as the modern 'heroes' is bitterly ironical and in that sense dialectical. They are as heroic as it is possible to be in such a situation, a situation not so much unheroic as anti-heroic. The society which can make a writer, even at the height of his creativity, only this kind of hero, makes him also 'a whore', one of Baudelaire's favourite figures for the writer. Benjamin cites many passages, both poetry and prose, where Baudelaire attacks the commercialisation of literature and compares himself as writer unfavourably with the prostitute. And Baudelaire is very definite that *la Bohème* includes both. Looking back from the standpoint of the revolutionary proletariat and making static comparisons, in the manner of the 'vulgar Marxists' attacked by Benjamin, would lead to unfavourable judgements: petit-bourgeois, lumpenproletarian, anticipating decadence, etc.

Benjamin sees this as a method alien to historical materialism. There was no way in which Baudelaire could express in his poetry the revolutionary standpoint of the proletariat. He was, rather, truly a 'secret agent' within his own class, the bourgeoisie. The poet was 'whorish' (as Baudelaire said, for example, of Lamartine) not only because he was more and more becoming forced to relate to people and to objects only in 'value' terms. The fact that there is a demand for a thing by the mass of others in the market changes that thing's character. Prostitution is the extreme of the incorporation of men and women themselves, quanta of labour-power, into these relationships. The poet drawn into this process can hardly avoid being embraced by things and experiences and words which have changed into something utterly 'unpoetic' (i.e., their qualitative and particular natures obliterated) just as life was unheroic. In Baudelaire's day this process was well under way but was not quite completed. By recognising and characterising this prostitution, and by giving the experience formed by its onset an incomparable expression through 'that empathy with inorganic things which was one of his sources of inspiration', Baudelaire made changes in the technique of poetry itself[39] which are more vital for defining the historical character of his achievement than any number of abstract judgements about his 'values'. That he could make these advances even while being unable to go beyond the horizons of the bohemian elements of his class, those who felt close to the lumpenproletariat (and it was to this that the bourgeoisie condemned its best sons in art and literature), is a measure of his greatness as a poet. Benjamin notes that the 'empathy' with commodities which is the secret of Baudelaire's *flâneur* (the stroller in the city streets and arcades) is again something with a strict historical limit. And here Benjamin clinches the argument by which he places Baudelaire historically:

> . . . insofar as a person, as labour power, is a commodity, there is no need for him to identify himself as such. The more conscious he becomes of his mode of existence, the mode imposed upon him by the system of production, the more he proletarianizes himself, the more he will be gripped by the chill of the commodity economy and the less he will feel like empathizing with commodities. But things had not reached that point with the class of the petty bourgeoisie to which Baudelaire belonged. On the scale with which we are dealing here, this class was only at the beginning of its decline. Inevitably, one day many of its members had to become aware of the commodity nature of their labour power. But this day had not as yet come; until that day they were permitted, if one may put it that way, to pass their time. The very fact that their share could at best be enjoyment, but never power, made the period which history gave them a space for passing time. Anyone who sets out to while away time seeks enjoyment. It was self-evident, however, that the more this class wanted to have its enjoyment in this society, the more limited this enjoyment would be. The enjoyment promised to be less limited if this class found enjoyment of this society possible. If it wanted to achieve virtuosity in this kind of enjoyment, it could not spurn empathizing with commodities. It had to enjoy this identification with all the pleasure and the uneasiness which derived from a pre-sentiment of its own destiny as a class. Finally, it had to

approach this destiny with a sensitivity that perceives charm even in damaged and decaying goods. Baudelaire, who in a poem to a courtesan called her heart 'bruised like a peach, ripe like her body, for the lore of love', possessed this sensitivity. To it he owed his enjoyment of this society as someone who had already half withdrawn from it.[40]

Certainly, then, Baudelaire could not produce a poetry of images which showed the contradictory future role of 'the crowd' in the big city — i.e., its concentration into a revolutionary mass — but he exposed a dimension of the crowd, a negative aspect, without which that contradiction, and the historical necessity of a new revolution, would not exist and could not be grasped. Where Hugo's romanticism found in the crowd, 'the hero in a modern epic, Baudelaire was looking for a refuge among the masses. . . Hugo placed himself in the crowd as a *citoyen*; Baudelaire sundered himself from it as a hero'.[41]

All these themes and many others are developed in detailed references to Baudelaire's work in Benjamin's monograph. Here we have only summarised some of the points at which Benjamin's approach yields different results from that of Lukács and Goldmann. Benjamin's method is further clarified by his reply to the criticisms of his 'Baudelaire' by Adorno in 1938, when the manuscript was submitted to him for publication. Adorno counselled Benjamin to be less anxious to prove himself a materialist, since that was leading (as Adorno expressed it elsewhere) to a too crude discovery of direct interconnections between works of literature and 'material tendencies and social struggles' rather than explicating these works in terms of the 'social whole'.[42] In his response Benjamin ignores the condescending advice that he should go back to being the very subtle not-quite-Marxist Walter they all knew and liked, and proceeds to tell Adorno what he means by a criticism which proceeds by thinking and work rather than by *a priorism* and 'applying' dialectical materialism. The material to be studied — in this case the poetry and prose of Baudelaire — must be appropriated rather than surveyed with a set of worked-out answers: 'I believe that speculation can start its necessarily bold flight with some prospect of success only if, instead of putting on the waxen wings of the esoteric, it seeks its source of strength in construction alone.'[43] This means starting with the work itself: '. . . the philological interpretation of the author ought to be preserved and surpassed in the Hegelian manner by dialectical materialists.'[44]

He goes on to explain how he proposes to achieve this 'preserving and surpassing', aiming at a historically concrete conclusion rather than the static, magical understanding rendered by philological textual criticism. In this summary Benjamin opens the way to a clarification of his distinction between historical materialism and historicism. The fixed, 'magical' character of the philologically interpreted text, its 'appearance of closed facticity', is broken by 'construing it in an historical perspective'. Previously, in 'The Author as Producer', Benjamin had written: 'For the dialectical treatment of this problem — and now I come to the heart of the matter — the rigid, isolated object (work, novel, book) is of no use whatsoever. It must be inserted into the context of living social relations.'[45] Like it or not, to construe historically means to bring the object into contact, into relation, with our own experience, our own historical tasks. And only in this relation is the object abstracted and made open to real historical understanding: 'Thus the object constitutes itself into a monad. In the monad everything that used to lie in mythical rigidity as a textual reference comes alive.'[46]

In the letter from which we are quoting Benjamin shows that it was by this method that he was able to juxtapose Baudelaire's poem *L'Ame du Vin* and the duty on wine, and not by the 'application' of materialist assumptions, as Adorno thought. The term 'monad' and the methodology here implied occur in another context in Benjamin, some two years later. It shows a striking consistency between his literary studies and his political and philosophical concerns:

Historicism rightly culminates in universal history. Materialistic historiography differs from it as to method more clearly than from any other kind. Universal history has no

Forsyth Library

Forsyth Circulation Desk
Ø7 NOV 1994   Ø5:2Ø PM LCR3

Item 2 1765 ØØØ 398 886

To   3 1765 ØØØ 337 89Ø

Due Ø2 JAN 1995

8Ø9.933

S631m;198Ø
Marxism, ideology, and
literature (Slaughter, Cliff)
198Ø

theoretical armature. Its method is additive; it musters a mass of data to fill the homogeneous, empty time. Materialistic historiography, on the other hand, is based on a constructive principle. Thinking involves not only the flow of thoughts, but their arrest as well. Where thinking suddenly stops in a configuration pregnant with tensions, it gives that configuration a shock, by which it crystallizes into a monad. A historical materialist approaches a historical subject only where he encounters it as a monad. In this structure he recognizes the sign of a Messianic cessation of happening, or, put differently, a revolutionary chance in the fight for the oppressed past. He takes cognizance of it in order to blast a specific era out of the homogeneous course of history — blasting a specific life out of the era or a specific work out of the lifework. As a result of this method the lifework is preserved in this work and at the same time cancelled; in the lifework, the era; and in the era, the entire course of history. The nourishing fruit of the historically understood contains time as a precious but tasteless seed.[47]

There is no better starting point in Marxist writing on literature than this passage, for the critique of structuralism. It shows the dialectical relation between the concept of structure as one moment of analysis and the dialectical process of history to which that analysis is directed, not in a purely contemplative and individual way, but from 'base-lines' of our urgent concerns in understanding a world which we must transform. Posing the question of 'reflection' in terms of the 'revolutionising practice' developed by Marx in his negation of Feuerbach and Hegel, Benjamin produces an original approach to realism. In the criticism of works of the past, as we see, his procedure is to 'construct' or 'construe' the work historically so that its real connections to the present through history are brought to light, as against the opacity of the usual confrontation between text and criticism. The result is something very different from that other procedure which looks more 'Marxist' than textual criticism but proves in the end to be equally formal: the juxtaposition of structure or content of the work with a preconceived notion of the structure of the possible consciousness of a class, or even the structure of the real world in which that class lives.

Whatever may have been the impact of Lukács's *History and Class Consciousness* at an early stage in stimulating Benjamin's turn to Marxism, he certainly arrived at independent conclusions on the relation between history, social consciousness and literary products, conclusions which could not have been more opposed to those of Lukács. This is easily confirmed if we recall the emphasis given by Benjamin to changes in the mode of perception and their effect on styles of artistic representation. Since the industrial revolution, these changes involve an atrophy of experience and the increasing role of 'shock' in the impact of the social world upon consciousness. Benjamin looked for a demonstrable continuity in the development of literary technique adequate to this change. Thus, from Baudelaire to Brecht, there was to be found a struggle to transform literary technique and style in order to go beyond a romantic critique of the destruction of the old type of 'organic' experience, to relive in art what men are forced to endure in social life and work, and to discover in this necessity the seeds of its negation: the 'universalisation' contained in the separation of things, of persons, of experiences, by capitalist production. Montage was for Benjamin the greatest innovation in modern artistic representation: utilising and transforming the technical developments in photography, it was able to take men into the objects which in experience flashed by or weighed down with an apparently incomprehensible, inscrutable form; and it explored relations between apparently quite separate things or events in a way which could open up men's mastery of the universalisation inherent in capitalist reification. Benjamin even regarded the change to sound films as a defeat for the revolutionary implications of the silent film.

Benjamin, along with Brecht, is usually characterised, even by sympathetic critics, as a pessimist, reacting to the crushing victory of Nazism over the German working class and to the bureaucratic degeneration of the Soviet state. Stanley Mitchell assimilates Benjamin's views to Romain Rolland's 'pessimism of the intellect, optimism of the will', a judgement which seems to be in no way borne out by Benjamin's works or by the analysis of them by Mitchell himself.[48] Rolland's formulation suggests that there is now no objective source for optimism, unless one calls the human will to survive an objective force. This is not Benjamin's position. As we have seen, he emphatically rejected the idea that the victory of Nazism was inevitable, and pointed to some of the sources, in working-class leadership, of the defeat. His last writings show an extraordinarily concentrated attention to the rigorous definition of a scientific historical method, despite the enormous pressure of the enemy and the consequent personal emotional crises. The search in history for the true tradition of the oppressed which must be liberated was not pursued in some idealist or utopian manner but consisted, for Benjamin, of a systematic analysis and construction. When Benjamin quotes Brecht's 'water getting the better of granite' he is not suggesting that survival and waiting for the old to be gradually worn away must replace revolution. There is a definite, objective truth in Benjamin's insistence that 'every second of time is the straight gate through which the Messiah might come'. In a revolutionary epoch (and every revolutionary epoch has counter-revolutions within it) revolutionary practice must be consciously planned and organised to extract or abstract from every 'living perception' the maximum which can be gained for the cause of the revolutionary class. It is not known in advance from which turn in the objective situation, from which particular new break of revolutionary theory and practice into the mass, a decisive development for the revolution might issue. Perception must be posited on the essence derived from past theory and practice, and only then is it possible to design new practices which will test whether or not particular events and actions are more or less decisive. Historical materialism is not an exact science, and certainly it is not a series of prophecies; it is a guide to action, a guide to acting in such a way as to be able to seize the revolutionary opportunity at that 'second of time' when liberation becomes objectively possible and necessary.

Benjamin's 'Theses on the Philosophy of History', independently of the immediate circumstances and personal moods surrounding their production, constitute a priceless contribution to this dialectical theory of capitalism and revolution. His work on literature and the role of writers and artists was as 'heroic' — in its relation to the attendant pressures of Nazism and Stalinism — as was the art of Baudelaire; and as rich a contribution to humanity's future.

7
Conclusions: Literature and Dialectical Materialism

In every work of literature the writer has reworked elements taken from experience, in such a way that interconnections between them and the whole from which they were 'abstracted' are revealed. The reader experiences a degree of shock. He is brought by the writer's struggle with his material to a confrontation with what effort must be made to make a step from illusion to reality. What he is brought to see in the artistic representation is not some example in verification of a logical generalisation (an example would be 'art' which illustrated the operation of a divine spirit in all human acts, or exciting 'structural' transformations between objects previously considered uniquely different one from another) but rather the *actual* relation between particular (individual) and general (universal), which is very different from this formal–logical one, with its dependence on the idealist notion of universals. If the relation between individual and universal is understood dialectically, then it renders more comprehensible the idea that the artistic consciousness grasps the world by taking a different route from the scientist's, and presents its results in entirely different form, requiring a different mode of reception. Universal and individual are opposites, but in the reality from which these opposite determinations are abstracted they are at the same time

> . . . identical: the individual exists only in the connection that leads to the universal. The universal exists only in the individual and through the individual. Every individual is (in one way or another) a universal. Every universal is (a

fragment, or an aspect, or the essence of) an individual. Every universal only approximately embraces all the individual objects. Every individual enters incompletely into the universal, etc., etc. Every individual is connected by thousands of transitions with other kinds of individuals (things, phenomena, processes), etc.[1]

In the natural sciences the general laws of these mutual interconnections are abstracted and given quantitative form; their limits in relation to other laws are established. They must be stated in testable and falsifiable form. In the arts images which present this same unity of opposites are created. And it is precisely the unity of universal and individual as *interconnection* and transition, rather than as abstract similarity of discrete individualities, which is highlighted by the concentration of art on the particular, the individual. In the artistic image the limits of the individual, limits necessarily defined and overcome by its very individuality, are shown concretely, through interconnections. The particular is transcended not mystically but in sensuous images; its very individuality is the key to its necessary transition to its other, to the universal. If a thing (particular) is to be related to others only by the possession of some common feature, then the actuality of its identity with the universal is entirely missed. Between two *identical* things there is no movement, no source of contradiction or change. The particular relates to, contains, expresses, participates in creating, the general by its interconnections with and transitions into other particulars. Between them there is a unity constituted by these very real interconnections, mutual transitions and transformations. The universal or general is not some mystical, immanent reality existing in a different sphere from the concrete particulars: 'the unity of the world consists in its materiality' (Engels). Once the particular is seen in its connection and transition to the general, then it is already seen as in process of transformation into other. Its internal contradictions are not static polarities, to be classified as 'structures', but are particular forms of the universal motion of matter, developing dialectically not as 'examples' of that universal but constitutive of it, in such a way that to understand this development requires comprehension of the material interconnections to the larger whole(s). It is not a question any longer of abstracting general characteristics, in order then to classify the particulars in some way, but of discovering and demonstrating this interconnectedness and its many phases: reciprocal action, cause and effect, etc.

The scientist does this by analysis, whether with the aid of experiment in the natural sciences or with other methods of controlled observation and measurement of error, plus abstraction, in the historical sciences. Art 'produces' the particular (whether it be individual character, historical situation or collision, or any other part of history or nature) in images built up of selected materials like language, sounds, paint and canvas, etc., or some combination of these as in drama or film. The values (meanings) conferred on these media by culture (culture in the sense of all the learned, non-natural behaviour to hand in the given society) means that they are not mere vehicles for meaning (not a 'mere form' for some other 'content') but are often called the content of the work by real interconnections, both material (natural) and cultural (historical, social).

Against the essentially generalising methods of science, art works with the image, in which the general or universal appears not as rule or law, quantifiable, but as the sensuous form of a particular which has such unique individuality that it is able to suggest to the feelings as well as to the intellect some of the vital transitions which lead to the universal (Max Raphael refers to 'aesthetic feelings', for example, as 'the inner aspect of perception').[2] When the social relations of capitalism reduce human relations to 'rational' i.e., quantitative relations, between things, art is therefore in a way predisposed to challenge the existing order, and does not begin only as a part of the ideology developed by capitalism itself. This is one meaning which can be given to Marx's remark that literature and art, like language, are part of men's *productive forces*. The same point may be stated in another way: the social totality confronting the writer in developed capitalist society confers upon each particular (individual character, situation) a meaning which 'leads away from life' (Lawrence), estranges men from nature, including their own nature; art will only challenge this totality and its meanings and be able to achieve real continuity with the art of the past (which is to say that art will only survive) if it can develop technique in such a way as to produce images which lead beyond and against the social totality to the contradictory unity of that totality and the totality of nature. Here again it may be seen that Benjamin's insistence on technical transformation rather than 'progressive' content rests on dialectical materialist foundations, and is not some species of vulgar technological determinism, as Adorno suggested.

In recent years the influence of Louis Althusser has resulted in the search for a 'scientific' basis for literary criticism. Marx's historical materialism and concept of ideology are interpreted ('read') as a system which has broken with the type of philosophical categories taken by Marx from Hegel. Instead, categories such as dominant structures, reproductive relations, overdetermination, structural transformation and so on are taken to be the concepts which, through a definite 'theoretical practice', will produce a scientific literary criticism.

The first chapter of a recent representative work of this school[3] concludes with the declaration that literary criticism 'must break with its ideological prehistory, situating itself outside the space of the text on the alternative terrain of scientific knowledge'. Eagleton seems to mean that criticism of a literary text must not restrict itself merely to making that text more comprehensible to the reader within the terms understóod or taken for granted by the author. To do that would be to ignore the ideological limits within which the text has been produced. Indeed, a literary work (text) conceals and contradicts in the very act of 'expressing' these ideological limits. The literary work carries all the marks of the way it was produced, but foremost among these marks is that the work constructs a mystification or particular way of obscuring the truth about its historical conditions of production. What could be the uses of a 'scientific' literary criticism as advocated by Eagleton? It would presumably lead us to a more accurate knowledge of and sensitivity towards the characteristic ideological forms of the class society in which the particular text was written — a knowledge, that is, of how that society's ideological self-defences are constructed.

Undoubtedly the scientific historical analysis of literary schools and literary works will contribute to a Marxist understanding of the formation of ideology. But if criticism is directed as Eagleton does, following Macherey, at the *omissions* from the text (as part of the specific means by which the work creates this 'self-oblivion'), will it not ignore the possibility that the dramatist or novelist or poet might penetrate, in some way and in some measure, to the source of this ideological structure, and thus be able to expose its contradictions (not merely be expressing these contradictions as their victim, something which can only be discovered afterwards, by what Eagleton calls a 'science of criticism')? From this question another follows: does the work of the artist reflect or express only the outlook of a given class (i.e., the 'world vision' of class which is for Lucien Goldmann the basis of the structure of every significant literary work) or is not art one of the ways in which man's objective knowledge is advanced, in and through the relative (ideological) phases of consciousness in particular societies?

Eagleton of course acknowledges that in the natural sciences the concepts produced are not simply ideological reflections of society but constitute objective knowledge (he cites the law of gravity, for example), but he never asks the same question about literature. It is difficult to see how any Marxist theory of literature can be developed from the foundations laid by Marx, Engels, Lenin and especially Trotsky without placing these questions of the theory of knowledge at the centre.

Eagleton's mentor, Louis Althusser, has propounded the idea that Marxism must be rescued from a Hegelian and 'humanist' bias. He asserts that Marx himself failed fully to understand the decisiveness and completeness of his break with Hegel, though his practice, and especially his 'theoretical practice', constitutes such a break, to science. This science has to be 'produced' by a reading of Marx (hence Althusser's *Reading Capital*). This anti-Hegelianism leads the Althusserians to mean by historical materialism something very different from what it actually was in the hands of Marx and Engels. Althusser believes that when Marx talks of 'essence' and 'appearance' in his economic and historical analysis he is mystifying, and that these terms are only a transposition of the idealist way of distinguishing between a thing (appearance, phenomenon) and the concept or thought of that thing (essence). Thus he rejects Marx's view that objective reality is a totality of dialectical processes, forms of matter in motion, in which essence appears in contradictory forms. In history the mode of production and its internal contradictions have many forms of appearance, and all products of consciousness are to be understood in the first place as such forms of appearance of the mode of production and the necessarily resulting class struggle. Thus Marx: 'If material production itself is not grasped in its specific historical form, it is impossible to understand the concrete nature of the intellectual production corresponding to it and the interplay of both factors.'[4]

It is their rejection of the materialist dialectic which makes the Althusserians (and, in this context, Eagleton) see history very differently, and in fact to return to the positions of Max Weber and neo-Kantians. For them there are many 'practices' (industrial, literary, natural—scientific, etc.), and then a mosaic of interconnections, congruences, mutual determinations and 'overdetermination' between them, which must be empirically discovered. What the source of all these 'practices' is, nobody knows. Temptingly, the entities posited by such a theory (entities, that is, like literary practice, economy, science) are more immediately measurable, definable, and accessible to classification and proof, than are the 'abstract' categories of Marxism. For all the Althusserians' raving against everyone else's 'empiricism' (by which they appear to mean a refusal to discuss endlessly a definition of terms), they themselves begin precisely from this fundamental concession to empiricism, with its 'operational' and 'quantifiable' concepts.

Eagleton's attack on Raymond Williams turns out to be a good example of Eagleton's own inadequacies, for his criticism of Williams can be turned against him. Eagleton complains that Williams rejects the historical—materialist concepts of economic base and ideological superstructure on the grounds that the distinction between them does not correspond to 'the social experience of culture'. Quite rightly, Eagleton comments: '. . . no one, surely, ever took the base/

superstructure distinction to be a matter of experience'. But Eagleton's separating out of a 'literary mode of production' among other such 'modes' is only a similar concession to empiricism, with its demands for operational definitions. Of course it makes sense to show the particular conditions of life of literary production in each society and at each stage of its development; to ignore these, and the specialised literary knowledge and traditions which serve as the immediate conscious starting point of the literary producers, would be fatally misleading. But to make of all this a literary mode of production is to introduce, in the guise of Marxist-sounding terms, utter confusion. One suspects that Macherey and his followers have been attracted by the following passage in the *Economic and Philosophical Manuscripts of 1844*: 'Religion, family, state, law, morality, science, art, etc., are only *particular* modes of production, and fall under its general law.' It seems clear, however, that Marx does not mean here that there are separate (moral, literary, family, etc.) 'modes of production' to which can be transposed all the categories he applied to the 'mode of production' in society. Eagleton even sees the 'literary mode of production' (LMP) as a unity of 'forces of literary production' and 'social relations of literary production' (and there will be several LMPs in any one society, one normally being dominant). The 'reproductive relation' between the LMP and the General Ideology (GI) of the society is called the 'ideology of the LMP'.

In this way the Marxist concept of ideology is completely misused, just as are mode of production, relations of production and forces of production. Eagleton is actually using the word ideology as Althusser uses it, to denote merely ideas, necessarily 'secreted' by social life, from which it follows that ideology is something which will exist in communist society just as it does in class society (in contrast to Marx's anticipation in *Capital* of a communist society of 'transparent' social relations). For Marx, in such contexts, ideology referred to a false consciousness, in which each sphere of thought was treated as independent and feeding on its 'own' material, thus obscuring its own character as product and mask of definite social relations of production. The consequence is that, while Eagleton or Macherey will make correct and interesting observations about particular writers or trends in literature, their overall conceptual framework is total confusion, because of this unwarranted, arbitrary argument by analogy (mode of production/literary mode of production, social relations of production/social relations of literary production, etc.) in place of scientific historical analysis. The relation between material means of production, social relations and consciousness in the mode of production of a given type of society (say, capitalism in its various nation—state developments and as a whole, a world system) is a relation which works through literature as through the several ideological forms. There is no separately existing 'base and superstructure' of literary production as such which somehow has the ability to interpenetrate another general sphere of production and ideology.

Not surprisingly, Eagleton produces a highly schematic and doctrinaire system. The literary text, we find, is the product of the 'complex historical articulations' of several 'structures' (General Mode of Production, Literary Mode of Production, General Ideology, Authorial Ideology, Aesthetic Ideology). The 'production' of literary works by these abstract 'structures' articulating with each other is nightmarishly reminiscent of the conclusion of Lévi-Strauss's 'science of mythology': that men are the mouthpieces through which the myths speak (not to mention the dreaded Hegel and his idea of the real world, including history, as the externalisation of the absolute, which turns out to be our old friend God). Eagleton's articulation of abstract structures to produce real 'texts' may prove to be no less divine, especially when he proceeds with a relativist view of the nature of truth which leaves a gap to be filled by some inevitably religious notion of ultimate reality. What else can result from the schema of complicated homologies, parallels, articulations and over-determinations between analogically constructed (and not scientifically abstracted) concepts? In the few places where Eagleton does make correct general points on the questions of the nature of art's and literature's way of apprehending reality, and its specific difference from science or historiography, we find him saying no more than can be found in Aristotle: an intelligent description of the way that, in contrast to other intellectual modes, art produces its own object; a description which is followed by a brief critique of the mystique of freedom surrounding this production in capitalist society.

This leads us to Eagleton's central idea, that the work of art, freed from any obligation to 'stick to the facts', is for this very reason more 'ideological', working up its images out of what are already ideological notions which only reflect the real society: 'The text takes as its object not the real, but certain significations by which the real lives itself . . . Within the text itself, then, ideology becomes a dominant structure.' We are back with the early Lucien Goldmann: the structure of literary works, their real content, is the world vision (ideology) of a particular class. This is the nearest Eagleton gets to an explanation of why ideology must be the central concept in a Marxist analysis of literature, in comparison with other spheres of analysis. Surely there remains, after all, the question of the objective content within the ideology itself as well as, possibly, within the literary work as against the prevailing ideology. The interpretation of literature purely as signifying ideological structure flies in the face of Marx's own notion of literature in 1874 as one of the *forces* of production, and certainly not as ideology ('acquired forces of production, material and spiritual, language, literature, technical skills, etc.')[5] Thus there are literary works whose imagery transcends the ideological justification of the contemporary world, in such a way as to clear the path for necessary changes in consciousness and action (through its affective or emotional as well as its intellectual components). Lenin, for example, did not rest content with a characterisation of Tolstoy's writings as representative of the Russian aristocracy through a noble individual with literary genius; he laid the greatest stress on Tolstoy's novels as a mirror of the historical changes brought about in the life and minds of the Russian peasantry between the emancipation of the serfs and the 1905 Revolution, a historical process in which all the old alternatives were exhausted.

Eagleton is not satisfied with such a view. It relies too much, he says, on the definition of Tolstoy as a great individual genius, and this, according to him, is a gap in Lenin's materialism. Yet it surely is not suggested that Marxism has a theory of how each individual writer came to be precisely what he was. That is what Sartre (*Critique of Dialectical Reason*) demanded of historical materialism, conveniently using the mechanical and vulgar 'Marxism' of the Stalinists in order to ignore the central questions of the scientific study of the laws of motion of society as the conscious basis of revolutionary practice. In fact this criticism of Lenin by Eagleton suggests again that yearning for a closed system, a doctrinairism, which is the other side of the coin to the descent into an empiricist pluralism in questions of method.

Trotsky's writings on literature come under Eagleton's hammer for suggesting that art appeals specifically to the feelings. Eagleton considers this a lapse into subjectivism on Trotsky's part. Again, this sounds highly 'materialistic' but it follows in fact from Eagleton's procedure of excluding all philosophical considerations, that is, all questions of the extent to which literature reflects the real world of history, of man's creation of his own world and his own nature through his productive relationship with nature, a relationship which depends on the discovery and recognition in practice of the laws of nature. The growth of this knowledge takes place whatever the alienated and oppressive forms through which men are compelled to struggle. It is in this context that Marxists see literature and all the arts as a struggle to understand and shape the response of men — men with feeling, passion and will, which are as essential as intellect in their purposive activity — to the struggle to control their own existence. It is a caricature of Marxism to reduce literature to just an ideological mechanism through which the ruling class establishes its hegemony, as Eagleton does:

> Literature is an agent as well as an effect of [national and class] struggles, a crucial mechanism by which the language and ideology of an imperialist class establishes its hegemony, or by which a subordinate state, class or region preserves and perpetuates at the ideological level an historical identity shattered or eroded at the political.

Such a definition could apply just as well to all manner of

cultural activities while offering no suggestion of what is specific to creative literature (novel, drama, poetry). It ignores the question of what it is that makes such works meaningful to men long after the disappearance of their functions as an ideological 'mechanism'. Without starting from Marx's revolution in philosophy it is not possible to begin to answer this question. Does not creative literature (like music and the visual arts), besides reflecting the contemporary ideology in particular ways, provide compelling and life-giving images for the inner struggle men must undertake in order to re-engage continually in the struggle to unite with nature, a unity and conflict of opposites? When Trotsky wrote *Literature and Revolution*, it was from this standpoint, which allowed him to start from the most specific problems facing the writers, readers and critics of the day, problems which together constituted the question of the whole historical meaning of the Russian Revolution as the beginning of the world socialist revolution, and the new way in which the thoughts and feelings aroused by this titanic struggle opened up to mankind the treasure-house of past literature. None of this is considered by Eagleton, restricted as he is to the ideological function of literature and criticism.

Eagleton contends that some writers who are politically reactionary (for example, T.S. Eliot or W.B. Yeats) achieve critical insights into social reality because and not in spite of their reactionary positions. Thus writers with a romantic yearning for some past organic, elite-dominated society will more easily criticise the way in which monopoly capitalism produces a collapse of values, and so on. The measure of truth in this argument is extremely limited, and if pushed beyond its narrow limits becomes an untruth. It is necessary to go beyond a writer's critical reaction to (in this case) the decay of capitalist culture, and ask if he has been able to move his readers to seek and identify those contradictory forces with which he must fuse his whole being in theory and practice in order to overcome the reigning oppression. Great art does this without the artist's necessarily grasping intellectually, theoretically, analytically, the historical contradictions and the tasks which flow from them.

The fact is that, even quite apart from the artificial analogy of 'mode of production: literary mode of production', the concepts of ideology, reflection, overdetermination and base superstructure as used by Althusser, Macherey and Eagleton become only crude descriptive and comparative categories, and certainly no basis for the 'science' which is claimed. In their haste to free Marxism of what they choose to call its humanism, they concentrate one-sidedly, even exclusively, on individuals as the 'bearers' of social relations, and turn historical materialism into another variety of pre-Marxian or mechanical materialism, i.e., a materialism in which the 'active side', man's practice, is neglected. Social relations are then conceived only as a 'second nature' or 'environment' in a conception fundamentally no different from that of the Encyclopaedists. Still more important, from the standpoint of dialectical materialism, the *objective content* of consciousness is left entirely out of account. This is why Althusser found himself saddled with a special 'theoretical practice', hermetically sealed off from the class struggle, as the realm in which 'science' lives. Here again he repeated the experience of the pre-Marxian materialists:

> The materialist doctrine concerning the changing of circumstances and education forgets that circumstances are changed by men and that the educator must himself be educated. This doctrine has therefore to divide society into two parts, one of which is superior to society. (Marx's third thesis on Feuerbach)

Even though Althusser gives art a different status from ideology in general, we find that it is only as a form of self-knowledge of ideology, and that there is no break from this closed circle, no break to the objective world in which men and their ideology live, a world which they change, and, in the course of changing it, change themselves. Whatever the mediations and obstructions to consciousness of necessity, the active, productive relation of men to nature, and to the social relations necessary for this production, must constantly be renewed. Consciousness, including art and literature, inescapably must confront the question of overcoming the frustrating effects of historically outworn relations and ideological forms. The most fundamental of the illusions involved in this process is that the efficacy of human activity appears to arise from the mental project with which the actor sets out. Here two things need to be said. In the first place, the mental project has a content and a form which result from the ways in which 'the totality of social relations' of the individual has given or denied him access to the experience, technique and knowledge necessary for the project. And secondly, the activity or labour upon which he engages to realise the project also has an objective content.[6] This latter has two sides: there is the vital question of to what extent the activity follows the actual contours of the object of the activity; and there is the fact that the activity takes place only in and through certain definite social relations of production, whose historical efficacy and ideological effects at the given stage of their development must be reckoned with. These elements of objective content in the initial project, and, even more important, in the activity, do not arise as such in the consciousness of the actor or producer: 'The Idea is. . . the Idea of the *True* and of the *Good*, as *Cognition* and *Volition* . . . The process of this finite cognition and *action* (NB) makes the universality, which at first is abstract, into a totality, whence it becomes *perfected objectivity*.' Having quoted this passage from Hegel's *Encyclopaedia* (the emphases are Lenin's), Lenin 're-reads it materialistically': 'The Idea is *Cognition* and aspiration (volition) (of man). . . The process of (transitory, finite, limited) cognition and *action* converts abstract concepts into *perfected* objectivity.'[7]

The image produced by the artist (in colour and line, in words) is the result of his activity, his practice, and is not of course identical with the image (or 'project') with which he set out to paint or to write. That initial image, an ideal representation of the material world transmuted into a form of thought, was itself not merely the imprint of some class's conception of its place in the world, but contained sensuous representations of the objective world. The artist's product may appear to him to be merely the manifestation of his inspiration ('project', initial image). Such inspiration is a genuine insight in so far as it concentrates into particulars a wealth of determinations which are real interconnections. The celebrated subjectivity of the artist has a degree of richness according to the wealth of his perception of this interconnectedness. Such perception is acquired by artistic experience and practice, as in the arts of war or of politics. The opposite view, and a highly influential one in literature, is that of Schopenhauer, who saw the artistic temperament as an exceptional, inborn ability to reflect a Being not contained in the life he must share with other men.

However, the work of art essentially conveys the struggle to achieve form; it communicates the passion of creating the work, as well as presenting an image of external reality. What was true (above) of the labour of the actor or producer in general, i.e., that it had an objective content, holds true equally for the creative labour of the artist. His techniques, his committed struggle to perfect form, embody the conquests of mankind, concentrated into the art he learns, practices and develops, along the road of educating men in their own passions and their place in the struggle to control nature. A Marxism which excludes the dialectical theory of cognition is 'a clock without a spring'. Goldmann's structural homologies between the images in the artist's work and the ideology of his class were the typical result of dispensing with the dialectics of cognition. They could no more take account of the objective content of consciousness than can the 'structuralist Marxists'.

If it is correct to point to the objective content of the artist's conceptions, and particularly of his artistic activity, then it follows that the material result of this activity, the work of art, is richer in content than the project or inspiration which, subjectively speaking, was its point of origin. Here is the epistemological source (there are other sources) of the process in which artists and writers bring out in their work an objective content which goes beyond and even flatly contradicts their own consciously formulated intentions or opinions of society and nature. We therefore need not be satisfied with the (nonetheless correct) characterisation of the writer as an 'honest' realist whose commitment to his craft overrides his preconceptions. As we see, there are good reasons why such commitment can produce something richer than the original conception. It is to this objective content of the artist's activity that Trotsky alluded in his reference to 'the accumulated experience of verbal craftsmanship'. Benjamin had the same thing in mind when he tried to turn discussion of the possible revolutionary content of art to questions of technique: '... the *writers who matter* — that is to say the best technicians in their particular branches of the trade ...'

We may note in passing that structuralism, including structuralist aesthetics, depends upon a theory of knowledge which is opposed in every respect to that of Marxism: following Kant, it starts out from the notion that the mind imposes order on the chaos of the world. When they speak of contradictions, these are formal contradictions, binary divisions into categories. The interest is not in development ('diachrony') but in 'transformations', i.e., in the realisation of the formal properties and their potential in the original structure. The idea of some combination of Marxism and structuralism is sheer utopia, given this Kantian basis. For the structuralist, works of art (and all the works of men) are essentially a closed system with internal rules of structural consistency and transformation. For Marxists, the structures of that world of the works of men are moments of a historical productive activity, an activity which not only breaks the closed circle of 'the mind' (as Lévi-Strauss says of the sphere of myth, 'the mind communing with itself') and its products, but actually stands at the initiation of all men's works, a starting point which is not just 'to be borne in mind' but which they must constantly actively renew if they are not to perish. The human individual, artist or anyone else, does not live, produce and think according to some properties of the brain (categories) which are programmed at birth as the body is programmed, but, on the contrary, has a type of brain which is capable of learning what the cultural heritage of society provides for the struggle with nature. Language is the principal material means of appropriating this heritage. There is no individual without the social relations and the learning process which each human being must enter. Society and culture are not the product of the aggregate of individuals with certain properties of mind, as must follow from Lévi-Strauss's Kantianism.

What 'happens' in literature and art is not the manifestation of inherent properties of mind but 'the aesthetic assimilation of the world', the development of that aspect of man's purposive activity (itself a 'nature-imposed necessity', as Marx put it) which requires a unity of thought, feeling and action. Here the contradictions are not formal and ideal but real. Again: 'the process of cognition and *action* converts abstract concepts into *perfected* objectivity'. It is in and through this historical process of action and cognition, the continual arising and resolving of contradictions, that man's needs are formed and developed on the original basis of his biological nature. Marx paid some attention to the aesthetic implications of this in some of his early work, with his remark:

> For not only the five senses but also the so-called mental senses — the practical senses (will, love, etc.) — in a word, *human* sense — the humanness of the senses — comes to be by virtue of *humanised* nature. The *forming* of the five senses is a labour of the entire history of the world down to the present.[8]

Literature and art undoubtedly share with all forms of cognition the characteristic of expressing ideology. The historical study of the ideological influences upon and ideological content of literary works is of course essential to any Marxist analysis. But cognition is not exhausted by ideological content. The social relations and the activity engaged in by the men of a particular society (from which, it goes without saying, cognition and ideology cannot be separated) are not to be comprehended solely in terms of the fact that they express or confirm that particular social formation. Ideological and 're-productive' functions are only part of cognition as a whole. They are *relative* to the growth of man's knowledge and control of nature and history. Literature must therefore be understood as a product which contains an absolute within the relative (the ideological). By absolute here is meant not some abstract essence of man but the whole world of men's activity, the development of their sensibilities, their struggle for control of nature, their ability to preserve and develop a material and spiritual heritage which more and more provides inexhaustible resources for the struggle to overcome the forces

of darkness and oppression that class society has always gene-
rated.

The true content of the most sublime works of literature
and art will no doubt be appreciated in new ways only possible
for the free men and women of a future classless society. The
meaning of these works today is stunted and distorted if they
are reduced to a means of creating a personal retreat from the
world from which they were won in so many bitter and noble
struggles. They take their rightful place only if they are
claimed as their birthright, defended and won back from the
oppressors, by all those who are driven to understand that all
those struggles to produce literature and art were and are one
with their own. This struggle is not only means but end. To
engage in it is to engage in the same fight to overcome petti-
ness and subjectivism, to survive and learn from even the most
hopeless and desperate situations, to combine will, intellect
and nobility of purpose, which was taken up by every great
writer and by every great revolutionary. It is the struggle for
the self-emancipation of the working class, the condition for
the emancipation of all mankind.

Notes and References

CHAPTER 1

1. G.Lukács, *Goethe and His Age* (London: Merlin Press, 1968). The work of Georg Lukács can only be understood critically, as a whole, by taking into account his adaptation to Stalinism and its profound consequences. However, we may leave these aside until later.
2. L. D. Trotsky, *Literature and Revolution* (Ann Arbor: University of Michigan Press, 1960).
3. R. Girard, *Deceit, Desire and the Novel* (Baltimore: Johns Hopkins University Press, 1965).
4. Cf. C. Slaughter, *Marxism and the Class Struggle* (London: New Park Publications, 1975) ch. 7.
5. Girard, *Deceit, Desire and the Novel*, pp. 90–1.
6. R. Nisbet, *Sociology as an Art-form* (London: Heinemann, 1976).
7. Erich Auerbach, *Mimesis: the representation of reality in Western Literature* (Princeton University Press, 1968).
8. Ibid., p. 13.
9. Cf. G. Thomson, *Studies in Ancient Greek Society*, vol. 1, *The Ancient Aegean* (New York: Citadel Press, 1965) p. 540.
10. S. S. Prawer, *Karl Marx and World Literature* (Oxford University Press, 1976).
11. Letter from Marx to Arnold Ruge, May 1843.
12. Max Raphael, *The Demands of Art*, Bollingen series (Princeton University Press, 1968).
13. K. Marx, *Economic and Philosophical Manuscripts of 1844* (London: Lawrence and Wishart, 1959).
14. K. Marx, *The Poverty of Philosophy, Collected Works*, vol. VI (London: Lawrence and Wishart, 1976) p. 159.
15. K. Marx, *Theories of Surplus Value*, part 1 (London: Lawrence and Wishart, n.d.) p. 276.
16. Prawer, *Karl Marx and World Literature*, p. 314.
17. L. Althusser, *Lenin and Philosophy and other Essays* (London: New Left Books, 1971) p. 204.
18. Marx, *Theories of Surplus Value*, part 1, p. 276.

CHAPTER 2

1. The publication of S. S. Prawer's *Karl Marx and World Literature* (Oxford University Press, 1976) has rendered it unnecessary to present a comprehensive survey of Marx's writings on literature. For writers and readers on that subject Prawer's work is indispensable.
2. Cf. István Mészáros, *Marx's Theory of Alienation* (London: Merlin Press, 1970) p. 113, and M. Lifshitz, *The Philosophy of Art of Karl Marx* (London: Pluto Press, 1973) p. 74.
3. K. Marx, *The German Ideology, Collected Works*, vol. V (London: Lawrence and Wishart, 1976) p. 292.
4. Ibid., p. 53.
5. Karl Mannheim, *Ideology and Utopia* (London: Routledge and Kegan Paul, 1954).
6. K. Marx, *The Holy Family* (London: Lawrence and Wishart, 1956) p. 52.
7. Ibid., p. 204.
8. K. Marx, *Grundrisse: Foundations of the Critique of Political Economy*, translator M. Nicolaus (Harmondsworth: Penguin Books, 1973) p. 296.
9. Max Raphael, *The Demands of Art*, Bollingen Series (Princeton University Press, 1968).
10. Marx, *Grundrisse*, p. 297.
11. G. Hegel, *Aesthetics*, vol. II (Oxford University Press, 1975) pp. 1051–2.
12. Mészáros, *Marx's Theory of Alienation*, ch. VII.
13. K. Marx, *Economic and Philosophical Manuscripts of 1844* (London: Lawrence and Wishart, 1959).
14. Cf. *Capital* vol. I, ch. VII, 'The Labour Process' (London: Allen and Unwin, 1946).
15. Marx, *Economic and Philosophical Manuscripts of 1844*, p. 76.
16. Cf. K. Marx, *The German Ideology* and 'Theses on Feuerbach', in K. Marx and F. Engels, *Collected Works*, vol. V (London: Lawrence and Wishart, 1976).
17. K. Marx, *Grundrisse: Foundations of the Critique of Political Economy* (Rough Draft), translator M. Nicolaus (Harmondsworth: Penguin Books, 1973).
18. Ibid., p. 496.
19. Ibid.
20. Lukács in *New Hungarian Quarterly*, vol. XIII, No. 47, 1972.
21. Marx, *Grundrisse*, pp. 161–2.
22. Ibid, pp. 156–7.
23. Ibid, p. 706.
24. Ibid, p. 172.
25. Preface to the First Edition of Marx, *Capital*.
26. The recent publication in translation of Marx's drafts of the first part of *Capital* should greatly facilitate the study of these questions. Cf. *Value: Studies by Karl Marx*, translated by A. Dragstedt (London: New Park Publications, 1976).

27. Ibid, pp. 58 ff.
28. Marx, *Capital*, vol. I, pp. 550—1.
29. Talcott Parsons, *The Social System* (London: Routledge and Kegan Paul, 1971).
30. Talcott Parsons, *Societies: Evolutionary and Comparative Perspectives* (Englewood Cliffs, NJ: Prentice-Hall, 1966).
31. *Capital*, vol. III, p. 805.
32. Ibid., p. 45.
33. Ibid., p. 807.
34. Ibid., p. 810.
35. K. Marx, *A Contribution to the Critique of Political Economy* (London: Lawrence and Wishart, 1971) p. 95.
36. István Mészáros, *Marx's Theory of Alienation*, p. 113.
37. Marx, *Grundrisse*, p. 226.
38. Ibid., pp. 225—6.
39. Ibid., pp. 221—2.
40. Ibid., p. 225.
41. Hegel, *Aesthetics*, vol. I, p. 267.
42. Mészáros, *Marx's Theory of Alienation*, pp. 206 ff.
43. Marx, *Economic and Philosophical Manuscripts of 1844*, p. 110.
44. Marx, *Grundrisse*, p. 497.
45. Marx, *The German Ideology* p. 66.
46. All quotations in this passage are from Marx, *Grundrisse*, pp. 295—7.
47. Hegel, *Aesthetics*, vol. I, p. 259.
48. 'Introduction' in Marx, *A Contribution to the Critique of Political Economy*, pp. 215—17.
49. Ibid., p. 215.
50. Cited by Lifshitz, *The Philosophy of Art of Karl Marx*, p. 35.
51. For an extended commentary on this passage from Marx, especially useful in indicating Marx's debt here to Hegel, Schiller, Herder and Fischer, see Prawer, *Karl Marx and World Literature* (Oxford University Press, 1976) pp. 280—7.
52. G. Lukács, *Goethe and His Age* (London: Merlin Press, 1968) ch. V.
53. Hegel, *Aesthetics*, vol. I, p. 26.
54. Cited by C. Taylor, *Hegel* (Cambridge University Press, 1975).
55. G. Hegel, *Phenomenology of Mind* (Oxford University Press, 1979) ch. VII.
56. Ibid., pp. 753 and 808, cited by G. Lukács *The Young Hegel* (London: Merlin Press, 1975) p. 508.
57. Marx, *Grundrisse*, pp. 471—514. (Previously published in a translation by Jack Cohen as *Pre-capitalist Economic Formations*, Introduction by E. Hobsbawm (London: Lawrence and Wishart, 1964).
58. Ibid., pp. 487—8.
59. H. Hess, 'Is There a Theory of Art in Marx?', *Marxism Today*, October 1973.
60. A. Hauser, *The Social History of Art*, vol. I (London: Routledge and Kegan Paul, 1968 [first published 1951]) p. 69.

61. M. Raphael, *Prehistoric Cave Paintings*, Bollingen series (New York: Pantheon Books, 1945) p. 2.
62. Marx, *Grundrisse*, p. 162.
63. Ibid., pp. 704—5.
64. G. Lukács, *Theory of the Novel* (London: Merlin Press, 1973).
65. Marx, *Grundrisse*, pp. 705—6.
66. Ibid., p. 712.
67. Marx, *Capital*, vol. I.
68. Marx, *A Contribution to the Critique of Political Economy*, p. 207.
69. Marx, *The Holy Family*, p. 181.
70. Ibid., p. 205.
71. Hegel, *Aesthetics*, vol. II, pp. 1052—3.
72. R. Girard, *Deceit, Desire and the Novel* (Baltimore: Johns Hopkins University, 1965).
73. G. Hegel *The Philosophy of History* (New York: Dover, 1956) p. 30.
74. Hegel, *Aesthetics*, vol. I, p. 196.
75. Karl Marx and Friedrich Engels, *Literature and Art* (Bombay: Current Book House, 1956) pp. 39—40.
76. H. Lefebvre, *Dialectical Materialism* (London: Jonathan Cape, 1968) p. 132.
77. Cf. F. D. Klingender, *Art and the Industrial Revolution* (London: Paladin, 1972 [first published 1947]).
78. Lefebvre, *Dialectical Materialism*, p. 165.

CHAPTER 3

1. See especially G. Plekhanov, *Art and Social Life* (London: Lawrence and Wishart, 1953), for the analysis of French eighteenth-century drama and the nineteenth-century aesthetic movement; and F. Mehring, *Die Lessing Legende* (Berlin: Dietz Verlag, 1953) and *On Historical Materialism* (London: New Park Publications, 1975).
2. L. D. Trotsky, *Literature and Revolution* (Ann Arbor: University of Michigan Press, 1960).
3. Raymond Williams, for example, writes that 'Marxism, in many fields, and perhaps especially in cultural theory, has experienced at once a significant revival and a related openness and flexibility of theoretical development' — *Marxism and Literature* (Oxford University Press, 1977) p. 1.
4. Trotsky, *Literature and Revolution*, p. 14.
5. Ibid., p. 170.
6. Ibid., pp. 218—19.
7. Williams, *Marxism and Literature*, p. 202.
8. Trotsky, *Literature and Revolution*, pp. 130—1.
9. Ibid., p. 132.
10. Ibid., p. 60.
11. Ibid., p. 61.
12. Ibid., p. 180—1.

13. L. D. Trotsky, *Class and Art: Problems of Culture under the Dictatorship of the proletariat* (Speech of 1924) (London: New Park Publications, 1974) p. 18.
14. Trotsky, *Literature and Revolution*, pp. 178—9.
15. Ibid., p. 180.
16. Ibid., pp. 242—3.
17. Ibid., p. 244.
18. Ibid., p. 225.
19. Letter of 30 December, 1922, in V. I. Lenin, 'The Question of Nationalities, or of "Autonomisation" ' (Moscow: Foreign Languages Publishing House, n.d.) pp.22—3.
20. Trotsky, *Literature and Revolution*, p. 225.
21. Ibid., p. 226.
22. Karl Marx and Friedrich Engels, *Collected Works*, vol. V (London: Lawrence and Wishart, 1976) p. 49.
23. Trotsky, *Literature and Revolution*, p. 227.
24. L. D. Trotsky, *Culture and Socialism and a Manifesto, Art and Revolution* (London: New Park Publications, 1975).
25. Ibid., p. 30.
26. Ibid., p. 33.
27. Ibid., pp. 33—4.
28. Ibid., pp. 32—3.
29. Ibid., p. 33.
30. Trotsky, *Literature and Revolution*, p. 152.
31. K. Marx, *The 18th Brumaire of Louis Bonaparte*, in K. Marx and F. Engels, *Selected Works*, vol. II (London: Lawrence and Wishart, 1942).
32. Plekhanov, *Art and Social Life*.
33. Trotsky, *Literature and Revolution*, p. 146.
34. Trotsky, *Class and Art*, p. 7.
35. Ibid., p. 18.
36. Ibid.
37. Ibid., p. 19.
38. Ibid., p. 9.
39. Trotsky, *Literature and Revolution*, p. 169.
40. Ibid., p. 179.
41. Ibid., p. 180.
42. Ibid., p. 173.
43. Ibid., p. 233.
44. Ibid., p. 137.
45. Terry Eagleton, *Marxism and Literary Criticism* (London: Methuen, 1976) pp. 50—1.
46. Trotsky, *Literature and Revolution*, p. 175.
47. P. Macherey, *Pour une Théorie de la Production Littéraire* (Paris: Maspéro, 1970).
48. Eagleton, *Marxism and Literary Criticism*, p. 51.
49. Trotsky, *Literature and Revolution*, p. 238.
50. Ibid., p. 79.

CHAPTER 4

1. Cf. B. Nagy, 'The Political Itinerary of Georg Lukács', *Fourth International*, vol. 7 (1971–2) nos. 2 and 3, and vol. 8 (1972) no. 1; and M. Löwy, 'Lukács and Stalinism' in *Western Marxism – a Critical Reader* (London: New Left Books, 1977).
2. Cf. in particular G. Lukács, 'Art and Society', *New Hungarian Quarterly*, vol. XIII (1972) no. 47.
3. Ibid., p. 49.
4. Ibid., p. 55.
5. G. Lukács, *Goethe and His Age* (London: Merlin Press, 1968).
6. Ibid., p. 108.
7. Cf. G. Lukács, *The Meaning of Contemporary Realism* (London: Merlin Press, 1963; German edition, 1957).
8. Lukács, 'Art and Society'.
9. Just how fatally 'tactical considerations' can get into the bloodstream is suggested by a purple passage in 1948: 'By a remarkable coincidence (if coincidence that be) I had just finished reading *Doctor Faustus* (Thomas Mann), when the Central Committee of the Communist Party of the Soviet Union published its decree on modern music. In Thomas Mann's novel this decree finds its fullest intellectual and artistic confirmation . . . ' – G. Lukács, *Essays on Thomas Mann* (London: Merlin Press, 1966) pp. 71–2.
10. Ibid., p. 50.
11. Ibid.
12. Ibid., pp. 50–51.
13. Preface (1963) to Lukács, *Essays on Thomas Mann*, p. 44.
14. Ibid., p. 11.
15. Isaac Deutscher, 'Georg Lukács and Critical Realism', *The Listener*, 3 November 1966.
16. Lukács, 'Art and Society', pp. 48–9.
17. G. Lukács, *History and Class Consciousness* (London: Merlin Press, 1971) p. xxvii.
18. Lukács, *The Meaning of Contemporary Realism*, p. 105.
19. Ibid., p. 128.
20. Lukács, *History and Class Consciousness*, p. xxx.
21. Ibid., pp. xxviii–xxix.
22. Ibid., p. xxxi.
23. F. Jameson (ed.), *Aesthetics and Politics* (London: New Left Books, 1977) p. 147.
24. Ibid., p. 143.
25. Ibid., p. 175.
26. Ibid., pp. 175–6.
27. Lukács, *The Meaning of Contemporary Realism*, p. 13.
28. Ibid., p. 14.
29. Ibid.
30. Jameson (ed.), *Aesthetics and Politics*, p. 69.

31. Ibid., p. 76.
32. Ibid., p. 78.
33. In Thomas Mann, *Adel des Geistes*, cited in R. Hinton Thomas, *Thomas Mann* (Oxford University Press 1956) p. 16.
34. Lukács, *Essays on Thomas Mann*.
35. Ibid., p. 133.
36. Lukács, *History and Class Consciousness*, p. 27.
37. In Thomas Mann, *Die Forderung des Tages*, cited by Thomas, *Thomas Mann*, p. 4.
38. Cf. Thomas, *Thomas Mann*, 82–3.
39. Lukács, *The Meaning of Contemporary Realism*, p. 92.
40. Lukács, *Essays on Thomas Mann*, p. 15.
41. Lukács, *The Meaning of Contemporary Realism*, p. 82.
42. Ibid., p. 89.
43. This viewpoint, fully developed in Lukács, *The Meaning of Contemporary Realism*, was anticipated long before, in his studies of Balzac in the 1930s. For example: 'The modern realists who as a result of the decline in bourgeois ideology have lost their deep understanding of social interconnections and with it their capacity for abstraction, vainly attempt by concretising details to render concrete the social totality and its real, objectively decisive determinants' – G. Lukács, *Studies in European Realism* (London: Hillway, 1950) p. 44.
44. Lukács, *The Meaning of Contemporary Realism*, p. 125.
45. Lukács, *Studies in European Realism*, pp. 63–4.
46. Ibid.
47. Ibid.
48. Cf. Lukács, *Goethe and his Age*.
49. Lukács, *History and Class Consciousness*, p. 197.
50. Ibid., p. 262.
51. Ibid., p. 81.
52. Cf. Lucien Goldmann, *Towards a Sociology of the Novel* (London: Tavistock, 1975). The abandonment of Marx's concepts of revolution was already explicitly stated in Goldmann's writings in *Les Temps Modernes*, published in *Recherches Dialectiques*, 1957.
53. Lukács, *Studies in European Realism*, pp. 59–60.
54. Lukács, *History and Class Consciousness*, p. 132.
55. F. Engels, Preface to Second Edition (1885) of *Anti-Dühring* (London: Lawrence and Wishart, 1977).
56. V. I. Lenin, *Philosophical Notebooks*, in *Collected Works*, vol. 38 (London: Lawrence and Wishart, 1961) p. 363.
57. Fredric Jameson, 'Reflections in Conclusion', in Jameson (ed.), *Aesthetics and Politics*, p. 202.
58. Ibid., p. 208.
59. Fredric Jameson, *Marxism and Form* (Princeton University Press, 1971) and *The Prison House of Language* (Princeton University Press, 1972).
60. Jameson (ed.), *Aesthetics and Politics*, pp. 212–13.

CHAPTER 5

1. R. Williams, in 'Introduction' to L. Goldmann, *Racine* (Cambridge: Rivers Press, 1972) p. xiv.
2. R. Williams, *Marxism and Literature* (Oxford University Press, 1977).
3. L. Goldmann, *Cultural Creation in Modern Society* (St. Louis: Telos Press, 1976) p. 58.
4. Ibid., and L. Goldmann, *Towards a Sociology of the Novel* (London: Tavistock, 1975).
5. L. Goldmann, *The Hidden God* (London: Routledge and Kegan Paul, 1964).
6. Ibid., p. 315.
7. Ibid., p. 99.
8. Goldmann, *Cultural Creation*, p. 81.
9. Ibid., p. 80.
10. Ibid., p. 79.
11. Goldmann's 'Introduction aux premiers écrits de Lukács', in G. Lukács, *La Théorie du Roman* (Paris: Editions Gonthier, 1963).
12. G. Lukács, *Theory of the Novel* (London: Merlin Press, 1973) part II.
13. In Lukács, *La Théorie du Roman*, p. 179.
14. Goldmann, *Cultural Creation*, p. 81.
15. Ibid.
16. Ibid., p. 58.
17. Reply by Goldmann in a discussion on the work of Geneviève Mouillaud on Stendhal.
18. Ibid.
19. L. Goldmann, *The Human Sciences and Philosophy* (London: Jonathan Cape, 1969) p. 19.
20. Williams, in 'Introduction' to Goldmann, *Racine*.
21. Goldmann, *Cultural Creation* and *Towards a Sociology of the Novel*, *passim*.
22. Goldmann, *Cultural Creation*, pp. 54–5.
23. Ibid., pp. 55–6.
24. Cf. Goldmann's review of the work of Fritz Sternberg in *Arguments*, vol. I (1957) no. 1.
25. Preface to First Edition, in *Capital*, vol. I (London: Allen and Unwin, 1946).
26. K. Marx, *Grundrisse* (Harmondsworth: Penguin Books, 1973) p. 162.

CHAPTER 6

1. Walter Benjamin, 'The Author as Producer', in Benjamin, *Understanding Brecht* (London: New Left Books, 1973) p. 103.
2. Ibid.
3. Cf. Adorno's letter to Walter Benjamin (10 November 1938) in F. Jameson (ed.), *Aesthetics and Politics* (London: New Left Books, 1977).

4. Benjamin cites Marx's *Critique of the Gotha Programme*, in K. Marx and F. Engels, *Selected Works*, vol. II (London: Lawrence and Wishart, 1942).
5. W. Benjamin, *Illuminations*, ed. H. Arendt, tr. H. Zohn (London: Jonathan Cape, 1970) p. 244.
6. Ibid., p. 243.
7. Ibid., p. 253.
8. Ibid., p. 220.
9. Ibid., p. 238.
10. W. Benjamin, *Briefe*, vol. II (1929–40) (Frankfurt: Suhrkamp, 1966).
11. Benjamin, 'The Author as Producer', p. 92.
12. Benjamin, *Illuminations*, p. 260.
13. G. Lukács, *The Meaning of Contemporary Realism* (London: Merlin Press, 1963) pp. 40–41.
14. In Benjamin, *Illuminations*, pp. 255–66.
15. T. W. Adorno and M. Horkheimer, *Dialectic of Enlightenment* (New York: Herder, 1972) p. xii.
16. Benjamin, *Illuminations*, p. 260.
17. Ibid., p. 257.
18. Ibid., p. 258.
19. Ibid., p. 262.
20. Benjamin, 'The Author as Producer', pp. 118–19.
21. Ibid., pp. 85–103.
22. Ibid., p. 101.
23. Ibid.
24. Ibid., p. 102.
25. Ibid.
26. Ibid.
27. Ibid., pp. 102–3.
28. Cf. Adorno's letter to Benjamin, in Jameson (ed.), *Aesthetics and Politics*
29. Benjamin, 'The Author as Producer', pp. 118–19.
30. Ibid., p. 98.
31. Ibid., p. 94.
32. Ibid., p. 95.
33. Ibid., pp. 97–8.
34. Ibid., p. 100.
35. W. Benjamin, *Charles Baudelaire: a Lyric Poet in the Era of High Capitalism* (London: New Left Books, 1973) p. 104.
36. Ibid., p. 103.
37. Ibid., p. 106.
38. Ibid., p 75.
39. Ibid., pp.98–100.
40. Ibid., pp.58–9﹒
41. Ibid., p. 66.
42. 'A Portrait of Walter Benjamin', in W. Adorno, *Prisms* (London: Neville Spearman, 1967) pp. 237–8.

43. Jameson (ed.), *Aesthetics and Politics*, p. 136.
44. Ibid.
45. Benjamin, 'The Author as Producer', p. 87.
46. Jameson (ed.), *Aesthetics and Politics*, p. 137.
47. Benjamin, *Illuminations*, pp. 264—5.
48. Introduction to Benjamin, *Understanding Brecht*.

CHAPTER 7

1. V. I. Lenin, *Philosophical Notebooks, Collected Works*, vol. 38 (London: Lawrence and Wishart, 1961) p. 361.
2. Max Raphael, *The Demands of Art*, Bollingen series (Princeton University Press, 1968) p. 217.
3. Terry Eagleton, *Criticism and Ideology* (London: New Left Books, 1976).
4. K. Marx, *Theories of Surplus Value*, part 1 (London: Lawrence and Wishart, n.d.) p. 276.
5. Cited in S. S. Prawer, *Karl Marx and World Literature* (Oxford University Press, 1976).
6. Cf. A. N. Leontyev, 'Activity and Consciousness', in *Philosophy in the USSR* (Moscow: Progress Publishers, 1977) pp. 180—202.
7. Lenin, *Philosophical Notebooks*, p. 195.
8. K. Marx, *Economic and Philosophical Manuscripts of 1844* (London: Lawrence and Wishart, 1959) p. 108.

Index